ASPECTS OF EDUCATION

ASPECTS OF EDUCATION

Selected papers from the Dartington Conference

Edited by
Mark Braham

JOHN WILEY & SONS

Chichester · New York · Brisbane · Toronto · Singapore

C C

Copyright © 1982 by John Wiley & Sons Ltd.

All rights reserved.

British Library Cataloguing in Publication Data:

Aspects of education.
  1. Education—Congresses
  I. Braham, Mark
  370'.1   L13   80–42315
  ISBN 0 471 28019 4
  ISBN 0 471 28022 4

Text set in 10/12 pt Linotron 202 Palatino, printed and bound in the United States of America

Contents

Editor's Foreword

This is a book for those who are interested in education. It contains a selection of papers from the Dartington Conference which is held each April at Dartington Hall, near Totnes, Devonshire, England.

Those who participated in the first three conferences—they began in 1976—will have known them by their original name of 'New themes for education'. The 'new themes' have by no means been lost, but the name has been changed to allow for greater flexibility and in recognition of Dartington Hall's role as the setting for this increasingly popular event.

Like the conference in which they were first presented, the papers in this book offer 'new themes for education': ideas, information, and knowledge that can contribute to the development of educational thought, programmes, and practices. This book, therefore, provides a range of material that anyone who is interested in education—parents, students, teachers, lecturers, or administrators—will find well worth considering.

Preface

When something turns out very differently from what was foreseen when it started there is a fair presumption that it may have chanced upon a change of climate. This was certainly the case with the initiative of the Dartington Trustees out of which this book has emerged. They were simply puzzled to know, in 1974, in which direction the future of their educational responsibilities should lie. To help them decide, they convened a conference which was to set this question in the context of contemporary thought. In the result, this conference has acquired a life of its own and has become a catalyst for the ingredients of what amounts to a new philosophy and which in a growing stream are challenging conventional assumptions at their roots. If Dartington has proved fertile ground for this process, it is perhaps because in its very existence—in the presence there, within one scheme of things, of numerous activities which would make no sense in the conventional world by being part of one another—it has long represented a standing challenge to those assumptions.

If the Trustees did not realize how the climate was changing, however, it is possible that Mark Braham did. He was working as a Scholar-in-Residence at Dartington and we seduced him from his writing (for which he has since exculpated us) to run our conference. Single-handed except for the dedicated help of Florence Burton, and subsequently of Mary Bride Nicholson, he established the series. Many people other than ourselves are in his debt as a result, and this book will surely add to their number.

MAURICE ASH

Acknowledgements

It is barely possible to produce any book, let alone one of this nature, without the participation of many people. Neither this volume nor the Dartington Conference upon which it is based would have been possible without the constant support of Maurice Ash, Chairman of the Dartington Hall Trust, and his belief in the endeavour, and the assistance of the staff of the Trust, the Dartington College of Arts, and the Devon Centre for Further Education.

Also, on behalf of the Dartington Society, grateful appreciation is extended to the Joseph Rowntree Memorial Trust, the Wates Foundation, the Elmgrant Trust, International Business Machines (UK) Ltd, and Marks & Spencer Ltd, whose kindness has also made the Dartington Conference and this volume possible.

Introduction

Mark Braham

Thunder within the earth
The Image of the turning point.
Thus the kings of antiquity closed the passes
At the time of solstice.
Merchants and strangers did not go about,
And the ruler
Did not travel through the provinces
I-Ching (Wilhelm's translation)

Imagery for winter? Yes, but also for more, for there is indeed thunder within the earth and it is commonplace to say that we are at a critical juncture, a turning point, in human affairs. Phrases such as 'a water-shed between two eras', 'the birth pangs of a new humanity', the 'new age', the 'age of Aquarius' endorse our sense of departure from a past in which life was supposedly more stable and harmonious, and an entry into a future that, on the one hand is viewed with bleak uncertainty with predictions of nuclear holocaust, geological cataclysms, and civil strife—a kind of cosmic winter of discontent—whilst on the other hand there are joyous visions of a golden age based upon the material and spiritual transformation of the human condition. Given the array of uncertainties, difficulties, and possibilities, we cannot but wonder at the human condition and how it has come to pass.

Wondering alone, however, is not enough, for the needs of our time are too urgent. Need they be spelled out? The continuing ecological crises that threaten the very web-of-life of the planet; the armaments race and international tensions that portend a doomsday scenario; inflation and unemployment, and the increase in urban decay and personal violence, and more. To note these as part of an introduction to a volume on education is not to say that this volume will reply to the problems, or that education holds all of the answers, but it is to suggest that there is more than just a slight connection between education and the present state of human affairs.

The connection rests, it seems to me, on the fact that we are a species of life which, in comparison with all others, is of very limited instinct and must, for the most part, learn in order to live. This is something that was probably as true for our earliest Cro-Magnon ancestors as it is for each child today, despite the vast differences in the range of circumstances and needs. The continuing problem, greater at some periods than at others, is that as populations have increased and the patterns of migration, intra- and inter-group communication, conflict and co-operation have spread, human environments have been faced with overall instability. Where, therefore, there has been the opportunity for a group to build up a cultural pattern for transmission to successive generations, there has also been, and undoubtedly will continue to be, the introduction of destabilizing factors that can raise the lives of the group to a new level of productivity and complexity (as with the case of the domestication of animals, or as it is now averred with silicon chip technology), or provide for its destruction (as with the introduction of the slave trade, colonization, gunpowder, and nuclear weaponry). Additionally, despite the overall fluctuations and, one might want to conclude, cycles, of cultural development and decline, humanity has been, and continues to be, an agent of that profound force which we still do not understand: evolution. Thus, although we do not speak of the continuing physiological evolution of the human species, we do speak about our cultural evolution, recognizing that our actions, thoughts, feelings, and intuitions are a part of the process guided less by the information encoded in our genes than by decisions derived from our heads and hearts.

Whilst lectern-thumping moralists may wish to point to our defection from good, and to our original sinfulness as the cause of so many human ills, the notion of sin can usefully be translated via Sanscrit as *avidya* or 'ignorance' and perhaps come closer to the truth. We may be born free, like Rousseau's Noble Savage or Joy Adamson's lions, but we are also born ignorant—without the necessary information and knowledge that we need to guide and govern our existence, and millennia of generations have carried our ignorance, our non-knowledge, around the globe. One says this with full regard for the centuries of folk-wisdom, arcane teachings, religious traditions, schools of philosophy, and the great expansion of science and technology in this most calamitous century.

This is not a matter of fault finding, although certainly faults can be found, but of description and the belief that things could have hardly been otherwise. Somehow, we have had the hope and the expectation that, even given the vastness of the planet and the relative recency of the primitive violence in what until the Middle Ages was tribal Europe, and then was a battle ground of feuding war lords in their clanking armour, we would turn within a few hundred years into reasonably gentle, considerate, knowledgeable people who could live in peace and harmony with man and beast having developed our potentialities and our wisdom to the full.

Instead, our evolution has involved the slow development of consciousness—of sentiency, awareness, trials and errors, successes and failures, rationalizations and superstitions, reflections and questionings, speculations and theories. Time after time we have had to doubt and to test the validity of our beliefs and claims to knowledge concerning ourselves, our group, other peoples, the nature of the earth and the fauna and flora that covers it, the atomic density of matter and the farthest planets. To undertake this has meant that instinct, which anyway has been for us in short supply, has had to be supplanted by a disciplined intelligence that enables us to give care and attention to the details of life in an orderly and organized way; to select the appropriate from the inappropriate, the life sustaining from the life destroying, so that we can continue to live in our environment at the same time that we, or others, are changing it. This has meant, therefore, learning and teaching: the organization, acquisition, and transmission of extra-genetic rather than genetic information for its application to, and the overall enhancement of, life—in sum, education.

That we find the world so rife with problems is in itself indicative of our educational strengths and weaknesses. Our weaknesses, due to the inadequacies, the inappropriateness, and even the non-existence of much teaching and learning, are a major source of our difficulties. Our strengths, on the other hand, have given us the expanding world-wide network of educational opportunity that, even with its failings, has produced the scientific and technical, although not always the moral, knowledge that is with us today, a knowledge, we should add, that has confronted us with our supermarkets of folly—the poisoning of our water resources, the destruction of our great forests, the exploitation of one another—that are now of so much concern. In sum, our lives are in large part expressions of the quality of our education.

What then of education? We cannot live without it. We cannot indicate precisely the point at which it begins, for it does so but faintly and gradually. We can only suggest that a beginning is to be found where sentiency transforms into awareness, and awareness leads to intentional action, which in turn gives rise to reflection, as inchoate and minimal as this might be. Perhaps a starting point, undoubtedly nebulous, is intra-uterine for the amniotic sac offers no proof against sensation, and the nervous system and brain are, anyway, functioning as they form, so that the near-term baby is already being affected by what is within–without. Certainly there are educational beginnings in the days and weeks that follow birth as each newly born human starts out on the long course of transactions with all that surrounds him.

Education may have no absolute beginning, but nor does it appear to have an absolute ending, except that of death itself. Yet, one wonders—given the very widespread interest in Eastern thought and the hypothesis of our undergoing 'life after life'—if we are so sure that the myth of the 'eternal return' or the 'weary wheel of rebirth', well known to Orphics, Pythagoreans, Platonists, and Gnostics, as well as to Hindus and Buddhists, and being investigated by scientists such as Stevenson, Guirdham, and Moody, is without any element of truth? Are the arguments about education as involving remembrance—recall Meno the slave boy—totally unwarranted? If there is a warrant, then our psychological and educational attitudes will require some fairly drastic revision. Unacceptable notions, perhaps, but then speculation always lies at the periphery of convention where even the unthinkable needs to be thought.

We know of no limits to our educational possibilities, maturational or temporal, beyond those of disability, circumstance, lack of interest or volition. Maturity carries with it the implication of limitation, of a terminal point reached in a developmental process. But, as is raised in the paper 'Education is natural', what are the limits, beyond those our genes and environment impose upon our physiology, of our emotional, aesthetic, mental and, some will also ask, our spiritual development? None that we know of, and thankfully so, for if the contemporary state of human consciousness with its explosive emotionality, its aesthetic shallowness (where do we find beauty, harmony, balance, order as regular features of our life and works?), its mental restrictedness and spiritual confusion, is the mark of our maturity, then we have reached the limit of our possibilities and the future—if there will be one—can be no better than the present, and education will have no role to play.

Age also is no necessary limitation upon our possibilities. Of course one recognizes the facts of ageing and senility. But senility may in part by due to an undeveloped mentality, and programmes such as those of Britain's Open University, let alone the present interest in 'continuing' or 'lifelong' education, attest to the realization that whilst it may not be possible to teach old dogs new tricks, older humans do not have to suffer the same confinement. From this point of view, education can be understood to be potentially continuous with life, although whether the sentiment that education is the same as life itself is valid is, I think, to be doubted. The reason for this doubt is that education calls for attention to detail, for reflection, for intentional transformations of thought and action, but our lives, as we know, can slip by in cycles of more or less passivity, in incessant turmoil, in variations on habitual themes, in fixed patterns of action in which education has no place except as a thought that it is something that we once had in our youth. And if one wants to think in terms of formal schooling, then we must recognize that much of the world's population knows little of it.

If education is an organically grounded process—which given our instinctual deficiencies and need for learning is one of the views taken in this volume—what of such customary definitions of education as 'leading out', derived from the Latin root *educare* (and purportedly preferred by 'progressives'), or 'bringing up', derived from the Latin root *educere* (and purportedly preferred by traditionalists)?

The notion of 'leading out' suggests that within each child becoming adult, and each adult creating the course of his or her life, there is a distinctiveness of quality and possibility that requires both provision and nurture. This position accepts no *tabula rasa* idea, espoused by the empirical Locke, 'supposing the mind to be, as we say, a white paper, void of all characters, without any ideas',[1] which was his argument against the theory of 'innate ideas' and, we could even say, against the rebirth hypothesis. It was the nineteenth-century idealist Friedrich Froebel who, instead, cautioned us to let life 'unfold from within', and although we cannot demonstrate the appearance of concepts that are either fully formed in fledgling minds, or appear from *ratio seminales* as St Augustine put it, it is one of the recognitions of twentieth-century behavioural science that every living thing—and every human being—is, by definition, self-organizing, infused from the outset, not perhaps with ideas, but with a patterning of developmental process that is intrinsic to itself.

There is little doubt that not only are we born with the propensity, for example, for sensory and conceptual organization, for the structuring and integration of experience, but that infant life itself involves an active 'outgoingness'—if one may use such a phrase—or to quote the title of a book of one of our authors, is 'born curious', in order to come to terms with the world. Thus, if we are to allow for life's development, we must respect its integrity and provide the necessary conditions.

John Newson who, with his wife Elizabeth, directs the Child Development Research Unit at the University of Nottingham, describes, in his paper, the processes of infant–adult communication. He emphasizes the point that 'human babies characteristically exhibit a variety of intrinsic activity patterns which serve as a basis for communication competence'. 'Even at birth', he says, 'it is possible to detect gesture-like actions which are complex co-ordinations of arm and hand movements, head and eye orientations, mouthings and vocalizations. This activity of the infant is not formless but highly integrated. . . .'

Yet, given the intrinsic organizational and communications character- istics in infancy, there is neither learning nor education in isolation from an environment, and there is no such thing as an organism that is not in transaction with, and thus affected by, its environment. Thus, the *educere*, 'bringing up' point of view has its place. In fact, if the development of our consciousness happened of its own accord, if life was just an unfolding from within, then education would not be present in our lives and there would be no need for the patience, care, and attention that it requires. Our life and our learning may well start off as a bio-physio-psychological activity, but it rapidly becomes psychosocial, or cultural, involving parents, siblings, relatives, neighbours, and a whole gamut of humans including teachers who at once present both the support and the demands of the society into which we are born.

Elizabeth Newson has devoted a considerable period to elucidating the nature of these interchanges. In her paper 'Child and parent, school and culture' she says, 'It is not possible to envisage a culture-free child. . . . long before he is necessarily aware of a world beyond his family, the child's notions and expectations are shaped by an enormous variety of manifestations of his culture, as mediated by his parents. . . .'

In his paper 'Growth to autonomy within a system of conventions' John Shotter asks how humans 'may become masters of their ways of life rather than being slaves to them'. The child, he suggests, 'is an active agent who, from the moment of his birth, in the course of interchanges with others, is engaged in the task of making himself into a being able to take his own "place" amongst them'.

It is often suggested, though not always happily accepted, that schooling and teaching do not necessarily provide for education, by the same token, perhaps, that medicine and doctors do not necessarily provide for healing, or our religious institutions for spiritual develop- ment. Without putting the case in such stark terms, Sir Alec Clegg in his opening paper drops us right into the classroom. He writes about 'loaves' and 'hyacinths', an intriguing variation on the *educere–educare* theme. There is something intrinsically ineffable, not easily, if at all, measurable, about our 'hyacinth' nature. It is the 'feeling', the 'affective' side of our consciousness. There is something much more definitive, measurable, categorical, in our 'loaf' nature, our rational side. Most schooling, tied as it is, and has been, to the practical, the technical, and the mercantile (although with a dosing of theological morality to keep things within bounds), has given little attention to the development of feeling. Says Sir Alec: 'We ruthlessly emphasize the cognitive side of our learning by an examination system which is so costly that it consumes a sum equal to half the amount that a school has to pay for its books, stationery, and apparatus.' He offers us this verse for our thoughts:

> If thou of fortune be bereft
> And of thine earthly store hath left
> Two loaves sell one and with the dole
> Buy hyacinths to feed the soul.

Maurice Ash, the Chairman of the Dartington Hall Trust and long concerned with the fates and fortunes of Dartington Hall School,[2] one of the early educational attempts in Britain to give credence to the child as an individual in his or her own right, writes of 'The progressive inheritance and its renewal'. He reminds us of Rousseau's insights and his inconsistencies as well, and seeks to find ways of bringing the school life of the child in closer touch with human need, with 'growth in wisdom, which is what any development of the person must be concerned with'.

James Henderson, not unsympathetic to the progressive ideal, questions the progressive school movement's ability to have met it. In 'A Metaphysics for Education', he points out how the progressive schools, in their neglect of 'Being as contrasted with Knowing', and their failure to discriminate between sexual knowledge and the enlightenment of love, between good and God, between mistake and sin, between maladjustment and evil, and between putting up with life and coming to terms with death have fallen short of their ideal. Indicating that our progressive attempts, like our traditional ones, also suffer from a lack of balance, he proposes 'a pedagogical system embracing time, love, evil, tragedy, death and hope'.

James Hemming in 'The unawakened mind' explores some of the implications of the lopsidedness of much of our school programming and experience which Sir Alec Clegg has raised and the progressive movement has sought to, but has not yet, overcome. Following up some of the recent research into the two hemispheres of the brain in which our cognitive dispositions tend to be functions of the left hemisphere (in right-handed people) and the affective dispositions are of the right hemisphere, he draws up a list of some of their respective functions:

Left hemisphere	*Right hemisphere*
Logical thinking	Intuitional thinking
Analysis	Synthesis
Linguistic skill	Musical skill
Abstract thought	Imaginative thought

and so forth. He writes: 'Unfortunately, traditional secondary education consistently overvalues left-mode functions and consistently under-values right-mode functions so that its products have a poor chance of ending up well-balanced . . .. This leads to the vicious circle that much of secondary and higher education has been designed by left-moders for left-moders', indicating the need for 'hemispheric integration'—or, as Robin Hodgkin puts it in his paper 'Things for use and things for meaning', 'an adequate educational theory should be interested, at least marginally, in wholeness, even in holiness', and he turns to the child's world of toys, tools, and symbols as a wellspring of educational resource.

Frank Musgrove writes: 'I conceive education as liminality, the threshold state; it is a movement across boundaries, intrinsically am-biguous, always potentially dangerous—sometimes a journey into forbidden reaches of the mind', and this, to my mind at least, raises a Pauline question. St Paul, it will be recalled, said that it is 'the letter that killeth, it is the spirit that giveth life'. The letter is the law, the form, the routine that is established for its believed appropriateness in its time and place. The spirit, however, is the very energy of growth and development, of evolution, pressing everything that lives to-wards—although not necessarily achieving—the fullness of its possi-bilities. Spirit turns into form, as for example the religious spirit turned into the form of the church; but in time, form tends to encapsulate, perhaps even to incarcerate spirit, so that if the growth is to continue the boundaries must be transcended and new forms created. The same is true of our schools. Designed for the educational ideas of one era, they too often become limitations upon the educational possibilities of the next, withering the spirit or causing it to rebel. Frank Musgrove writes of 'the sheer waste and desolation of contemporary mass school-ing . . .. We have constructed a vast national network of bear-pits called classrooms; and our job in teacher training is to give patience and endurance to baited bears', and goes on to describe some of those—restless and searching—who walk perilously along the margins of contemporary culture: artists, members of a Sufi commune, de-votees of Hare Krishna, and others.

There are others, however, who do not even get the chance to explore the outer reaches of their minds but instead are confined by circum-stances from which they have little chance of escape. These are the 'problem' children and adolescents whose straying from the 'straight and narrow' has led them into institutional care; they are the children who have been reinforced in their deviancy by the very social conditions that have caused it. Spencer Millham writes about them in 'The dustbin

men', a title he has taken from a song a group of these children have
written about themselves:

> We are the dustbin men
> Born in 'em
> Kept in 'em
> And when we get out
> We're going to empty 'em.

Ivan Illich wrote about 'deschooling' society, something that has
seemed to be a somewhat doubtful notion, short of having national
disasters to make the possibility an inevitability. Education like every
human activity requires some form of organization, some range of
facilities, and some number of competent personnel. Whether the forms
of organization, the facilities, and the kinds of personnel we have at
present are appropriate is another, although no less important, question. Were we to turn to our work-places, to oceans, fields, and forests
as proper environments for education's expression, we would still have
schooling, albeit under another name.

Schooling for what? To provide for education. For whom? For all
human beings to the extent of their interest and abilities. Why? For the
fullest elaboration of human consciousness. Why? To improve, according to our understanding, the human condition: to develop the nature of
man, and man's place in nature. Do we believe it?

Colin Ward, who seriously questions our intentions, wonders about
that holy trinity of Western liberal democracy: Equality, Liberty, and
Fraternity. The French Revolution was fostered on it. The American
Revolution was supposed to achieve it, and a socialized British society
has envisaged its expression. For many a sincere social reformer free
public (state) schooling is the instrument. But Colin Ward says, 'The
universal education system turns out to be yet another way in which the
poor are obliged to subsidize the rich.'

Finally, because our institutions are very much with us, yet tend to
reflect the ideas, ideals, and ideologies of the time of their establishment, they must always be subject to revision and renovation. To fail to
do so is to run the risk of becoming but historical objects perpetuating
past performances that have little relevance to present conditions. This
is no less true in education than elsewhere, for as R. F. Goodings and
Joseph Lauwerys once wrote about schools, 'Institutions rapidly acquire
a quasi-life of their own . . ... They acquire traditions and habits which
stand them in lieu of instinct and thought. They resist any kind of
pressure which might change or modify their structure and the hierar-
chies of individuals of which they are composed.'[3]

Because it is extremely difficult to get schools to change, to become more adequate agencies or institutions for education, to be continually open to the needs of human consciousness, new schools, acting as new models, largely freed from past constraints and able to work out new patterns and possibilities (until they become steeped in their own conservatism), are required. Michael Huberman writes in detail about a new school, l'École Active in Geneva, which he helped to create and direct and has extensively studied, in 'Teaching, learning, and coping in "progressive" schools'.

Is there any more to be said? Yes, but as this is not a book of recipes for pedagogical kitchens, but rather a gathering of ingredients, the final word must be the reader's. Do you recall the words of *The Prophet* by Kahil Gibran?

Then said a teacher, Speak to us of Teaching.
And he said:
No man can reveal to you aught but that which already lies half asleep in the dawning of your knowledge.
The teacher who walks in the shadow of the temple, among his followers, gives not of his wisdom but rather of his faith and lovingness.
If he is indeed wise he does not bid you enter the house of his wisdom, but rather leads you to the threshold of your own mind.[4]

Notes and References

1 John Locke, 'An Eassy Concerning Human Understanding', Book II, ch. 1, in Edwin A. Burtt, Ed., *The English Philosophers from Bacon to Mill* (New York: The Modern Library, 1939), p. 248.
2 For a full description of Dartington Hall, see Anthony Emery, *Dartington Hall* (Oxford: The Clarendon Press, 1970), and V. Bonham-Carter, *Dartington Hall* (London: Phoenix House, 1958).
3 R. F. Goodings and J. Lauwerys, in G. Z. F. Bereday and J. A. Lauwerys, Eds, *The Year Book of Education* (New York: Harcourt, Brace & World, 1964), p. 478.
4 Kahil Gibran, *The Prophet* (London: William Heinemann Ltd, 1926; New York: Alfred A. Knopf, 1961), pp. 56–57.

The Authors

Sir Alec Clegg has had a lifetime of experience in education. Coming from a family of teachers—his father was his own headmaster—Sir Alec began his career as a language teacher. In time he turned to educational administration, becoming ultimately the Chief Education Officer for the West Riding of Yorkshire. By no means restricted to schoolroom activities, Sir Alec has served on the Council of Industrial Design, the School Broadcasting Council, the Central Advisory Committee on Education, the Social Science Research Council, and the Governing Council of the Open University. He is Chairman of the Governors of the Centre for Advice and Information in Educational Disadvantage, and is a Trustee of the Dartington Hall Trust. Sir Alec Clegg received an M.A. degree from Clare College, Cambridge, an Honorary LL.D. from Leeds University, and an Honorary D. Litt. from both Loughborough University of Technology and the University of Bradford in England. He was knighted for his services to education in 1965.

Maurice Ash is the Chairman of the Dartington Hall Trust, Totnes, Devonshire, England, and Director of its associated companies and institutions. He farms land in Devonshire and East Anglia, is Chairman of the Executive of the Town and Country Planning Association, London, and of the recently formed Green Alliance ecology group. Maurice Ash's interests encompass philosophy—with a special concern for Wittgenstein—art, music, and literature, land use, ecology, and education. He is the author of *The Human Cloud, Regions of Tomorrow, Where are the Progressives Now?*, and *A Guide to the Study of London*. He received a B.Sc. degree in Economics from the London School of Economics.

James Henderson was a Senior Lecturer in History at the Institute of Education, University of London, where he taught from 1945 until his retirement in 1977. He had previously carried out social relief work as a conscientious objector during the war years, and prior to that was a teacher, with a period spent at Bedales School. Concerned with the international nature of education, he was until January 1979 Chairman of the World Education Fellowship. He is author of *A Bridge Across Time*, published by Turnstone Books, London, in 1975.

Mark Braham is a philosopher of education with particular interests in the philosophy of nature and its implications for education. Previously an Associate Professor of Education at Concordia University, Montreal, and Scholar-in-Residence at Dartington Hall, he was the Chairman, for the first three years, of the 'New themes for education' conference (now called the Dartington Conference). He is Secretary General of the International Association for Integrative Education, and Advisory Director of the Bridge Educational Trust, Dorset, England, and a member of the Council of the Teilhard Centre for the Future of Man, London. He received his B.A. degree from Goddard College, Plainfield, Vermont, USA, a Academic Diploma in Education from the University of Illinois, and a Ph.D. also in Philosophy of Education from Stanford University, Palo Alto, California, USA.

John and *Elizabeth Newson* are a husband-and-wife team who have been working together on long-term studies of child development since they met at the University of London. They are Co-directors of the Child Development Research Unit in the University of Nottingham. Their joint publications include *Patterns of Infant Care in an Urban Community, Four Years Old in an Urban Community, Seven Years Old in the Home Environment, Perspectives on School at Seven Years Old*, and *Toys and Playthings in Development and Remediation*. John and Elizabeth Newson are concerned about the role of play in early child development, a concern that has extended to the design of children's toys. They are consultants to a well-known toy manufacturing company. John Newson received his B.Sc. and Elizabeth Newson her B.A. from the University of London, and their Ph.D. degrees in Child Psychology from the University of Nottingham.

John Shotter is a Lecturer in Psychology at the University of Nottingham. His early concerns were with mechanisms and computers until, in 1969, he began to devote himself to studying the properties of social life. With a basically philosophical approach to psychology he has published *Images of Man in Psychological Research* and *Human Action and its Psychological Investigation* (with Alan Gauld). He gave the principal address, 'Models of man' at the British Psychological Society Conference, Cardiff, Wales, in 1979. John Shotter received his BSc. degree in Psychology and Mathematics from the University of London.

Robin Hodgkin began his professional career as a geographer, became a teacher, was Head of the Rural Institute of Education in the Sudan, and Headmaster of Abbotsholme School in England. Until his recent retirement he was a Lecturer in Education at the Department of Educational Studies, Oxford University, with a particular interest in the philosophy of Michael Polanyi and its implications for education. He is also a mountaineer who has climbed in the Karakorum and Caucasus ranges. His publications include *Education and Change, Reconnaissance on an Educational Frontier,* and *Born Curious.* He received his B.A. degree from Oxford University.

James Hemming is a clinical psychologist working in industry, and education, and with adolescents. He is widely known as a broadcaster and author, with an interest in human development and brain physiology. He is a member of the Educational Advisory Committee of the United Kingdom Commission for UNESCO; President of the British Humanist Society; Educational Advisor to the World Education Fellowship, and Chairman of the Community Development Trust. He received a B.A. in English, a B.A. in Psychology, and a Ph.D. in Psychology from the University of London.

Frank Musgrove is the Sarah Fielden Professor of Education at the University of Manchester, England, recently the Dean of his faculty, and previously was Professor of Education at the University of Bradford, Yorkshire. He has been concerned with the nature of society and the sociology of education, and more recently has turned with a sympathetic understanding to the study of the counter-culture. He is author of *The Migratory Elite, Youth and the Social Order, The Family, Education and Society, Society and the Teacher's Role, Patterns and Power and Authority in English Education, Ecstasy and Holiness: Counter Culture and the Open Society,* and *Margins of the Mind.* He received his B.A. degree from the University of Oxford and his Ph.D. from the University of Nottingham. Professor Musgrove wishes to acknowledge the research assistance of Roger Middleton and Pat Hawes for his contribution to this volume.

Spencer Millham is a former schoolteacher who has turned his attention to the problems of the children and adolescents whose 'social offences' have led them into institutional custody. Director of the Dartington Social Research Unit, and Senior Research Fellow at Bristol University, he was previously a Research Officer at the Research Centre, King's College, Cambridge University, England. He is author of *The Hothouse*

Society, A Manual to the Sociology of the School, The Chance of a Life-time (with R. Lambert and R. Bullock), *After Grace—Teeth* (with R. Bullock and P. Cherrett), and *Locking Up Children* (with R. Bullock and K. Hosie). He holds an M.A. degree from Cambridge University.

Colin Ward is the Environmental Education Officer for the Town and Country Planning Association, London, and Director of the School Council project, 'Art and the Built Environment'. He is Editor of *BEE, the Bulletin of Environmental Education*. Having left school at the age of 15, Colin Ward worked in an architectural office and later qualified as a teacher. An early social critic, he became the Editor of the journal, *Anarchy*. He is also author of *Anarchy in Action, Vandalism, Tennants Take Over*, and *Housing: An Anarchist Approach*.

Michael Huberman is Professor of Education and Head of the Department of Research and Training in Educational Psychology at the University of Geneva, Switzerland. Formerly on the staff of UNESCO, Michael Huberman prepared a vital but suppressed criticism of its educational activities. Committed to educational innovation, he is the Co-founder and previous Co-ordinator of l'École Active in Geneva. He was recently a visiting scholar at Stanford University. His publications are *Solving Educational Problems, Understanding Change in Education*, and *Permanent Education: Some Models of Adult Learning and Adult Change*. He received his B.A. from Princeton University and his M.A. and Ph.D. from Harvard University.

Aspects of Education
Edited by M. Braham
© 1982 John Wiley & Sons Ltd.

Chapter 1

The Development of Education in the Twentieth Century

*Sir Alec Clegg**

Any education service at any time in its history will be subject to a variety of pressures. There will be, for example, the intention of government; there will be contemporary attitudes and prejudices; there will be pedagogical innovations; and there will be the convictions of individuals, be they philosophers, administrators, or teachers. And of course some of the pressures will be helpful and some harmful.

I propose to look at some of the *attitudes* which have influenced what we do, even if they were generated in the last century, as they may put us on our guard.

Then I think it is worth looking at some past *practices* even if they are odd, as we must constantly bear in mind no generation has had a monopoly of educational folly.

We should remind ourselves also of the good or ill that individuals can bring about in the education service.

And finally we should, I think, look at some of the things we now do in the light of current attitudes and prejudices.

Attitudes

How powerful can attitudes be and how are they influenced by the conditions of the day?

It was not, I think, unreasonable in the sixteenth century for one Richard Pace to say, 'I swear by God's body I would rather my son

---

* Formerly Chief Education Officer, West Riding of Yorkshire.

should hang than study letters. For it becomes the sons of gentlemen to play the horn well, to hunt skilfully and elegantly and to carry and train the hawk, but the study of letters should be left to the sons of mean people.'

Three centuries later this attitude has been reversed and a distinguished bishop said, 'It is safest for the government and for the religion of the country to let the lower classes remain in that state of ignorance in which nature has already placed them', and a certain Dr Whitaker said that 'translations from the Latin were not needed by gentlemen and they were no concern of others'.

This attitude continued well into this century. When I first started teaching in 1932, conditions were much as they are today and the May Committee cut our salaries by 10 per cent. They were appalled at our national extravagance and put their prejudice in these words: 'The education provided by the State is sometimes superior to that provided for children of middle class parents.'

Yet nearly a hundred years before the May Committee's statement was made, one of Matthew Arnold's colleagues, HMI Henry Moseley, had said in his report to the Lords of the Treasury, 'Education is not a privilege to be graduated according to men's social condition but the right of all in as much as it is necessary to the growth of every man's understanding, and into whatever state of life it may please God to call him an essential element in his moral being.'

When our present century began, prejudices and passions on educational matters were at their most vehement and, although the government had taken the momentous step of allowing secondary schools to be built at public expense, what really set the country ablaze was the idea that the public purse should support church schools. Now in my view the compromise that was reached at that time on this matter was one of the wisest and most sensible steps ever taken in education administration in this country and it saved us from much of the administrative cost and duplication which one still finds in Canada, Australia, the United States, and elsewhere.

In the early years of the century feeling was violent. Lloyd George said of the 1902 Education Bill that it 'was originated by a wily Tory Cardinal, promoted by state clergy, who accepted Protestant pay for propagating Catholic doctrines', and added that its advocacy 'was the last act of treachery in the career of one who had sold most of his principles'. The County of Glamorgan said they would not operate the Act, and indeed for some time refused to do so. In the West Riding, Alderman Willy Clough said, 'We propose to administer the Education Act in so far as we think it wise and leave the administration of those parts of the Act that we think are not wise. This is not violating the Act, it is simply not carrying it out.' The debate on the Bill lasted from 16 October to 11 November when the guillotine was applied, and on one night between 11.00 p.m. amd 3.00 a.m. there were no fewer than 22 divisions. On another occasion one third of the government supporters walked out of the House.

What was involved here was public passion, and both my grandfathers had their silver teapots distrained by the bailiffs because they refused to pay the rate.

But the Act was passed, church schools were paid for out of public funds and secondary schools were built.

The building of secondary schools brought in more passion and prejudice. How were the children to be selected for them? Were they to be the children whose parents could pay or were they to be gifted pupils who could pass a minor scholarship examination?

It was decided to accept both on stated proportions, and for the next half century we battled with the belief that a magic device called the Intelligence Quotient would enable us to pick out at the age of 11 the children who would prove to be the most academically able four or five years later—and the superstition still persists.

Having looked at a few prejudices, let us turn to practice

What went on in the schools? Why did we, for instance, in my youth talk not of classes or forms but of standards? By 'standard' we meant a group of 40 to 60 children in an elementary school.

My grandfather as a boy had to express £5.5.6¼ and 1/20 of a farthing as a decimal of £7.10.8¼ and 11/14 of a farthing. There might have been some virtue in this, but he had also to know what an illative co-ordination is, and there is probably only one person in the world who knows this and 'that's me', or if you are doing 'O' level English 'I am he'. He had also to sing moral songs, such as 'All I drink is water bright', and in Coles's *History of the Education of the Working Classes* in the City of Leeds there occurs the sum: 'Solomon had 100 wives and 300 concubines, add the concubines to the wives and state the result.' This is what today we might call integration of mathematics and religious education.

My grandfather also parsed. I once calculated that he did some 200 vertical yards of parsing between the ages of 10 and 15 but, although he became what was known in his day as a Queen's Scholar, he did not write at the age of 15 any more effectively than his great grandson who never parsed anything. What, one must ask, was the purpose of his parsing?

Incidentally he had also to learn what a copulative conjunction was and, when asked, would answer, 'Also, likewise, moreover, further, and furthermore.'

This kind of learning became a rigid part of the system and continued well into this century. Most people who attended secondary schools and are now in their fifties prepared for School Certificate English by learning from Nesfield's English Grammar all about metonymy and synecdoche and that 'he lay all night on a sleepless pillow' was a transferred epithet.

It is perhaps worth looking at a detailed example of this. Let me quote one I came across in a book of William Cowper's verse in which was written this extract:

> The cattle mourn in corners where the fence
> Screens them and seem half petrified to sleep
> In unrecumbent sadness. There they await
> Their wonted fodder not like hungering man
> Fretful if unsupplied but silent meek
> And patient of the slow paced swain's delay.

A delicate piece of writing, but one which produced this strange effect in the classroom:

'Where the fence screens them' is an example of an adjective sentence intro-duced by an adverb. Here 'where' equals 'in which'. 'Half petrified' is an adjective qualifying 'they' understood and forming an enlargement of the subject. 'To sleep' is a gerundial infinitive, adjectival in tone, qualifying 'they' predicatively and forming the complement of the copulative verb 'seem'. The epithet 'unrecumbent' is transferred from the 'cattle' themselves to the 'sadness' which is associated with them, hence this is an example of hypallage.

And so the child learns to enjoy good poetry.

I am fairly sure that when our grandchildren go through our 'O' level and 'A' level examination papers, and particularly when they investi-gate the subjects of some of our educational researches, they will be at least as astonished by, and critical of, what we do, as we are as a result of some of the examples I have quoted.

These then are some of the effects which attitudes and pedagogical practice have produced and few would deny that some of the practices of the past, to say the least, now seem to us a little bizarre. But before I take a look at our current education, let me say a little about the achievements of certain individuals merely to remind ourselves that individuals can bring about change for good or ill in the education process. I mention only a few and these are people in whom I have had a particular interest. Let me start with one who I believe did great damage.

One of the great characteristics of our education service has been, and still is, that we overemphasize and overvalue what we can measure, and neglect and undervalue what is not susceptible to measurement. I suspect that the origins of this lie in the standards which formed the Code of the last century. The idea was first put forward by the Newcastle Commission of 1861 and was eventually promulgated by Robert Lowe in his scheme of payment by results. I go back to this because I think that it has affected and probably still affects our twentieth-century education. Robert Lowe it was who said:

I do not think it is any part of the duty of Government to prescribe what people should learn except in the case of the poor where time is so limited that we must fix on a few elementary subjects to get anything done at all. . . . The lower classes ought to be educated to discharge the duties cast upon them. They should also be educated that they may appreciate and defer to a higher cultivation when they meet it, and the higher classes ought to be educated in a very different manner, in order that they may exhibit to the lower classes that higher education to which, if it were shown to them, they would bow down and defer.

These, let us remember, were the views of the founder of our public education service in this country, and as a result of these views what had to be taught was set down in yearly doses, and whether it had been learned was, as you all know, measured by HMI. Children were graded in standards according to their ability to master each yearly dose, and the school was not given a grant for the pupil unless he could so master it.

We may think that this was a development of excruciating stupidity, in that it ignored the variations in background and ability and a host of other limiting factors. But it still happens. The way I found it happening within the last year seems to me far more ludicrous than anything Robert Lowe did, though the similarity between them is obvious. I collected these American examples in Michigan:

By the end of the pre-Kindergarten experience 90 per cent of all children will demonstrate their recognition of at least 3 of the 5 basic emotions (fear, anger, sadness, joy and love) in self and others as measured by a future Michigan Educational Assessment Program pattern of tests.

By the end of the pre-Kindergarten experience 90 per cent of all children will demonstrate increased understanding of the concept of sexuality.

By the end of the 3rd Grade children will create vocal or instrumental

accompaniments to songs using combinations of melodic, harmonic or rhythmic patterns as measured by a minimum criteria on an Objectives Reference Test.
> Example:– While the class sings the chorus of 'Oh Susanna' the child plays the tambourine any way he chooses.

By the end of the 3rd Grade students will voluntarily choose linear media to interpret personal feelings as measured by a minimum criteria on an Objectives Reference Test.

It is easy enough for us to draw fun out of this kind of thing, but let us not forget that the fashionable movement in this country nowadays is once more accountability. We have ceased to pay by results, we have ceased to revere the Intelligence Quotient as we once did, but the same danger is likely to last in whatever form accountability may take in the future.

Having said this, we must not forget what wiser individuals have done. I think, for example, of the benefits we have drawn within this century, from people like the Macmillan sisters, from Susan Isaacs, from Rudolf Laban and Kurt Hahn who, without the recognition from us that they should have received, virtually recast our practice and use of physical education. I think also of Cizek and our own Marion Richardson, who did for art what Laban and Hahn did for physical education. There were some like John Dewey whom I think we misinterpreted, and others such as Thring of Uppingham and Armstrong of the City and Guilds of London Institute. I cannot resist quotations from these two—we have not yet caught up with them. First of all Thring, writing nearly 100 years ago:

Marvellous computers can be imagined of force bodily and intellectually able to carry on when set in motion every process of mechanical skill. These computers would figure as agents of a high order, busy with innumerable problems of calculation and statistics, science, measuring other people's thoughts and exercising all kinds of coercive power as well as all the fact collecting power in the universe.

But powerful and honoured as these computers would be they would be separated eternally from the feeblest tenderest birth of human thought and feeling requiring man to think and feel it. The distinction is very vital and it cannot be disregarded in education.

Mental factory wheels and the scintillations of life are different in kind and might belong to two different worlds, though both are packed into man's being.

I have of course cheated here—Thring used the word 'automata' not 'computer' and there is, I suppose, a difference.

But Armstrong, who was writing at about the same time—perhaps just into this century—I find as moving as Thring. These few comments seem so apt if applied to the good primary school methods of our day:

The whole policy of the teacher's duty is summed up in one little word yet the most expressive in the English language—it is to train pupils to 'do'. Gradually I would have nearly all classrooms converted into workrooms—teachers would constantly move about noticing what is being done, criticising and giving brief directions to one group of pupils after another . . . when such a system is adopted an effective punishment will be a few days' banishment from the workroom to the bread and water solitary confinement atmosphere of the old-fashioned classroom.

We pride ourselves on our new invention of team teaching but Armstrong said years ago:

The advantage being that the teacher—or teachers, where several combine to take a composite class—could find time to pass round the class and criticise the doings of each pupil. To make such teaching effective, the account of the work done should be most carefully written out by the worker as the work proceeds— the dictation of notes by the teacher being regarded as a criminal offence.

Finally:

As to apparatus, it should be gradually provided to meet requirements as they arise and every effort should be made to utilise ordinary articles . . . and to construct apparatus in the workroom; a carpenter's bench and tools, vice and files and a small lathe and anvil and even a small forge should whenever possible form part of the equipment. Infinite injury is done at the present day, invaluable opportunities of imparting training are lost by providing everything ready made.

Fears and hopes

Well now I have said something about the attitudes and practices of the past which have influenced development of our education service. I have mentioned as examples some of the individuals who have made their imprint on the service, and others where wisdom at the time failed to make its mark. May I now turn to the present and mention the things that make me fearful and the things that give me hope.

It is idle to pretend that our civilization is all that it ought to be. We can congratulate ourselves on flight, electronics, the moon landings, the reduction of poverty, and a whole host of achievements in which education has played a major part. But education has also contributed to the two bloodiest wars in history, to genocide, napalm, and lethal bacteria, to the technology of crime, to dull conveyor belt occupations, to pollution, to the squandering of resources, and so on. And when we talk of education we tend to forget the most important side of it. We think what a marvellous thing is nuclear power, but education also has to do with the use and abuse of it and we are seldom as clear about this distinction as we should be. It is a distinction which I once saw expressed in a curious little verse burned with a poker into a piece of plywood. It is a repellent practice, but this was the verse:

> If thou of fortune be bereft
> And of thine earthly store hath left
> Two loaves sell one and with the dole
> Buy hyacinths to feed the soul.

Loaves and hyacinths.
Notation and fine music.
Reading and the enjoyment of fine books.
Historical facts and the visions of evil and greatness that history reveals.
The Bible stories and honesty and compassion.
The law of the Old Testament and the love of the New.
Scanning and analysing a poem and enjoying it.
The making of the bomb and the decision against whom to release it.

In the past, and indeed almost up to the present, education has consisted of emphasizing the loaves which can be measured—the cognitive, as we call it in the jargon—and minimizing the significance of the hyacinths—the affective.

We have overvalued the technician's side of the teacher's job, the teaching of the facts, and undervalued the professional side, which consists of the ability to detect and remove the impediments to learning and to foster and encourage all that will stimulate and promote it.

Yet in any class we go into anywhere on God's earth one child will be the most shy, one will have the least support from home, one will like his teacher least, one will be least liked by his teacher, one will have the worst health, one will be the least articulate, and all these deprivations and many others as well are likely to do far more damage to his learning than will the teaching methods used by his teachers.

We ruthlessly emphasize the cognitive side of our learning by an examination system which is so costly that it consumes a sum equal to half the amount that a school has to pay for its books, stationery, and apparatus.

But this is not the worst that we do. In far too many schools concern for the child diminishes with his ability. The gifted will succeed and bring credit to the school so they must have the best teachers, the smallest classes, the most lavish resources, while those who stand most in need are bereft. In short, give all to those who can manage the loaves.

Then there is the lamentable practice of turning the hyacinths into loaves. Art must be marked so you must award marks for its technical skill, and immediately its creative and expressive force is diminished and it has less power to develop the child as a person. I came across a powerful example of this recently. Admittedly it was prescribed a long time ago but the practice, though disguised, is not dead. HMI's instruction on Drawing for Infant Boys in the 1890s:

I am to inform you that drawing may be taught to infant boys on the lines of the Froebel system. Slates ruled crossed lines making squares $\frac{1}{4}''$ each side should be used and on them children should be made to draw perpendicular, horizontal and diagonal lines. Interest may be given to the exercises by making figures or patterns out of the combinations developed in this practice but the main object of the teaching should be the training of the hand to execute with nicety and precision and the eye to discern degrees of variation in the straight lines from the perpendicular or horizontal and to compare and judge the relative lengths of the lines and the angles made by their junction.

We are not as bad as this nowadays, but the tendency to turn a hyacinth into a loaf which can be weighed and measured is undoubtedly still there.

To complete my threnody, I must mention one other lamentable fact of our system. At the beginning of this century we used to select 10 per cent or fewer of our youngsters for secondary education. They consisted of those parents could pay and those who could pass the county minor scholarship. Their selection was seen as a reward or privilege and it did not greatly disturb the remaining 90 per cent. Now, however, that we are selecting not 10 per cent but 50, 60 or 70 per cent for some form of higher education, we are not giving a reward to the few who are selected, we are inflicting ignominy and disregard on the 20 to 30 per cent at the other end of the ability range who see themselves passed over. And we wonder why they vandalize. As one youngster put it to me quite simply: 'Well you've got to make your mark somehow, haven't you?' What is happening is that we are caring for the afflicted, the blind, the deaf and the subnormal, we are caring for the gifted and the average, but to the group of less able normal children we are saying: 'You don't matter because we don't need you even to hew wood or draw water.'

Where lies hope?

There is no doubt in my mind that the greatest steps forward have occurred in our infant schools, and this has happened because the teachers there are forced to take note of the way in which the home has influenced the child. If the child is miserable, or will not talk, or is frightened, the teachers have to put these matters right in order that they can begin to teach. The junior schools and the secondary schools have a much poorer vision of these personality problems.

But the junior schools also—or some of them—have made vast steps forward. They accept that every child must succeed and they have dropped the practice of grading pupils in a way which ensures that 20 per cent of them are continual failures who constantly live down to the lowest expectations of them.

They act on simple but powerful principles, that a child will talk and write and paint more effectively about something he has done than something he has merely heard of; that a child will be more eager if he is allowed some choice, albeit a choice carefully arranged by his teacher; that he will be helped if he can work at his own pace rather than have to mark time or hurry to catch up. Above all, they have realized that all subjects cannot be taught in the same way. The loaves and hyacinths are not evenly distributed in them.

Two plus two equals four is a matter of loaves—the child gets it right or wrong.

If a child learns the 'Ode to Autumn', the accuracy of his memory is a matter of loaves, but his joy in it and his powers of expression are matters of hyacinths.

If a child writes or paints or models as a result of a moving experience, the context is pure hyacinth.

It is this latter point that in personal writing, painting, modelling, dancing, the child does his own thing that has made so much difference to our junior schools, and where this expressive work is well done the academic side, the loaves, is far better handled and the discipline is something which comes from the children themselves. On these points I have no doubt whatsoever. But there is a mystery about this, and I cannot fully solve it. I do not know how it comes about that teachers with no expertise themselves in the use of a medium, and who also have a conscientious objection to giving instruction in the use of that medium, nevertheless can produce pupils who develop extraordinary skill and sensitivity and most powerful endeavour. And I must repeat that whenever this happens academic standards rise and discipline difficulties disappear.

On our secondary side I draw comfort from the fact that the examination system is becoming so grotesque that radical reform is almost bound to emerge, and I am encouraged to find so many schools where attention, genuine and concerned attention, is being given to the slower learners. Any time now we shall find out what is the best that can be done for them, and there may well be as a consequence a complete reform of the subject packaged system which we now enforce on the gifted.

I am also encouraged by the fact that there is more vitality in the further education field. I certainly know of one or two schools which are open for longer periods during the year for further education than they are for school purposes and what is even more significant, more and more the local people, small neighbourhood groups, are being given the responsibility for organizing what they do.

The old school practice of 'this is what you have to do, this is how you have to do it, do it or else' is on the way out.

The old further education practice of 'this is the programme we are putting on for you, take it or leave it' is also on the way out. But there are dangers against which we must guard.

We now have a lot of junior schools working in the new ways. Some are doing it badly and they are, as a friend of mine put it, 'like a wet play-time all day'. When they do it badly the press and the broadcasters pick them out and expose them, and some of the mud sticks on to those schools which are doing a good job, and the backlash sets in.

Then there are always those who say: 'Suffer little children with an IQ of 130+ to come unto me for they shall add most to the gross national product.'

There are also those who promote the cult of management and who believe that accountability will be the answer to all our problems.

What I hope for is that the balance of our education will change and that the hyacinths will flourish, but we shall need continual vigilance if they are to be fully nourished.

Aspects of Education
Edited by M. Braham
© 1982 John Wiley & Sons Ltd.

Chapter 2

The Progressive Inheritance and its Renewal

*Maurice Ash**

My subject regretfully, can be accommodated only in the widest of frames—of civilization itself. This is not just because education is the transmission by one generation of all that matters to the next. It is also because within our civilization there is a perennial tension, one which haunts that process of transmission. This tension is that between the person and the world: in other words, the ultimately religious question about the Self and its surrounding immensity. It will be my theme that what we call 'progressive education' takes sides in this relationship, and is therefore as enduring as that tension itself: and further, that philosophy is today forging a tool to give intellectual respectability again to an educational stance which has largely been written off as staled romanticism.

The trouble with this approach, I know, lies not just in my own possible inability to paint on so broad a canvas, but also in the scepticism rightly growing towards all the grand theories of life: all the emptiness in which our idealizations of the world have ultimately left us. In extenuation, then, I would only say that I want, not so much to paint on this large canvas, as to clear away some of the nonsense on it; and that I am concerned, not so much with some interpretations of life, as with the meanings to be found in what we make of it.

When I speak about our civilization I am thinking of what the Koran calls 'The Peoples of the Book'—that is, Jewry, Christendom, and Islam. Perhaps I should add the Greeks, whom Islam excluded, and for the very good reason that therby it excluded the problem. The problem, I mean, of personality. For the scandal of Christianity, for Islam, was that

---

* Chairman, Dartington Hall Trust; Chairman of Executive, Town and Country Planning Association, London.

13

it had divided God, who is indivisible; yet Christianity had done this—and therein, I think, lay its very potency—because through the Trinity it resolved the contradiction between the Jewish Jehovah, remote and law giving, and the humanism of Greek civilization with Man's personal sense of himself. If, then, today Islam with its rhetoric, its poetic caravan of Man, its very irrationality, is the proselytizing religion (as it is) we in the West remain irredeemably burdened with our rational self-consciousness. We are thus back almost where we began.

Moreover, in all practicality, we have to resolve this problem of personality—why it possesses us—in our own terms, even though there has been much turning towards the East for guidance over recent years. Buddhism, it is true, is much about the same problem—the problem of the Self and how it should be conquered—and there are affinities between some Buddhist thought and the latest phase of Western (i.e. post-Wittgenstein) philosophy that seem to me profoundly moving. But, in practice, we have to start from where we are—so to speak, unconverted, and condemned each to live with his idea of himself. Moreover, if I have carried you thus far in setting my stage, I must not push my luck.

What I have to do next is to locate in our own times—by which I mean, in our era of the Christian civilization—where the 'person' is to be found in our everyday scheme of things. Immediately, however, I would entertain the view, ever more widespread, that we are at a watershed between eras of ideas. Indeed, this is the justification for my now taking such wide bearings on our lives, and not least on education. By the inverse of this token, however, I would excuse myself from any discussion of Plato—conventional as this would be in any survey of Western educational thought—except to say how deeply I sympathize with Robert Pirsig's views in *Zen and the Art of Motorcycle Maintenance* (a philosophical journey, incidentally, as deeply moving as it is personal) that Plato perpetrated the biggest deception in all history. By this, I simply mean his successful suppression of the Sophists' case, that Man is the measure of all things. My own view is that the era we are entering is precisely the one that could make restitution for that crime. This, of course, is to raise an educational hornet's nest.

In my search, therefore, I start with Descartes, because without question his rational idealism marks the beginning of the modern mind. I should perhaps first justify my tracing a course (primarily, though not exclusively) in terms of ideas rather than, say, of historical events. Yet, if I start by recalling the philosophers, my thoughts are bent towards action. We have, however, got so far lost in our times that we must pick our bearings from the markers we have left behind, and amongst these are a few ideas which have touched whole generations of practice. In doing this I risk being insufficiently academic for some (which I do not mind) and too abstruse for others (which I should much regret). I must take this risk, however, not just for the economy of effort it offers me, but rather because I am sure we have to forge a new language of education. We cannot do this without some understanding of what lies behind the discourse. For this reason, also—and for all my bent towards action—do not expect any blueprint from me at the end, no sensational successor to deschooling, say. Rather, excuse my allusiveness! For one person cannot make a language on his own, he can only reconnoitre for contact with others, and action itself may better wait until the new discourse is in being.

Moreover, for modern philosophy my particular theme has been crucible. I think this theme was also evident enough in history— particularly, say, in the French and American Revolutions—and in culture, with the Romantic movement and its central cult of the Hero; and I am quite sure that today—subsumed under such terms as 'identity', 'alienation'—it is critical to everyday life. I suppose one might usefully argue that the tide of history itself was what precipitated the modern philosophical discourse: the Protestant era, that is, with Man's sense of his direct responsibility to God, and the whole Renaissance concern for personal integrity, as expressed in Shakespeare's 'This above all—to thine own self be true'. Anyway, Western Man's con-sciousness of his Self, and hence his puzzlement as to how he can know other than himself, has arguably provided the main thread of modern philosophy.

A secondary excuse for my building on the history of ideas would be that there have always been strong links between philosophers and educational thought. I need only refer to Locke, Rousseau, Dewey, Russell, and Whitehead, together with the whole school of Herbartian pedagogues stemming from Hegel. I suppose the connection between knowledge, learning and education must suffice to explain this. Be that as it may, I can assure you my purpose is not to magnify the philosophers, but only to use them to get our bearings. It may help in this to bear in mind that, in the rather poor vocabulary of progressive education, the most accepted description of it has been that it is 'child-centred', and, to that extent, its relationship to the crucial concern of post-Cartesian philosophy must be obvious.

For Descartes, the Self was a thinking substances: 'I knew that I was a substance the whole essence or nature of which simply was to think.' His very body and the whole external world, was outside that incor-poreal substance. The universe was thus knowable, and was found to be governed by mechanistic laws. One might, with hindsight and charity, forgive Descartes the spurious philosophic doubt upon which this self-consciousness was founded. Perhaps he had to go through such a show because of the authority, spiritual and temporal, of which he stood realistically in fear. But from that doubt has stemmed the essential egocentricity of modern thought, and for us this must already foreshadow the question of whether the child-centredness of progressive education does not dangerously partake of the same quality.

The British empiricists in due course weakened the Cartesian foundations of the Self, together with the authority of the Church on which it rested, and in the process Locke did much to establish the educational ideal of the liberal English gentleman—his position founded less on hereditary privilege than on his capacity for experience; an ideal that perhaps survived longer and more potently in the United States, through Jefferson and others in their rural Athens of Virginia, than in England. But Hume, perhaps sensitive to the Industrial Revolution's growing inhumanity of man to man (though he did the most to reassert human intervention in the processes of the world as we may know it) could not put Humpty Dumpty together again, and retired into a baffled scepticism. He could not, that is, reconstruct from his demolition of Descartes, for example, a plausible idea of the Self. This because Kant's purpose—as arguably, his actual achievement: his self-proclaimed 'counter-Copernican revolution', with Man himself (but a much enhumbled Man) exercising his necessary judgement at the centre of the known universe.

Yet Kant's triumph was stillborn, for the Romantic movement was already upon him. This, of course, is where we ourselves as the chorus of progressive educationalists also come on stage, with Rousseau's *Émile*. First, however, to give Kant his due perspective he welcomed the dynamic that Rousseau brought to the idea of the Self, whilst giving warnings (surely justified) of the unself-critical, aesthetic basis of the Romantic movement. Certainly it is said that the only day Kant ever missed his constitutional was that on which his copy of *Émile* arrived. For here indeed was a whirlwind to fill the vacuum left by Hume's scepticism; a marvellous polemic to justify the idea of the person, albeit in the form of a child.

For myself, when I speak of 'the progressive inheritance', it is above all *Émile* I have in mind. By contrast, one should remember that Locke had said the mind begins as 'white paper, void of all character, without any ideas', and he had concerned himself as schoolmasters will with how it should be furnished. In this task Locke was liberal—his pupil would have 'a mind free and master of itself and all its actions'—but paternalistic. 'The affection and tenderness which God hath planted in the breasts of parents towards their children make it evident that this is not intended to be a severe arbitrary government but only for the help, instruction and preservation of their offspring.' Locke, then, thought of the child as an individual, rather than as a person from birth—seeing him, that is, mechanistically fitted to his place in society. 'I have always thought that to direct a young gentleman's studies right, it is absolutely necessary to know what course of life—either by destination of his quality or fortune or the choice and determination of his parents—he is designed to.' (Rousseau, by contrast, was to say that Émile might make neither a priest, a lawyer, nor a soldier, but he would be a man!). Locke was thus liberal, not radical—for that is what, in my educational vocabulary, marks the difference between the conventional and the progressive. Thus, though Locke was no believer in chastisement on principle, yet when the tutor to his correspondent's son fell short of expectations (Locke having, on balance, advocated home education rather than boarding) he suggested in frustration the boy might be sent to 'Westminster or some other severe school, where if he were whipped soundly while you are looking out another fit tutor for him, he would perhaps be more pliant and willing to learn at home afterwards'. (Maybe that strikes a sympathetic chord here, for have we not sometimes asked, 'What do they know of Dartington who only Dartington know?') Yet, compared with all this, how fresh and radical Rousseau still sounds!

Let me remind you of the savour of *Émile*:

Childhood is the sleep of reason.

Childhood has its own ways of seeing, thinking, and feeling.

They are always looking for the man in the child, without considering what he is before he becomes a man.

What a poor sort of foresight to make a child wretched in the present with the more or less doubtful hope of making him happy at some future day. [*Prophetic shadows of our examination treadmill!*]

Every stage, every station in life has a perfection of its own.

Émile should remain in complete ignorance of those ideas which are beyond his grasp.

Reading is the curse of childhood . . .. When I thus get rid of children's lessons I get rid of the chief cause of their sorrow. [*And yet, even in Bacon's time, virtually without benefit of schools, it seems three fifths of the population of England could read.*]

Work or play are all one to him, his games are his work, he knows no difference.

I hate books, they only teach us to talk about things we know nothing about. [*Between Rousseau and the Black Papers, there's no doubt who wins on rhetoric. It is nice to remember he also wrote* **In Praise of Ignorance!**]

Mankind has its place in the sequence of things, childhood has its place in the sequence of human life, the man must be treated as a man and the child as a child. Give each his place.

You must make your choice between the man and the citizen, you cannot train both. [*Meaning, I take it, between the person and society.*]

The art of teaching consists in making the pupil want to learn.

Let him know nothing because you have told him, but because he has learnt it himself. [*Rousseau in effect suspended the curriculum, and said, 'Teach by doing whatever you can, and only fall back upon words when doing is out of the question.'*]

While he fancies himself as a workman, he is becoming a philosopher.

And so forth, all, to my mind, at once limpid and outrageous stuff, and still authentic. Our modern intellectuals seem to understand nothing about Rousseau. (I could think of various reasons why.) But perhaps it is only his own fault. In the end, he could not make it all add up. For society was as much concern to him, of course, as was the person. And must these not, surely, somehow be of one stuff? Rousseau, himself, was loath to choose between the two. So, in the end, he had to resort to the mischievous banality of forcing men to be free; a banality that has come to seem very sick, a sickness—perhaps, the sickness—with which we are still living. In education itself, moreover, the logical contradictions of Rousseau's position could result, not just in his barbarous ideas for the upbringing of Sophie, Émile's feminine counterpart, but in his proposals for Polish education, subordinating all personality to the emergent state as completely as could be imagined.

Sadly, indeed, the symptoms are already there in *Émile* itself, and it is time we recognized this, for all the foregoing quotations come from Émile's childhood. With his adolescence. Rousseau's ebullience deserts him—shades of the prison-house close round the growing boy with a vengeance. The early years will have had their negative value, of course, and Émile will confront society, the external world, the more successfully for being the more himself. We today, however, are all too familiar with the problem of introducing progressive education at the secondary level. It remains a great rarity, because of the social risks, the oppressive claims of society. And yet, as truancy shows, that is when progressive education can most readily be justified. In fact, in the very form of ideas which Rousseau himself introduced—the organic form, in which the Self is immanent in a world organically conceived—it is only in childhood that any separate place for the person as such can at all plausibly be found. And this will not prove adequate.

Perhaps it is for this reason that the nineteenth century seems to me so devoid of educational interests—though of course it is rich in pedagogy. I confess, the Victorian era is to me like a huge blind alley, back out of which, after two world wars, we are only now emerging to take up again the theme of civilization, and against which the best people of the time (I mean, such as Ruskin, Morris, Kropotkin, Tolstoy—I don't mean the Great Victorians) could merely react, more or less hopelessly. This may be only subjective, but it fits my theme. Hegel had it too much his own way—even whilst one has to say that the artist, the Romantic artist, became the surrogate 'person' of the age.

Yet the artist did so, as we know, at the cost of becoming ever more divorced from ordinary life and people, and with an arrogance sometimes above the law—a process that has continued to enfeeble both us and the arts to this day. Perhaps we should admit that art was the only space then allowed for the person in philosophy. In education there was Froebel, of course, with the idea of play—but such didactic and structured play! or so it seems to me. However, was not the German nation in the making and the Industrial Revolution being carried forward by the ruling method of thought, whilst Cartesian knowledge accumulated most satisfactorily? And what more could school be about? Certainly, this state of affairs conformed with the particularly English phenomenon of the egocentric academic as guardian of (supposedly) pure knowledge. Indeed, this remains the ground on which our universities stand, whence it pervades our whole system of schooling.

One must say that if, in our age, the idea of the Self is latently egocentric, then the Romantic movement surely intensified this state. The nineteenth century, despite its mass conformities, seethed with the idea which provided, as it were, the underlife of the period. We recognize now, for instance, that these were the springs of Marx's energies—and, at least in this respect, he was truly Rousseau's successor. Remarking of Hegel that philosophers explained the world (which, actually, they did not) but the task was to change it, Marx in effect made 'the worker' the person in his scheme of things. And of him he said, 'He is not at home when he is working, and when he is working he is not at home.' In other words, he is alienated from himself by the factory. Whatever the shortcomings of this social philosophy, with its virtual lack of a psychology, it is pertinent that Marx both gave his worker/person a discrete place in his universe, and (perhaps more important) turned him from the passive role of a thinker to an active role. (Activity, after all, is one of the hallmarks of progressive education.) In this, perhaps, Marx at least began our process of escape from egocentricity.

It is also worth noting, in my attempt to keep track of the idea of the person, that before *Das Kapital* Marx felt compelled to write (though it was actually unpublished for nearly a hundred years) his *A German Ideology*. In this he took issue, and at great length, with the anarchist views of a now forgotten writer, Max Stirner, who had drawn the logic of egoism to its full conclusion, idealizing the egoist. Anarchism, I suppose one might say, is the politics of the person, and, of course, this doctrine is once again being taken seriously today. It is true that Stirner's ideas seemed so extreme as to be harmless even to the Prussian censorship. But not to Marx! He, if not the authorities, could recognize a real threat when he saw it. Other writers like Kierkegaard, Dostoevsky, and Kropotkin kept the idea of the person alive against all the ominous uniformity of materialism. Ultimately, however, there came the, as I think, inevitable conception and development of psychoanalysis. The Self is indeed too integral to our sense than to have fashioned any other possible outlet for ideas in the circumstances of the nineteenth century.

Here, of course, we come closer to home, because there have always been links—some of them albeit very ill-conceived—between psychoanalysis and the progressive schools. But I do not want to dwell on this, because I do not think anyone would claim that the unconscious is the person itself. The unconscious matters, as the body matters, and if it is not in health one suffers. But, as its very name implies, it is not in commerce with the world, as the person must be. I would only suggest, therefore, that psychoanalysis provided the Self with a sympathetic refuge, and the fact that it has become so predominant in that most Cartesian of countries (as de Tocqueville perceptively described the USA) may illustrate my point.

All this only brings us to the turn of the present century, but thus to that period when what we call 'progressive education' actually began to be practised, and flourished astonishingly. At least, it seems astonishing to look back on those world-wide congresses of the New Education Fellowship with their thousands of delegates, and the dozens of its affiliated schools, in the United Kingdom and other countries. Today, after all, you could hardly say there is a movement. Yet conversely, that earlier movement scarcely drew upon the well of ideas I have been at pains to plumb. It did draw upon it, of course, but only haphazardly, perhaps because there was enough common practice—such as the bias towards activity rather than the academic, or the involvement of children in running their own schools, or an emphasis on the arts—to establish the network of a genuine movement. But it seems generally agreed that the movement, as such, was primarily reactive—that is, a revolt against conventional education—and in this, surely, there was a flaw. And it is because of this flaw, I hope you will understand, that I have just been taking my pains. (I believe, as I shall soon explain, that today we have a common idea, of great potency, ready for the picking.) What one can at least happily say, nevertheless, is that there was remarkably little Utopianism, little social engineering, about the movement in those days. It was always the child itself who mattered.

Of course, I am in no way decrying the marvellous practicality of, say, a Montessori, with whom the child always came before the system, let alone the skill and devotion of all that made for the NEF up to 1939, and beyond. To pursue my philosophical point, however, one is bound to ask, where was progressive education before the turn of the century? If the ideas were as available before that time as now, why was Rousseau not being invoked already? I suppose the answer must have to do with the provision of public education and the grounds—those of social, rather than educational, concern, of getting children off the streets and out of the factories—on which it was really established. I would hazard the guess, then, that progressive education always was taking place, but in the homes, particularly though not exclusively, of the rich. (It may be remembered that Rousseau said he took Émile from a wealthy home because he would be 'another victim saved from prejudice'. The poor, he thought, were nearer to life, and so in less need of saving. I myself have sometimes felt the same about the regimes of comprehensive schools in middle-class as contrasted with working-class areas today; in the one there is instruction, in the other education.) If there is force in my guess, then, it follows that the world was unprepared—educationally, not socially—for public education. In retrospect, indeed, it was logically absurd to base upon Lockean ideas of proconsular schooling an era of mass education. The only logical basis for public, and therefore equitable, education can be the progressive one: of education of the child as a child. Not surprisingly, then, to this general absence of ideas about public education, one has to admit the important exception of John Dewey.

I confess myself a little baffled by Dewey. I cannot claim to know such a prolific writer, nor to follow him from his Hegelianism to his Pragmatism. I must be circumspect, however, because Dewey had long been close to Dorothy Elmhirst in America, before she came here with Leonard in 1925 to start Dartington, and whatever she touched, I respect. He never visited here, but I am sure his imprint on the school was strong. This school was, in fact, in its earliest days quite extraordinary, consisting as it did of the following departments: Garden, Farm, Forestry, Building, Workshop, Crafts, Music, Drama, Publishing, Language, Social Studies, Geography, History, Government, Health, and Accounts. Dewey, like Rousseau, was uninterested in knowledge as the conventional curriculum structures it. The purpose, rather, was to use the activities of the Dartington Estate as a learning resource, whilst the first prospectus announced in Deweyesque tones that the school was not a preparation for life, but life itself.

Things came unstuck rather quickly and I am reminded of the time when Leonard and Dorothy came back from abroad to find that, as a result of a democratic revolution (of which one might have thought Dewey would have approved) the Head Gardener was in charge of the school. Benevolent paternalism was quickly restored, yet I always treasure the enigmatic comment of Mr Calthorpe, the said gardener, 'Now Mr Elmhirst, we understand what you want.' Of course, it would be ridiculous to blame Dewey for that episode, but I do wonder if it does not tell us that the Dewey scheme of things was incompatible with the heady air of personal freedom at Dartington in those days.

My own amateur view, at least, is that Dewey's theory with its American origins, is really to do with social engineering, not the person, and that in his case there is more than a whiff of Utopianism. His 'person' was a synthetic creature, hopefully animated by aesthetic sensibility and liberal social attitudes, but all deterministically arrived at with the aid of a social science in which, with hindsight, hopeless overconfidence was placed. The child, for Dewey, was ultimately an object, and material for detached observation. I am not sure how much this matters, because one is so often in sympathy with Dewey's practical, non-didactic ideas. In practice, moreover, I suspect he himself really was on the side of the child. Yet the point is still important, in so far as his thought, above all, must have set the climate of the comprehensive movement in Britain, and its intellectual limitations therefore remain worrying. To complete the story so far as Dartington was concerned, however, the point is immaterial because with the appointment of W. B. Curry, who became the really formative head of the school in 1931, the influence passed from Hegelian Pragmatism (or whatever it was) to Russell's Atomism, and therewith the school became committed to that child-centred stance in which its perpetual revolution—its renewal through encouragement of the child's personal life—still courageously continues. (However, having said that, I am bound to admit it has been contended that the person, as conceived in Russell's philosophy, logically could not communicate with another person, as such.) Yet, in changing the direction of the school's philosophy, Curry effectively took received knowledge for granted, reducing progressive education to an alternative route to a given end. We are at least lucky, and unique perhaps, at Dartington in having had two such rich educational experiences from which to draw our lessons. It remains for us somehow to draw these distinct streams together.

Now I hope you will have followed the categories of my thought, for they constitute my excuse for calling some holy cows in question. I have arrived at the point of saying that our culture still provides no way of reconciling our ideas of the person and of the world in one and the same conceptual framework, and the debates of the past 20 years on the Left, vainly seeking some reconciliation of Marx and Freud—let alone the titanic dispute between Russia and China—provide some independent confirmation of this view. The discrepancy seems endemic. I am also saying, in case it has not been clear, that what we have called 'progressive education' has been a discourse concerned with the person, or the Self (or the Soul) rather than the world (in this confusion of language games that our culture has become). By this I mean, you can test in any instance where someone starts from (and, in any experience, you have to start from somewhere), whether from the personal or the institutional position, no matter how liberal that may be; and the 'progressive' in education starts from the person. But I, too, am not content with this stance because, no matter how central it has been to our civilization, the tension it maintains seems to me ultimately negative and ruinous of us all.

Briefly, I agree with John MacMurray: 'The central crisis of the present is indeed the crisis of the personal.' I agree with him, also, that this is a problem of escaping from the static and therefore egocentric idea of the Self, and that contemporary Ordinary Language philosophy—because language is two-way—holds the key to this. It is in this that the absolutely radical character of post-Wittgenstein thought consists: the prospect it holds of resolving the tensions upon which Christianity is founded; the tension between the person and the world. God and Caesar are not essentially incompatible, as language at least. That many others also agree about this dynamic reciprocity in the nature of the person is shown by the growth of Existentialist thought, for which Martin Buber's two contrasting basic words—'I–Thou' and 'I–It'—may represent the case. (He, incidentally, was a contributor to the NEF between the wars. May education attract such great men again!) To my mind, these developments in philosophy argue very well for the kind of education for which I am concerned. But let me risk trying to put in a nutshell why I think, the tide of ideas is running our way, such that at last we shall no longer need, against such odds, to borrow soiled concepts in order to make our case.

If I say (as I do) that Wittgenstein's thought is the philosophy of our

times, I do not mean this in any technical sense. I simply mean it is in
tune with the needs of the age, just as Descartes's was instrumental in
overthrowing the decadent Schoolmen. By facing the fact, then, that
words do not (cannot) reflect the world's reality, that rather 'the
meaning of a word is its use in the language', Wittgenstein shifted the
ground of philosophy. He has shifted it from knowledge to meaning,
and he has done so at a time when the value of knowledge is no longer
self-evident, when we are all coming to call in question knowledge
which only leads, through endemic specialization, to the dangerous
despoliation of Nature, to the degradation of work into a mere relationship with the pay packet, and to our loss of identity in lonely
suburbs. In doing this, it seems to me, Kant's counter-Copernican
revolution has been achieved. Man is back at the centre—though,
perhaps, only if he stays silent of what he cannot speak, and is
accordingly humble in himself. Since words (or languages, rather) are a
matter of reciprocity, and so Man is a game-playing animal—not *Homo
sapiens* at all—we can now see that Rousseau need not have strained so
hard to show that the child is somehow a physical reality, nor have
overcompensated in doing so. Not just the child, indeed, but also the
person is not something to which the whole natural world needs to
conform, just so long as our discourse about him makes sense in
whatever situation it occurs: whilst, as for knowledge, it cannot be
'pure', it does not exist for itself, but must find its place in life. And that,
it seems to me, is what progressive education has always been about,
the place of knowledge in life; the meaning to the child of what he or she
learns, the living situation of his experience and the 'doing' rather than
the 'knowing'. Think of Pestalozzi, but also of Tolstoy and Tagore, of
Neill (whose own prized possessions were his tools), and—yes!—
Dewey and Montessori and all the others who in a variety of ways have
evoked the meaning that experience has for a child!

I think, therefore, that with these new instruments of thought our
kind of education can be aggressively espoused as it has not been for
years, whilst conventional education will find itself more and more on
the defensive. (I take it as axiomatic that the Cartesian division of
knowledge into the 'subjects' of the curriculum must—for all the
structures of power it secures—collapse under its own absurdities.) It
was not at all a coincidence, incidentally, that between his two great
periods of work on philosophy, Wittgenstein taught in Austrian village
schools in the 1920s. He did so directly under the influence of the School
Reform Movement in Austria and its anti-authoritarianism: its concern
to give meaning to children in school. These same intellectual tools,
however, call on us to review our own practices.

Let me begin, then, by trying one or two crude heresies. I suggest we have to rid ourselves of the sense of the separateness of childhood—yes! even in Rousseau's sense, and as it now constitutes the glory of our primary schools—because otherwise, alas, we shall never break through the barrier this only builds up before the self-consciousness of adolescence. Next I say, let us forswear any primacy the arts may claim as the way to self-realization in education, along with the egoism they foster. (I really do not want to repeat Black Mountain College here—for all its supposedly glorious, but as I think squalid, failure—at Dartington College of Arts, and I do not think we shall.) For my part, I refuse to accept the opposites of feeling and intellect, or find in the arts a refuge. Somehow, the person must relate to the world, not just to change it, but to be an agent in it.

If these proposals shock, please allow that I know where I start from! My concern is to escape from the ghetto into which our practices at present drive us. My purpose, rather, is to claim the world as now it might be ours. But these are merely reactive and negative proposals; you will want me to be positive. I have, then, two simple basic demands: I want children to earn, and I want them to talk.

When I say I want children to earn, I do not mean I want to deschool them. I think children must, of course, be protected, or sheltered. But I also want school to be where earning occurs. For earning will not take place unless certain disciplines are observed. These, as I think, are the disciplines needed to counteract the egocentricity of the child, seen passively as a child, that produces soft-centred 'progressivism': the disciplines of survival, but administered with the love of which so many people are imbued in their working lives yet never have a chance to show. So I want school to be partly, if not in the factory, then in the workshop or on the farm, and I want the workers to be amongst the teachers. Also, I think there could be a continuum through the ages of childhood in which this earning takes place. Thereby, I would see the too rigid barriers between one age of childhood and another—and, particularly, self-conscious adolescence—being broken down. Perhaps it is worth remembering that both Locke and Rousseau advocated the learning of a trade by the child. To recall Rousseau again: 'Keep the child dependent upon things only', and Dewey said you could concentrate the history of mankind into the making of clothing. It is the extra dimension of earning, though, which should provide 'schools' with its context of realism. Let no one underestimate, however, the difficulty of intermingling the structures that have grown today around the practices of earning and learning, of Industry and Education respectively. My simple precept requires a revolution.

Next, why do I want children to talk? Don't they do that anyway? Not personally, I think. Not so very much as person to person, using the 'I–Thou' word, not the 'I–It' word. The very subjects of the curriculum are conceived in the 'I–It' mode, as knowledge to be 'mastered', for us to lay our rules across, and with even Man treated as an object. (You have only to read between the lines of Descartes's *Method* to see the hatred of Nature that comes through. Perhaps, when life was nasty, brutish, and short, this was admissible. But now . . . now it is our symbiosis with Nature that matters.) To 'talk', in my sense of it, you have to be involved with what you are learning, and that is why the environment is so important, because you cannot learn about the environment abstractly, as a subject, but only by concern with some issue in it. It will be obvious from this, that I am in general sympathetic to the school without walls, to programmes rather than institutions. I know my sort of talking must arise from respect between the parties to it, and as such is already taken for granted in progressive schools. But I think there is much more to it than that, especially in terms of the curriculum—and, anyway, I want all children to have the verbal ability, and hence the skills, which this respect confers.

I will stop there, because there is no point in building castles in the air. We, here at Dartington, will do what we can—and we will have our debates about it—in our own beleaguered educational patch. The Dartington Estate is committed to life as a learning process—and we are glad Recurrent Education is elsewhere making progress too: the only (slight?) difference is that we have always tended to consider school an extension of life, not life of school and hence of academic learning. But until the public system abandons its monolithic structure, no significant change can occur, for this monolith is established on and determined by the module of subjects in a sixth form spanning the spectrum of 'knowledge'; and what I am pleading is the abandonment of that sacred cow, along with all the push-button expectations of the schooled society. I can see nothing in the public system as such which would disallow this step, and in the end I think it will have to happen. Admittedly, it could not be justified in quantitative terms, because implicit in my whole discussion has been a return to respectability of what is qualitative in life. I do not see, for instance, how you could measure growth in wisdom, which is what any development of the person must be concerned with. But really that does not matter, because it is less with *Homo sapiens* than with *Homo ludens*—with the serious or joyous interplay of persons, as the human occupation, and the mode of our understanding—that the future lies.

Perhaps I should conclude with a saying of Wittgenstein's: 'The difficulty in philosophy is to say no more than you know, e.g., to see that when we have put two books together in the right order we have not thereby put them in their final places.'

Chapter 3

A Metaphysics for Education

*James Henderson**

1. Being and Knowing

What a pretentious and presumptuous title! Not really, not if we stick closely to *Oxford English Dictionary* terms, in which metaphysics is defined as 'that branch of speculative enquiry which treats of the first principles of things' (in this case education) as 'the ultimate science of being and knowing' (in this case as it is applied more or less consciously to the ways in which the elders of a society bring up their young). It is, in the language of Gabriel Marcel, 'reflection trained upon mystery' (Marcel, 1965) and especially, in the words of Sir Alec Clegg, the mystery of teaching. Now, because there can be no knowing without a correspondingly adequate state of being, because 'we only understand on the basis of what we are'[1] and because this is a truth which the secular humanism of the West seems to have mislaid, it is chiefly about the Being side that it is necessary to confer. The need for such a dialogue has arisen from certain historical circumstances, which are now compelling forward-looking educationists to ponder whether the direction in which they have been looking is as forward as it once seemed to be. Such a suspicion is confirmed by a quick glance back at the recent educational past.

Is it not the case that Progressive School Movement of the early decades of the twentieth century in general and Dartington in particular constituted the first stirrings of protest against that previous, educational orthodoxy which was enshrined in Christianity and the English Public School gospel of being a 'decent chap'. The protest took the form on the one hand of secular, moral earnestness and on the other of varying degrees of permissiveness in the spheres of sexual mores and manners

* Formerly, Chairman, World Education Fellowship and Senior Lecturer in Education, University of London.

altogether. Both had their protagonists flaunting the banner of child-centredness in the face of the pedagogical establishment and challenged the content and perhaps even more the methods of its policies and practices. It is my contention that, while it undoubtedly rendered essential and valuable services to the cause of Progressive Education at the time, it nevertheless neglected to cultivate Being as contrasted with Knowing: for instance, it failed to discriminate between sexual knowledge and the enlightenment of love, between good and God, between mistake and sin, between maladjustment and evil, between putting up with life and coming to terms with death. The poverty of its metaphysics began to show up under the cruel spotlights of totalitarianism, the Second World War, the Cold War and the violence-spawning aridity of the nineteen-fifties and nineteen-sixties. By the nineteen-seventies violence and terrorism had become an all-too-frequent feature of the public life of nations.

For Progressive education to have a future, it needs to have an identifiable goal towards which to progress that is not imprisoned in the Sartrean dungeon of time, in Musgrove's 'bear-pits',[2] or Barnes's 'Shadow and Thief'.[3] It needs to look in a direction that will include in its educational terrain the necessary corrections to what we are now just beginning to recognize as its inadequacies and aberrations. These corrections will include a pedagogical system embracing time, love, evil, tragedy, death and hope. This in turn demands a metaphysics of education with regard to the learning process, namely one that accepts a science of learning—of learning in order to do—and therefore of teaching derived from a balanced partnership of Being and Knowing. For it is from such a partnership, out of the play between the two, that consciousness is born and can develop. The educative function of play has to be appreciated in its double sense, that of recreation and that of the sustained tension of conflict fully accepted. George Lyward of Finchden Manor ('Waiting consumes my life' and 'Never make a bargain with a child') and C. G. Jung ('No man is whole without negative qualities') were prophets of this creed. The supreme intuition of Eastern philosophy is now required to complement our Western one, a merging which Haas has epitomized brilliantly at the beginning of his profound study on *The Destiny of Mind*

The author remembers being seated on the terrace of a country house overlooking a wide prospect toward a range of high mountains. He was discussing metaphysics with an Indian visitor . . . Suddenly the Indian, pointing at the flowers which grew in abundance in the garden before our eyes, turned to me with an unexpected and seemingly meaningless question. 'Against what background do you see those flowers?' he asked. 'Against the background of those

shrubs,' I answered. 'And against what background do you see those shrubs?'
he continued. 'Against the background of those trees.'

'And against what background to you see those trees?' Again I answered, and
so one question and its manifest answer followed the next until the query came:
'Against what background do you see those clouds moving behind and beyond
the mountains?' The answer was of course: 'Against the sky.' And then came the
final question uttered with the same calm as those preceding: 'And against what
background do you see the sky?' I was left stupefied without an answer. The
Indian turned to me and said with his soft voice: 'I will tell you: against the
background of consciousness.' This was certainly more than an escape man-
oeuvre. Nor was it an ingenious bluff. It was a counter-attack on the Western
way of thinking . . . for it placed consciousness above reason as the ultimate and
superior datum. And it intimated that the development of consciousness might
lead up to quite other results than the investigation of reason.[4]

The metaphysics of education, which will now be outlined, is also 'a
counter-attack on the Western way of thinking', perhaps a redressing of
the balance between right and left hemispheres of the brain or between
'divergent' and 'convergent' thinkers, or in Robin Hodgkin's concept
respecting the need for ambiguity and delay in the educational process.[5]
It too places consciousness above though not against reason as the
ultimate and superior datum, and its cultivation can lead to quite other
results than our present system.

2. History and consciousness

Because of early training and experience, it so happens that my own
step forward into this metaphysical dimension was dictated to me by the
problems I encountered when trying to learn and teach history. These
gradually forced me to formulate a theory of the art of historical study
which I have described elsewhere.[6] All I need do here is to emphasize
the notion in it of the mobility of consciousness in both space and
time—the idea that quite often we are not consciously 'all there or here',
and hence the accompanying need to define history as the record of the
growth of human consciousness. The justification for studying history
in this way is that it can provide an essential ingredient in the means
whereby our levels of consciousness are raised. This happens as we
grasp from the scrutiny of historical events that they are not merely
knots in a string of chronological sequence, but symbols of a transcen-
dental human experience, as valid globally as it is locally, and as such
constituting a vital part of the educational curriculum stretching right
across the planet. 'There is a universality, which is not of the conceptual
order . . . the only possible victory over time must be fidelity as one of
its factors.'[7] It is that universality and that fidelity which are key
components in the only metaphysics of education that matters today,

namely the education of that 'global village' which science and technology have compelled us to inhabit.

Let me try and put some flesh on these dry bones by taking an actual historical happening: in its pedagogical interpretation there are three elements present, the facts themselves, my own capacity for being able to understand them, though only on the basis of what I am, and thirdly the state of Being of a particular age and intelligence of a group of pupils.

John Fines, Principal Lecturer in History at Bishop Otter College of Education, has described excellently the metaphysical dimension of such a history lesson; he is speaking of that intoxicating occasion on which teacher and taught find through history their consciousness extended beyond time and space: 'It is an urgent, vibrant moment, one of those eccentric trips over the edge of time into another level of experience, a level that ignores death and decay and joyfully recognizes the infinite, the extra-terrestrial, the immortal'.[8]

Let us attempt a not too 'eccentric trip over the edge of time' and remind ourselves of the story of Dorothy Osborne (1627–1693) and Sir William Temple (1628–1699). This man and woman lived through most of the seventeenth century in England, never far from the headlines of history but never for long in them. Dorothy was a daughter of Sir Peter Osborne, who fought and suffered for the Cavalier cause in the Civil War, being forced after the Parliamentary victory to live in impoverished seclusion at his family home of Chicksands near Bedford. There, as his sole companion, the girl spent her young womanhood—lonely, stately, delighting in the beauty of the countryside, not altogether unhappy. Then, in 1648, she had a brief first encounter with a young man called William Temple. They fell deeply in love, but both his and her family opposed the match, so that for many weary, long years they had to wait and pine—'Shall we never be happy?', she wrote to him. In the end their constancy was rewarded, their families reluctantly relented, Dorothy came up to London and plunged into the social round, and then on the very eve of her wedding in 1655 was stricken with smallpox and lost her looks. However, they accomplished their goal of marriage, although they did not live happily ever after. Temple was too much away from home on his diplomatic duties for that: 'Mild Dorothea, peaceful, wise and good' (according to Swift) presided over their household at Moor Park. Yet only one of their six children, 'Little Jack', reached manhood, and then he drowned himself in a fit of madness aged twenty-one. Answering a letter of condolence from a nephew, Dorothy wrote:

The strange revolutions we have seen might well have taught what this world is, yet it seems it was necessary that I should have a near example of the uncertainty of all human blessings, so that by having no tie to the world, I may the better prepare myself to leave it and that this correction may suffice to teach me my duty must be the prayer of your affectionate aunt and humble servant, Dorothy Osborne.[9]

Those are the historical facts, which however I can only properly understand on the basis of what I myself am, i.e. my own experiences of expectation, frustration, fulfilment, resignation and transcendence of the body-ego attachment, my own ability to relate these personal, these time-bound, twentieth-century happenings of mine to a period three hundred years ago, and, vice versa, to build a bridge of consciousness over that period and be able to cross it to and fro. This means my being able, from my own acquaintance with it, to recognize and extend deep bonds of intimacy—Herder's *Einfühlen*—existing between lovers even when their bodies and their fortunes have to meet the onset of death and decay. This, the story of Dorothy Osborne and William Temple, can help me to do, for I can identify with their entanglement in the politics of their day as well as its social and moral conventions, which neither of them were prepared to flout openly, but which their loving constancy ultimately circumvented. I can, through something exceeding mimesis, enter into their joys and anguish and at last begin to perceive, as Dorothy did, how all human love, vital and essential as perennial romance declares it to be, is finally driven on to the rocks of shipwreck and decease.

It is by reflecting on the great lovers of history that we can be introduced through our own emotional experiences of attraction and repulsion to a deep and therefore more progressive conception of the nature of the sexual bond, one no longer based on the frantic and futile attempts of two egos to resolve the discords of themselves and their times, to which their very own intimacy is cruelly conducive, but on the calm meeting in mutuality of two personalities, both of whom have discovered and are living from their own, no longer egocentric mid-points but instead from that true midpoint of personality, which Jung called the Self and Martin Buber 'the redemptive third' in a genuine I–Thou relationship.

From studying this piece of history I too receive 'a near example of the uncertainty of all human blessings, so that by having no tie to the world, I may the better prepare myself to leave it'. Just in that one phrase alone lies a pointer to the dramatic and challenging fact that love and death are closely and necessarily and blessedly interlinked, and any genuine education must be able to demonstrate this. By learning and teaching history in this manner, fully exploiting its literally inexhaustible store of objects for empathy, by exposing ourselves to the brutal sequence of mere chronological time (one damn thing after another), but also to the solace of time-transcending love, which triumphs over mere sequence, we may restore a metaphysical dimension to educatioin. True, that for most of us this metaphysics is no longer the Christian one, which inspired Dorothy's convictions, but because its shape is different, its reality need be no less, as this brief study may have helped to show.

3. Evil—tragedy—death—hope

So far then, with the help of the Osborne–Temple story, we have been able to conceive how two components in a metaphysics of education can be restored to the curriculum. First, there is the cultivation among teachers and pupils of an attitude to time that embraces both a sequential, profane and a revelatory, sacred quality. Secondly, there is the deliberate fostering of an attitude to love that validates it both as an expression of the attachments of body-egos to other body-egos, and also as the transcendence of that kind of attachment through the recognizing and reverencing of the reality of our deep selves, redeemed from time.

It will now be necessary to consider the pedagogical treatment of four other factors, each of them central to man's Being, each of them requiring to be known and not just known about. For, as Kierkegaard once remarked, 'There are two ways: one is to suffer; the other is to become a professor of the fact that another suffers'.[10] Indeed there are two ways of education: one is to learn; the other is to become a professor of the fact that another learns, and then of course one has ceased to be a teacher. With regard to the first of these factors, evil, Edward Crankshaw wrote in a review of Solzhenitsyn's *The Gulag Archipelago*, '. . . for a number of generations Western man had lost the sense of evil. Faced with manifestations that were clearly evil, his instinct was to treat them as aberrations. But, now, we know that evil can be everywhere at once.'[11] It is that sense of evil as distinct from a mere awareness of social misfit or economic injustice or personal misfortune, capable of correction by rational means if sufficient attention is paid to them, which we have to educate our pupils to recognize, resist, and at the same time accept. For this achievement they need to be introduced to that sense of evil which is manifested for example in Dostoievski's *The Brothers Karamazov*, Nadezha Mandelstam's *Hope against Hope and Hope Abandoned*, and, above all, in Solzhenitsyn's own observations when he writes:

In keeping silent about evil, in burying it so deep within us that no sign of it appears on the surface, we are implanting it, and it will rise up a thousandfold in the future. When we neither punish nor reprimand evildoers, we are not simply protecting their trivial old age, we are thereby ripping the foundations of justice from beneath new generations. It is for this reason, and not because of the indoctrinational work that they are now growing up indifferent.[12]

and again:

It was granted to me to carry away from my prison years on my bent back, which nearly broke beneath its load, this essential experience: HOW a human being becomes evil and HOW good.[13]

'Men', wrote George Steiner, 'are accomplices to that which leaves them indifferent.'[14] Here then we have a sentence or two of cutting analysis and indictment, which challenges us as educators to offer to our pupils a convincing metaphysics of evil, and this we can only do to the extent that in our own Being we have come to recognize the inseparability of our so-called good and bad impulses, to grasp that there does exist our shadow side, whether individually expressed as in malice or violence to our associates or collectively as in mob violence and concentration camps. We must train our pupils to detect the evil, not just the crime, which does not appear on the surface by not being afraid to 'punish or reprimand evildoers'—otherwise we shall indeed be 'ripping the foundations of justice from beneath new generations'. Considerations such as these have many implications for the content of school curricula, but as many also for methods of teaching, best summarized once again by George Lyward's prescription of 'stern love' as the essential condition of honest learning, one incidentally which he applied with a marvellous degree of success to those in the category of Spencer Millham's 'Dustbin Men',[15,16].

We may take a further leaf out of Solzhenitsyn's book of wisdom by reflecting on the connection which he quite rightly detects between 'the lack of a sense of evil' and 'the abuse of power':

Power is a poison well-known for thousands of years . . . But to the human being who has faith in some force that holds dominion over all of us, and who is therefore conscious of his own limitations, power is not necessarily fatal. For those, however, who are unaware of any higher sphere, it is a deadly poison. For them there is no antidote.[17]

The force to which the new metaphysics of education may invite the young to appeal, which does hold dominion over all of us and therefore does compel us to recognize our own limitations, is constituted of what we, because of our human limitations, have to perceive and describe as light and shadow, good and evil. It is constituted of the two of them together but also transcends them: it lies beyond good and evil. When it cannot be believed in, it can be responded to. Such a recognition is the needed antidote, which can be most readily and richly gained through the second ingredient we must now restore to its rightful place in the curriculum, namely a sense of the tragic, for tragedy is seed time. Yet again we may follow Solzhenitsyn: 'The imagination and the spiritual strength of Shakespeare's evil-doers stopped short at a dozen corpses. Because they had no ideology'.[18] In other words, for them there was still at work the antidote of Christian and early humanist beliefs about the sinful nature of man and his dependence on spiritual grace, which in our times are no longer available, at any rate in their orthodox forms, hence the ice-cold abstraction of totalitarian evil and our susceptibility to ideological manipulation. Shigalov's prophetic words in Dostoievski's *The Devils* have proved only too true: 'starting from unlimited freedom, I arrive at unlimited despotism'. As the rhyme has it,

The permissive society works in this way,
I do as I like—you do as I say.[19]

Free discipline can easily slip into anarchic licence and/or totalitarian tyranny—a situation of which some of our large comprehensive schools are already symptomatic.

We may now consider how a study of *King Lear* may conduce to the re-establishment of a valid sense of the tragic element in our educational scheme of things. From many different levels of interpretation, one at least is that the play is a study in the abdication of authority. Lear, we are told by Regan in Act I, Scene 2, 'hath ever but slenderly known himself', and this is a clue we may follow. He has not known himself to the extrme extent of his being unable and unwilling, because of his divided and immature personality, to take the responsibility for his royal prerogatives and duties which his kingly office demands. Indeed, as the drama unfolds, there is revealed to him a petulant, almost childish psyche within an old man's body—hence the foolish notion of his dividing up his kingdom while retaining for himself some of the perquisites, and his infantile reaction to Cordelia's admittedly brusque and stubborn responses to his expectation of the daughter he called his joy. The tragedy which ensues is the price Lear and others have to pay for his previous neglect of his duties, and eventual redemption is only gained through suffering. This includes his and our reluctant acknow-ledgement of the power of evil to the extreme paradoxical degree that however we act and however much we strive to act rightly, we are as human beings necessarily involved in doing evil as well as good and must learn to live with the consequences. As Cordelia remarks (Act V, Scene 3):

We are not the first
Who, with the best meaning have incurred the worst.

In fact this is, as Professor Herbert Butterfield maintained in his definition of history, the nature of the human predicament. It is by means of the vicissitudes suffered by Shakespeare's characters in *King Lear* that we begin to learn two vital pedagogical truths: one, that adults in their responsibility for non-adults, as kings for their subjects, cannot shuffle off authority; two, that the only legitimate seat of such authority lies at the midpoint of the personality which transcends the body-ego claims, and further that it is only through love and suffering that this Jewel in the Lotus can be won. 'Lear makes our 'tough-minded' modern plays, those niggling studies in 'absurdity' and 'hopelessness' and gratuitous violence, look what they are, lifeless scribblings on a small-town lavatory wall.'[20] The lesson can be learnt through a meditation on *King Lear* that, because there can be no resolution but only catharsis in human conflict as it straddles our path from birth to death, it is possible and essential to take into our educatioinal theory and practice a metaphysics of death. Otherwise 'unaccommodated man' (Act III, Scene 2) is naught but the victim of 'capricious cruelty'; otherwise the child is cheated of an education for death; he is denied the means whereby to learn how not to die by achieving identity with his timeless self and so is unable to make sense of life.

This can only come with the acceptance of a fully integrated philosophy of life and death as twin, complementary aspects of reality, and this in turn depends on our willingness to accept the truth of some of the new insights of parapsychology and the recognition and realization of the Self, the midpoint of the personality, the Atman of the Brahman, as the core of Being, the ultimate touchstone of reality. As the following lines proclaim, that entity is 'birthless and deathless and changeless'.

Never the spirit was born, the spirit shall cease to be never:
Never was time when it was not, end and beginning are dreams:
Birthless and deathless and changeless the spirit endureth for ever,
Death does not change it at all, dead though the house of it seems.[21]

That sublime insight of the *Gita* has somehow or other got to be made to suffuse our, at present, totally inadequate, too exclusively Western outlook about what concerns man ultimately. This implies quite deliberate teaching to the effect that man, as long as he is defined merely as a body-ego entity, is not the measure of all things, but that there is a core or kernel to him which is. We need to affirm with William Penn that 'Death cannot kill what never dies'.

In the realization of that truth lies out last metaphysical component, hope, and 'the only genuine hope is hope in what does not depend on ourselves'. And by 'what does not depend on ourselves' Gabriel Marcel meant 'the mystery as opposed to the problem of Being'. His metaphysics of hope is linked to 'a certain virginity untouched by experience . . . . it belongs to those who have not been hardened by life . . . it is untarnished by catalogued experience'. Incidentally, how much of our present education has got to be written off as just so much catalogued experience! 'Hope appears as though piercing through time: it does not see what is going to happen, but it affirms as if it did.'[22]

So we should take as our final focus the relationship of our last and our first ingredient in a metaphysics of education, 'hope piercing through time', thus making comprehensible for us humans the experiences we undergo of love, evil, tragedy and death as they occur to all of us on the horizontal track of sequential time. Such an educational philosophy is free of sentimentality, once defined as sympathy based on insufficient knowledge: on the contrary, it is rooted in the only real knowledge available to us through our being in and out of time, in and out of love, while with our negative qualities, appreciating the comedy of life by means of our acceptance of its tragedy, dying our own proper death. This mystery of being, as Marcel pointed out,

is perfectly well able to affect souls who are strangers to all positive religion of whatever kind . . . it in no way involves the adherence to any given religion, but it enables those who have attained to it to perceive the possibility of a revelation in a way which is not open to those who have never ventured beyond the frontiers of the realm of the problematical and who have therefore reached the point from which the mystery of being can be seen and recognized.[23]

In his latest, most profound and amusing novel, *Humboldt's Gift*, Saul Bellow has approached this kind of enlightenment: 'The old philosophy distinguished between knowledge achieved by effort (ratio) and knowledge received (intellectus) by the listening soul that can hear the essence of things and comes to understand the marvellous'.[24] Can we, progressive educationists, cater for the listening soul? Obviously only if we ourselves are listening! Elsewhere in the same book Bellow has a direct message for us:

And if there is one historical assignment for us, it is to break with false categories. Vacate the personae. I once suggested to her (his mistress, Renata): A woman like you can be called a dumb broad only if Being and Knowledge are entirely separate. But if Being is also a form of Knowledge, one's own Being is one's own accomplishment in some degree.[25]

This entire paper has been an effort to establish just that point, namely that Being is not only a form of Knowledge, but that there can be no knowing without a correspondingly adequate state of Being. I have tried to bear witness to the availability of such wisdom and to plead for its reinstatement in school, but this will only happen to the extent to which we are prepared to venture beyond the frontiers of the realm of the problematical by embracing a metaphysics of hope and teaching it in the classroom.

Notes and References

1 Marcel, Gabriel, *Being and Having* (London: Collins/Fontana, 1965).
2 See Musgrove, Frank, 'Education in a Plural Society', this volume, Chapter 10.
3 See Barnes, Kenneth C., *Energy Unbound* (York: Sessions Ltd.; 1980).
4 Haas, W. S., *The Destiny of Mind* (London: Faber, 1956), p. 10.
5 Hodgkin, Robin, 'Things for Use and Things for Meaning', this volume, Chapter 8.
6 Henderson, James L., *A Bridge across Time* (London: Turnstone Books, 1975).
7 Marcel, Gabriel, *An Essay in Autobiography* (London, 1947), p. 33.
8 Fines, John, 'The Narrative Approach', *Teaching History*, vol. IV, no. 14, November 1975, pp. 97–104.
9 Cecil, David. *Two Quiet Lives* (London: Constable, 1948), p. 73.
10 Kierkegaard, Søren, *The Journals (1834–1854)*, edited and translated by Alexander Drew (London: Fontana, 1938).
11 Crankshaw, Edward, in *The Observer*, 30 November, 1975.
12 Solzhenitsyn, Alexander, *The Gulag Archipelago*, vol. I (London: Collins/Fontana, 1976), p. 178.
13 *Ibid.*, vol. II, p. 597.
14 Steiner, George, *Language and Silence* (London: Faber, 1967), p. 175.
15 Burn, Michael, *Mr. Lyward's Answer* (London: Hamish Hamilton, 1956).
16 Millham, Spencer, 'The Dustbin Men', this volume, Chapter 11.
17 Solzhenitsyn, Alexander, *op. cit.*, vol. I, p. 147.
18 *Ibid.*, vol. I, pp. 173–74.
19 Masterman, J. C., *On the Chariot Wheel: an Autobiography* (London: Oxford University Press, 1975), p. 242.
20 Enright, D. J., *Shakespeare and the Students* (London: Chatto & Windus, 1970), p. 66.
21 *The Bhagavad Gita*, quoted from *The Testament of Man* (London: Gollancz, 1936), p. 66.
22 Marcel, Gabriel, *Homo Viator—Introduction to a Metaphysics of Hope* (London: Gollancz, 1951), p. 51.
23 Marcel, Gabriel, *The Philosphy of Experience*, p. 31.
24 Bellow, Saul, *Humboldt's Gift* (London: Secker and Warburg, 1973), p. 306.
25 *Ibid.*, p. 404.

Chapter 4

Education is Natural

*Mark Braham**

The title of this paper will to many be at best proclaiming the obvious, and at worst but a tautology. At the risk of having stated no more than many already believe, let me begin with man's naturalness and do so because as educationists, man is, after all, the subject and object of our concerns. Man, in the form of human infant, child, adolescent, and adult undergoes, for good or ill, what we choose to call education. Man, as an image or as an idea, is the very object of our educational thoughts, programmes, and practices. Thus, we start with man, and wonder about ourselves.

This wondering has led, in the past, to the belief that we humans are some special sort of creation, unique, and above all very superior to anything else in the universe. True enough, as it is said in Genesis, we do have dominion over the fish of the sea, the birds of the air, the cattle, and every creeping thing—although with regard to the latter our contests end up more as draws than successes. But certainly, as the diminished schools of fish, flights of birds, and herds of wild animals could testify, we have dominion over them to the point of nearly dominating many of them out of existence.

What this has to do with us, human beings, is that in seeking to comprehend our place in the scheme of things we eventually arrive, not so much at the recognition of being some special and separate form of life, but at the realization that we are intrinsically woven into the whole fabric of Creation.

But then Creation is too large a word for us. Not only does it imply immensities, but also a Creator, and some kind of Grand Design, all of which are perfectly acceptable within the confines of the world's

---

* Philosopher of Education, and founding Chairman, 'New Themes for Education' conference, Dartington Hall, Totnes, Devon.

religions, but in an epoch that doubts the conflicting claims of theologies, and seeks substantial evidence to support its beliefs, it is not always fitting to talk about a Creator, although the advent of 'Jesus Christ Superstar' and the proselytizing disciples of Buddhism and Hinduism seem indicative of a return to metaphysical ideas that a recent positivism has been all too ready to deny.

Let us, however, somewhat shift our perspective. Let us take a somewhat smaller word than 'Creation', and speak of 'Evolution' instead. Here, the problems of teleology, of substantiating the idea of purpose in the universe, and of looking for a 'First Mover' can be set aside, in favour of a more rational approach to the nature of our existence. With evolution, it is not Divine Providence and a myriad life forms created in a septenate of days that confronts us, as a zealous reading of the Genesis account would suggest, but rather, natural selection, random mutation, and the survival of the fittest populations.[1] Whether this really dispenses with a Creator is, I think, open to doubt. The esoteric Gurdjieff looked upon the evolution of life as but a lengthy series of divine experiments, carried out until a vehicle fit for the habitation of that consciousness we call 'human' could be developed.[2] The American philosopher of science, O. L. Reiser, recognizing that every form of life requires information in order to exist, is quite prepared to regard the informing of life as ultimately being caused by a Source which he calls the 'Cosmic Lens', a focusing agent that transforms an infinite flow of free energy in the universe into the myriad objective forms of seemingly inert, as well as of obviously active, matter.[3] But these are speculations that take us from our main point. That point is that human existence is inseparable from the totality of life on earth and, to whatever extent it exists inseparable from life within our galaxy; and thus from the universe's infinity.

We speak of this infinite universe as 'nature', although it has been customary to regard nature as something that particularly belongs to our earth. Our earth is clearly but one small planet among many, and the composite of them is but a region among other regions in the immensities of space. There are no known boundaries.

Nature, therefore, is taken to be the field of our experience and our concepts. All is nature, all is in nature. There is nothing outside of nature from the minutest particles to the widest ranging activities of human minds, and even as J. G. Bennett suggested, to the possibility of intelligences other than human.[4]

To speak of nature in this fashion is to include far more, then, than the inorganic structure of the earth, its green cover, and the life that moves among it. It is to speak of a feature that is now becoming far more widely recognized than heretofore: that nature is a dynamic system of interacting parts that at once belong to, and generate, a vast hierarchy of increasingly complex forms, each caught up in continuous processes of transformation and energy exchange with all that surrounds.[5] Thus, from micro-molecules to macro-molecular aggregates—from organelles, cells, tissues, organs, and organ systems to individuals, communities, and at the human level to institutions, concepts and idea systems—and outside of these to the spiral nebulae, all is nature, and we are part of it.

To say this calls for a caveat. It is customary to consider systems as closed, and attached to this custom is a fairly widespread reaction to, if not resentment of, even the idea of systems. They are taken to be something determinate, functioning in a machine-like way. But nature is to be understood as an 'open system', a pattern of interpenetrating and interacting relationships giving rise to new and unique modes of action that in time either find their place as participants in and contributors to the development of the whole, or gradually pass away, leaving their remnants as perhaps interesting, but no longer as essential, features of present conditions or possibilities.

The implication of this view of nature is that we cannot speak of anything as being 'non-natural', or even as 'super-natural'. We can speak only of a vast differentia of natural properties: a property being understood as any process or product. Thus, every human process and product is natural, as are the processes and products of other animate, as well as inanimate, systems. The so-called 'super-natural' implies, not a field of action 'above' or 'outside' of nature, but rather (a) processes and products that are not yet amenable to the general state of human cognition, scientific method, and its accompanying technology;[6] (b) hallucination, and (c) illusion. Hence, we should even cease to speak of the mystical as a non-natural, or unnatural event[7] (although it may well be unusual). We should instead note our ignorance concerning what may be matters of fact, and the imperfection of much of human perception and conceptualization, an imperfection which, because it is ours, is also nature's incompleteness.

This position requires, then, a psychological shift on our part. We must cease to think, and to act, as if we humans exist in a separate realm from that of nature. Note, for example, Asimov's comment:

The unity of present life is demonstrated in part by the fact that all organisms are composed of proteins built from the same amino acids. The same kind of evidence has recently established our unity with the past as well. Biochemists at the Carnegie Institution in Washington showed that certain 300 million year old fossils contained remnants of proteins consisting of precisely the same amino acids that make up proteins today. None of the ancient amino acids are different from the present ones.[8]

Actually, our sense of separation from nature rests not on our biochemistry and paleontology, but on our particular kind of consciousness: one that enables us to regard ourselves as subject, and the not-self, which in this case is the rest of nature, as object. As a consequence, our general 'Westernized' attitude, marked by that Cartesian sense of the indubitability of the self, is to objectify the rest of nature, to hold it at 'arm's length' as it were; to classify, to analyse and pollute it, but to fail to recognize any identity with it.

To regard human consciousness from a naturalistic perspective does not commit us, as earlier naturalisms have done, to a position of absolute determinism, for nature is not completely deterministic. Nature is an evolving system in which determinism appears in the forms of patterns of action that have been established and maintained over long periods of time. I believe that one may safely state the rule: the older and simpler the form, the greater the degree of determinism; the younger and more complex the form, the lesser the degree of determinism. If we set ourselves a scale from, let us say, amoeba to man, I think that we will find that, in terms of evolutionary time and in terms of the complexity of form and function, not only does man stand out as the youngest of all species on earth, but also the most complex and, significantly, the least complete. Were we complete, we would find ourselves in equilibrium with our environment, maintaining a careful balance between metabolism and catabolism, between syntropy (or negentropy) and entropy without our fitful struggles to find a place for ourselves in the world. This equilibrium would, if it were necessary, have been achieved, and not if we needed it not. We would be in a steady state.

But, as the labours of psychologists attest, we are a species in search of our reference points, in search of harmony, unity, and balance. We are marked, thus, by a deficiency of determinism and an open field of action in which new patterns of action have continually to be developed, elaborated, and refined. It is this opportunity for self-determination that lies at the root of human problems and possibilities, and signifies the fact of freedom.

Nature is thus neither a system existing apart from us, with which we have commerce but no identity, nor a system that has given rise to us, but from which we have since departed. Nature manifests itself through us, as it manifests itself through every form at its particular level. Nature is not just something 'out there'; it is 'here' as well. Julian Huxley and

Teilhard de Chardin are both echoed in the statement by Victor Weisskopf: 'Nature, in the form of man, begins to recognise itself.'[9]

We cannot speak of nature for long without having recourse to evolutionary theory, the 'history', according to Goudge, 'of all populations on earth'.[10] Without entering into the niceties of evolutionary theory, the Darwinian interpretation and its various theoretical formulations, I think that, like Huxley, we can accept that there have been three main evolutionary phases with regard to the earth: 'the inorganic or cosmological', the 'organic or biological', and 'the human or psychosocial'.[11] These are modified by Teilhard de Chardin in terms of 'geogenesis' involving the formation of the barysphere, lithosphere, hydrosphere, and atmosphere; and a 'biogenesis' providing for the 'living membrane of the fauna and flora of the globe', which by virtue of its sentiency becomes a 'psychogenesis'. This 'psychogenesis' marking the rise of psychism or consciousness led to man and a 'neogenesis' the birth of thought, marking 'a transformation affecting the state of the entire planet'.[12]

Existence in the inorganic phase involves powers of attraction and repulsion among and between relatively simple forms. In the organic phase, stimulus and response appear as a basis for action. With the emergence of the human—the psychosocial or cultural—phase, stimulus and response are increasingly mediated by reflection; by the consideration of meanings, of consequences, and alternate patterns of action. Thus, determination rather than predeterminism appears as an increasingly dominant mode of human life. Teilhard asks: 'Are we to say then, that the evolution of man ceased with the end of the Quaternary era?' (That is to say, with post-glacial man of some 25,000 to 10,000 years ago.) He answers:

Not at all. But without prejudice to what still may be developing slowly and secretly in the depths of the nervous system, evolution has since that date overflowed its anatomical modalities to spread, or even at heart to transplant itself, into the zone of psychic spontaneity both individual and collective.

Hence it is in that form almost exclusively that we shall be recognising and following its course.[13]

Now, psyche and culture are indispensably linked features of human existence. To say that they have evolved together is a truism, if not a tautology. Together, they represent the successive adaptations to, participation in, contribution to, and transformation of the environment on the part of an evolving humanity. As we, by our very sociability, are environmental to each other, the increase in the human population has meant the progressive humanization of our environment. Our environment for the most part is now psychosocial or cultural.[14]

Each individual and, collectively, every population, must develop those behaviours that are environmentally adaptive, although adaptiveness is not necessarily the sole criterion for a behaviour. The development of a new behaviour pattern is an addition to the complexity of the individual and the population. It is also an addition to the complexity of the culture. As the culture increases in complexity, it in turn calls for new behaviour patterns on the part of its members. This again adds to the complexity of the individuals and their cultural milieu. Thus, a spiralling reciprocity is set up resulting in the mutual complexity of individual and culture.

Through this reciprocal and 'complexifying' action, human consciousness, rather than biological determinism, becomes recognizable as the agent in the evolution of humanity. Moreover, by virtue of its place as the latest, freshest and still evolving species in nature, the human being also stands as the agent for the contemporary evolution of nature. We find ourselves as the 'growing tip' of the tree of life, and our uncertainties and difficulties are precisely because we, as nature at the human phase, have to determine the future:

The future of progressive evolution is the future of man. The future of man, if it is to be progressive and not merely a standstill or a degeneration must be guided by a deliberate purpose. And this human purpose can only be formulated in terms of the new attributes achieved by life in becoming human.[15]

The evolution of the psyche and its cultural attributes and effects has paralleled the evolution of the human brain and the highly complex nervous system that underlies it. The nervous system provides for the reception and transmission of information; the brain provides the locus of integration and the source of intentionally directed activity. It also functions as a vast memory bank. In many ways, the computer is its analogue.

The evolution of brain capacity is often given as an indication of the progressive cerebralization of hominids. In itself, this is insufficient to be regarded as the most important correlative of psychosocial evolution as there appears to have been no change in the cubic capacity of *Homo sapiens* brain cases for the past 25,000 years. Neanderthal and Cro-Magnon man both had a brain capacity that slightly exceeded the 1,350 cc. average of contemporary man.[16] The significant feature appears to have been an evolution in the conformation of the skull, with a corresponding evolution in the parietal, frontal, and temporal regions of the brain. These, states Werner, 'are the regions which are considered of the highest correlation', that is, concerning the integration of human thought and action.[17] For psychosocial purposes, the most important region of the brain is the frontal including the pre-frontal. Upon it depends the 'increasing differentiation and refinement of mental phenomena and functions'.[18] Here is Sherrington's 'roof-brain', *par excellence* that organ where motor act and finite mind get in touch with one another'.[19]

From the standpoint of the interaction of brain and culture, we have Wallace's statement:

The immediate source of culture change is the brain itself, in which changes of state within the lifetime of the organism lead to changes in overt behaviour, which are the visible substance of culture change. Hence, without evolutionary advance in the brain as an organ, culture cannot exceed a certain degree of complexity because the necessary innovations cannot be made.[20]

At this point, I believe, we reach what is generally regarded as the terminus of known biological evolution. As far as we can tell the evolution of the human physical frame has become stabilized such that we are able to speak of the physical maturity of humans, and regard this as being reached somewhere between the twenty-first and perhaps the twenty-eighth year. After this time one does not normally expect any further growth, although changes, without major deviation, to the general shape of individuals of course go on.

But what of the evolution of the brain, and especially of the forebrain? Do the same maturational considerations that affect the body apply? Can we, in fact, speak of a mature brain?[21] And if cognition is regarded as a function of the brain, can we point to cognitively mature individuals? Can we state the criteria for cognitive maturity, for example? If we can demonstrate what is a mature brain, then by definition we are stating the end-term of a series of innate and inherent processes. Since these processes provide the structure for cognitive processes, and these, in turn, are interconnected with cultural processes, we should then be able to designate the end-term of human evolution at the psychosocial or cultural phase. Moreover, by so doing we shall also be designating the end-term of the evolution of nature at the psychosocial or cultural phase.

Clearly, this is something we are unable to do. The contemporary concerns for 'self-realization' and 'self-actualization', the struggles of individuals for integration, the painful processes of human history, with its legacy of personal and social chaos and a concomitant search for order, underscore the immaturity of the human species from a cognitive (and one may as well add an affective) point of view. We are immature precisely because we do not know what it is to be mature, and we do not know what is maturity in this dimension because no end-term is yet explicit in our development. We are unfinished, and because we are unfinished we may conclude that nature, too, is unfinished. And here, of course, is the locus of the human predicament. Our species' evolution, compared with that of our predecessors', is apparently too recent for us to have become totally determined or 'programmed'. Our future descendants may eventually be able to bestow a total maturational scheme upon their progeny. We must content ourselves with the task of working out our own destiny.

Our incompleteness may also be inferred on other grounds. Of all known forms of life, humans are the most deficient in instinctual adaptive patterns, and require the lengthiest period of postnatal nurture and training. One can, for example, note the ability of young alligators to make their way unaided to water minutes after their hatching. We may note how rapidly calves and foals rise to their feet to suckle and run soon after birth. Most animals are capable of self-support within weeks or months after their birth. But this is not the case with human young. In Western industrialized societies one can increasingly point to the requirement of up to 25 or even 30 years of postnatal nurture and training before many an individual is capable of self-support. There was a time, 2000 or more years ago, when it made sense for the Jewish boy upon reaching his thirteenth birthday to proclaim from the Temple at his Bar Mitzvah ceremony, 'Today I am a man.' In this more complex age, this proclamation, still enunciated, is a quaint relic of simpler times. Owing to the very reciprocity we have indicated between psychic and cultural complexity, we may, in fact, state the rule: *postnatal nurture and training among humans increases in direct proportion to the increase of cultural complexity.*

Prior to the human phase, instinct (or unconditioned reflex),[23] signifying patterns of action that have been selected and maintained over time, predominates in the organization of individual and species life. Instinct appears as well in human life, but to a far less degree. Infants suck, swallow, and cry without being taught. Our heart beats and our lungs respire according to an ancient rhythm not of our own choosing. In this sense, mechanism, or determinism, governs a considerable portion of our lives, and necessarily so. It leaves us with the opportunity—with the requirement, in fact—of paying attention to our cognitive and affective processes. What is not already governed by our history demands our attention.

Beyond the physical and perhaps a limited range of affective and cognitive responses, human action requires constant attention until established patterns of action or habits, secure our adaptation, and provide an orientation for our direction. Instinctual patterns and processes blur with learned, or culturally rather than genetically acquired, behaviours. Unconditioned reflexes are overlaid by conditioned reflexes. Through the auspices of our 'roof-brain' reflection, abstraction, and protection emerge as our thought-life. Between the stimulus and the response, the psyche makes its claim.

Our very deficiency in instinctual behaviours calls forth a constant demand for 'learning': for the acquisition of information and the establishing of subsequent responses to environing conditions. It is the intentional organization of learning that we imply when we speak of 'education'. Education is the formal link between a developing individual and his cultural milieu. Through the process of education, successive generations of human young learn the necessary adaptations for living in their culture. Through education, they also develop their individual repertoire of information and responses that enables them to participate in, and to contribute to, their culture. As there are no identical (although there are similar) responses each individual, through his education, adds to the content of his culture; a minority become dynamically transformative.

By the same token that there is a constant reciprocity between psyche and culture in the course of evolution, there is a constant reciprocity between psyche—perhaps 'personality' is a better term—education, and culture. These three then appear as a basic triad in evolution at the human phase.

To this we may add the observation that in the course of human history, the complexity of educational processes has increased with the increase in cultural complexity. Societies have deemed parents insufficiently competent to provide for the education of their young, and hence we have had the establishment of formal educational systems, or schooling, to take over the task that parents have given up as cultural life has evolved. There is every indication that the complexity and extent of education will increase markedly over the next decades, and this factor may be one of the causes of the widespread unrest and concern about educational aims, methods of instruction, and the nature of schooling at all levels.

In summary, we arrive at the conclusion that education appears in the human situation as a matter of natural or, we may say, evolutionary necessity. This is the case, for without learning in general, and the intentional organization of learning in particular, evolution at the psychosocial phase would not have been possible, and we could not speak of culture or, for that matter, any kind of abstract discourse.

Education, defined in part as the intentional organizational of learning, is not simply the result of cultural demand or personal interest, but is primarily called for by the instinctual deficiency and immaturity of the human brain, and consequently the immaturity of our thought and emotional life.

If maturation would be implied in our genetic programme, and if our development was straightforwardly orthogenetic, the intentional organization of learning and the vast institutions and programmes that have been developed for this purpose would not only be unnecessary, they would not have been created. Since this is not the state of affairs with regard to humans, at least, we require education which, differing considerably in its content and structure from culture to culture, is the prime agency through which psychosocial evolution proceeds.

Now, there is need to uderscore a distinction between education when used as a catchword for a vast assemblage of badly to well done human activities in the learning field, and education as a necessary process in nature. Both dimensions of education are natural in that they occur in nature, but the former is an attempt to carry out tasks that are required by the latter, by a necessity that extends far beyond that of culture or personal fiat. Thus, we can make the not very astounding statement that schools and schooling may, or may not, be educational depending on whether or not they are in keeping with their naturalistic function. A restricted definition for education is therefore implied which subsumes it under evolution, while schooling and schools represent better or worse attempts to respond to mankind's educational needs.

The implication of this position is that anyone who seriously regards himself as an educator has become, whether he recognizes it or not, a prime agent in the evolution of humanity, and as a consequence is directly caught up in the evolution of nature.

An examination, then, of the place of education in human life suggests that it involves four developmental tasks. These, if they are accepted as justifiable, may be regarded as general criteria for our educational activities. A failure to adhere to them, where education is the espoused intent, would be tantamount to declaring such non-adherence as non-, anti-, or even mis-educative. Thus, we may take the position that schools are not necessarily educational institutions, nor are teachers necessarily educators, depending on the degree of their adherence or non-adherence to such criteria.

The criteria for education as conceived here are:

1. the criterion of adaption to the environment;
2. the criterion of participation in the environment;

3. the criterion of creative contribution to the environment;
4. the criterion of constructive transformation of the environment.[24]

The term environment is used here to designate the external milieu, human and non-human, within which the individual exists.

The criterion of adaptation

By 'adaptation' we may understand the 'fittingness' of the individual to his surroundings. More explicitly, one may say that that individual (or organization) who functions in his milieu with the minimum wastage of energy—that is to say, with greater economy of action, or with greater thermo-dynamic efficiency—is better adapted than another. In less technical language, we use such phrases as 'settling down', or 'fitting in', when referring to an individual's adaptive behaviour.

The human infant, like the young of other species, is born as a dependent being who must be cared for. His earliest activities are basically concerned with his survival in a post-uterine state and with the differentiation and integration of his total organic system. His body must be able to assimilate new food; it must accommodate itself to a host of micro-organisms; and as cognition develops the child must learn to function within the multifold conditions of his environment. Without learning, the child could scarcely continue to exist beyond a gastro-intestinal state.

While the child's adaptive behaviours begin below the threshold of cognition, lacking any intentional intervention on his part, by his first year his activities show considerable self-determination. During the first four or five years of his life, the child, under the direction and guidance of parents and members of the immediate—and, where existing, the extended—family, learns what and how to eat, to dress, to speak and understand the local language, and to know and respond to the expectations of an increasing number of people. He begins, in sum, to identify with and to acquire his culture.[25]

While it is common to speak of this period of a child's learning in terms of 'education', we should do so with the recognition that his learning is, for the most part, informally arranged. While certainly there is intentional organization of the child's learning (through, for example, approval and disapproval of behaviour), this organization is not necessarily clearly conceived or grounded in particularly justifiable concepts of child growth and development, except, perhaps, where professional assistance has been employed. In whatever manner it is brought about, the child's ability to adapt to his environment is a necessary condition of any further development.[26]

The criterion of participation

By 'participation' we may understand the individual's engagement in activities that, for the most part, are conducive to the maintenance and continuity of his culture. While adaptation continues to be a concern of the individual, at least until the parameters of his environment (phenomenally rather than geographically speaking) have become stabilized, it is far from all there is to his life. Adaptation, we might suggest in the light of our previous pages, is essentially egocentric or autocentric for it concerns essentially the organism's need to survive. Participation, within which adaptation must be included, is essentially socio-centric or allo-centric, concerning as it does the continuity of the culture to which the individual has had to adapt.

It is probably not too much to say that from about the age of 5 children the world over are placed under increasing pressure, not only to continue their adaptive learning, but also to participate in group and communal activities. For this purpose, the organization of a child's learning becomes far more intentional and systematic; it becomes more formally educational.

In hunting, fishing, and even more complex agrarian styles of life, daughters are generally relegated to household duties under the tutelage of the women, while sons undertake designated chores under the tutelage of the men. A girl, for example, learns to clean, weave, sew, and cook; a boy to hunt, fish, herd, plant, cultivate, and harvest. In industrial societies the complexity of adult tasks (and in many cases the appearance, as well, of political legislation) have transferred the child's learning from direct participation in the work of the community to a period of specialized instruction in the institution of the school. It is here that the child is expected to acquire the basic competencies in requisite fields before he is permitted to engage directly in an occupation.

In either case, whether the learning is provided for through schooling or through direct participation in the adult world of work, the child's education involves the gradual acquisition of lore, method, rule, and ritual that in some cases have been transmitted from generation to generation, and in other cases represent recent innovations. Whatever its source, the community, rightly or wrongly regards this information as essential for its own continuity.

Any extensive failure to provide such information to the young in a given culture means the inevitability of that culture's decline. There is evidence for this, for example, in the deterioration of North American Indian and Eskimo cultures, and in the paucity of a North American Black culture owing to the historic separation of the Negro from his African heritage.

From the point of view of the individual, the lack of opportunity to acquire his culture means increasing psychosocial maladaption and dysfunctionality, a condition not unknown to North America's native and Black populations and to many an individual who, uprooted from his own culture, has not been given the opportunity, or has not been able, to adapt to another.

The overall increases in world population, the multifarious migrations, the banding together of families into tribes and permanent settlements, the growth of villages, towns, cities, and nations, have given rise to a vast diversity of specialized work patterns. Meanwhile in the life of simpler communities (and one can point to the Soviet khokolz, the Israeli kibbutzim, and the North American communes as recent examples) there exists what might best be termed a 'totipotency' of roles. In this, other than for sex differentiated activities, each member of the community is expected to be capable of carrying out a wide variety of tasks. As communal complexity increases, however, task competency tends to demand increasing specialization or, in biological language, a functional specificity of behaviour. Of necessity, task specialization has also meant an increase in the kind and extent of instruction such that in technologically advanced cultures a few years of pre-adolescent schooling is no longer sufficient to prepare the younger members for participation in the work of their culture. Schooling continues, instead, not only through adolescence but, for many, into the first and second decades of adulthood, to say nothing of the increasing practice of 'adult' or 'continuing' education for those who wish to acquire or advance their educational opportunities well into, if not throughout, their adult years.[27]

The criterion of creative contribution

In terms of the foregoing, education has been seen in its adaptative and participatory functions. Quite apart from their naturalistic sanction, these functions are also culturally sanctioned as irreducible requirements for cultural survival and continuity. If these were the only requirements—and hence criteria—of education we could stop here, but there are good reasons for suggesting that there is more to be considered.

The evolution of culture, as that of nature in general, is two-fold; general and specific. General evolution concerns the continuity of life through successive levels or stages of complexity; specific evolution concerns the amplification of general evolution into adaptative specializations that have functional efficacy within a given space–time locus.[28] Once a mode of behaviour becomes adaptively specialized, it tends towards self-maintenance, or a 'steady-state', and this tendency becomes prepotent over pressures for continuity unless conditions are such that dysfunctionality and decline are immanent. As there is no preprogramming to shift a culture out of its adaptive specialization back into the stream of general evolution, the recognition both of stasis and of possibilities for continuity rests on the membership of the culture. But again, this recognition does not exist of its own accord, but is a result of the state of consciousness of individuals. If their learning has been such to canalize their consciousness into purely adaptive and participatory modes of thought and action, we then find that the possibilities for innovation and thus personal and cultural continuity are restricted.

The logic of our position, then, is that the continuity of a culture's evolution rests on the continuing development of its members; the continuity of the development rests, in turn, on their ability to harness their own tendencies and powers for continued development which can take them beyond the *status quo*.[29] As, however, the recognition and harnessing of such tendencies and powers is learned, it is implicitly an educational problem. The problem is that our schooling, for the time it has existed and to the extent that it does exist, has concentrated on the tasks of shaping the young for adaptative and participatory activities and has disvalued creative and innovative activities, such that the creative individuals in our cultures are liable to have succeeded despite, rather than because of, our general educational institutions. And, while the facts of individual success despite our educational deficiences cannot be denied, the possibilities of providing for a wider base of creative contributions to the culture through intentional educational provisions cannot be overlooked.

Now, by creative contribution, we may understand the application of novel responses to continuing or new circumstances, such that these responses become part of the general fabric of the culture, and— according to some measure which we cannot possibly develop here— provide for an improvement over what constitutes a normal pattern of thought and action, or in some way indicates possibilities for the future.

This implies that there is more to creativity than merely a spontaneously novel response to a situation, for such a spontaneous response is but the indication of possibilities. Creativity emerges as a vital factor when it becomes organized and directed towards the solution of problems and to the elaboration of new possibilities for human arrangements, whether we are dealing with artistic, literary, philosophical, scientific, political, legal, technical, or other features of life. For a creative idea to be contributive, it must be grounded in a recognition of the cultural conditions to which (and within which) it is to be applied. Such objectivity is scarcely possible much before adolescence.[30] Except in rare cases, therefore, we would not expect to find culturally contributory activity (to the extent that it is provided for) emerging much before middle or later adolescence. Hence, while the impulse to innovate and create is certainly available and requires supporting throughout childhood, we must turn to adolescence and to secondary schooling as the locus for guiding creative talent for culturally contributive activities.

To summarize the educational consequences of our criteria thus far (i.e. adaptative participation and creative contribution), while not in the least espousing mutually exclusive practices that are restricted to particular educational stages, we would suggest that the emphases (or central tendencies) might be as follows:

1. adaption to the environment—Early Childhood Education (comprising the sensori-motor and pre-operational periods of thought);
2. participation to the environment—Middle and Later Childhood Education (comprising the period of concrete operational thought);
3. creative contribution to the environment—Adolescence (comprising the first period of formal thought).

The criterion of constructive transformation

While the creative contributors of individuals add to and enrich the prevailing cultural structure they tend, on the whole, to find acceptance in so far as they are not in conflict with, or at least are not perceived as a threat to, the life-style of the culture-at-large or to the vested interests of dominant individuals or groups. If, however, the prevailing structure cannot, or will not, accept further creative contributions, we find pressures building up towards cultural transformation on the one hand, and for maintenance of the *status quo* on the other. If the pressures for continuity are strong enough, a period of cultural conflict is inevitable, until either stasis or continuity succeeds.

It should be made clear that all pressures towards cultural change are not necessarily constructively transformative. Where the impetus is for a 'negative' freedom from restraint, without a 'positive' orientation towards a clearly conceived good, we are not in a position to speak, except perhaps after the fact, of constructive transformation. Destructive transformation is always a possibility.

Our interest here is for constructive transformation, for that which experience and reflection suggests will prove for the optimization and increased self-organization of individual and, by extension, of social life. Our problem is that unless the members of the culture have been prepared to be constructively transformative, which means that they are cognizant of the prevalent conditions and limitations of the particular culture dimensions which are their concern, and have the competency to conceive and carry out constructive activities, we are liable to find ourselves caught up in change for the sake of change, and not for justifiably conceived purposes.[31]

In the secondary period we find but the 'birth' of objective and reflective thought. It is hardly likely that we would find, or could expect, the intellectual proficiency at this stage for the awareness of prevailing conditions, the rational search for alternatives, and a concern for the possible consequences of action in adolescence. Rather, it seems at this juncture of my thought on the matter that the task of assisting individuals to become constructive transformers of their culture belongs to the adult stage of education. By this is meant, not so much the elementary and secondary schooling that is provided for those adults who did not acquire such schooling in their childhood and youth, but undergraduate, graduate, and continuing educational opportunities that can enable socially aware and concerned persons to develop the expertise that can constructively transform the culture by intent towards defensibly desirable goals, rather than rely purely on chance and the possibilities of the right leaders emerging at the right time true to the messianic tradition.

Unfortunately, this is neither a study in value theory nor in curriculum design. We therefore cannot pursue this matter further and deal with the controversies that it raises, nor with explicit recommendations at this time. We must leave it, in fact, with a paradox. The position that is taken here calls for a dynamically orientated education that at once can provide for cultural stability and yet can further provide for the continuity of cultural evolution and individual development.

Notes and References

1 For a contemporary discussion of evolutionary theory, see P. Handler, ed., *Biology and the Future of Man* (New York: Oxford University Press, 1970), ch. 12.
2 G. Gurdjieff, *All and Everything* (London: Routledge, 1950).
3 O. L. Reiser, *Cosmic Humanism* (Boston: Schenkmen, 1965).
4 J. G. Bennett, *Systematics*, **IV** (3), December 1966, 181–201.
5 See, for example, E. Laszlo, *A System's View of the World*, (New York: Braziller, 1972).
6 Ordinary philosophic language would regard 'process' and 'product' as

'states-of-affairs'. They, rather than 'state of affairs' will be used in this study as they more accurately depict the dynamics of nature with which this study is concerned.

7 There is also a tendency for us to equate the 'natural' with the 'normal'. This is a fallacy for from one standpoint what appears in nature, i.e. a fact, may not be a normal observation for any individual observer or group of observers. From the perspective of the naturalism in this study, natural is an ontological category, while normal is purely an *epistemological* one. While the normal is natural, the natural is not always normal.

8 Isaac Asimov, vol. 1 of *An Intelligent Man's Guide to Science* (2 vols., New York: Basic Books, 1960), p. 676. See also V. Weisskopf, *Knowledge and Wonder* (Garden City, New York: Doubleday, 1963), p. 198:

> Chemical analysis has showed beyond a shadow of a doubt—that living objects consist of the same kind of atoms as non-living things. In fact, living matter consists mainly of the four elements carbon, oxygen, hydrogen and nitrogen, with traces of other elements such as iron, phosphorous, and magnesium. There is not the slightest indication that living matter contains any special material or that the laws of interaction between the atoms are different. The phenomena of life, therefore, must be the result of ordinary interactions between atoms and molecules—very special molecules to be sure, of a structure and complication that distinguish them strikingly from the molecules of lifeless matter.

9 Weisskopf, *op. cit.*, p. 270.

10 T. A. Goudge, *The Ascent of Life* (Toronto: University of Toronto Press, 1961), p. 34.

11 J. Huxley, *Evolution in Action* (New York: New American Library, 1953), p. 10.

12 Teilhard de Chardin, *The Phenomenon of Man* (London: Collins, 1959), p. 202.

13 Teilhard de Chardin, *op. cit.*, pp. 181ff.

14 We must, of course, note the simple fact that the degree of psychosocial or cultural content of our environment depends upon the size and kind of human population that is involved. For the explorer, the space-traveller, as for the backwoodsman and the plainsman, the environment, containing definite psychosocial or cultural elements as it does, is still largely non-human.

15 Huxley, *op. cit.*, p. 577.

16 See A. F. C. Wallace, *Culture and Personality* (New York: Random House, 1961), ch. II.

17 See H. Werner, *Comparative Psychology of Mental Development* (New York: Science Editions, 1961), p. 49.

18 Werner, *op. cit.*, p. 51.

19 C. Sherrington, *Man on His Nature* (Cambridge: Cambridge University Press, 1963), p. 182.

20 A. F. C. Wallace, *Culture and Personality* (New York, Random House, 1961), p. 65.

21 Of course, on a purely statistical basis one can speak of maturity from the standpoint of the amount of growth one normally observes within a given population, with the understanding that the maturational processes are innate. But this cannot disclose, except over vast periods of time, if further

development is going on or not. This problem applies to the total physical frame of man, as well as his brain. However, on the grounds given for suggesting the immaturity of human cognitive and affective behaviour, I think we may conclude that at least the fore-brain in humans is incomplete.

22 By maturity, we mean the end-term of developmental processes that are innate. See W. C. Olsen in *Encyclopedia of Educational Research*, ed. C. W. Harris (New York: Collier-Macmillan, 3rd ed., 1960), p. 373:

> The term maturation is confined frequently to sequences and patterns which are innate. Users of the term recognise the fact that frequently the nervous system anticipates a new function, that is, the environment does not create the function. The progression is assured by internal factors and the environment supports the changes but does not generate them.

23 Th. Dobzhansky, *Mankind Evolving* (New Haven, Conn.: Yale University Press, 1962), p. 203.

24 See also R. B. Perry, *Realms of Value* Cambridge, Mass.: Harvard University Press, 1954), p. 411: 'In short, the purpose of education is threefold: inheritance, participation, and contribution.'

25 See N. Beck, *Modern Science and the Nature of Life*, London: Penguin, p. 40: childhood, it then appears, is the prolonged immaturity we *must* have in order to imbibe our culture and learn what went before us, before we can become a part of it in one or another of its aspects.

26 See W. B. Brookover and D. Gottlieb, *A Sociology of Education* (New York: American Book Co., and ed., 1964), p. 100: 'The basic social processes of socialising the members of society in the appropriate common behaviour patterns and allocation to specific roles are primary functions of education.'

27 See also G. D. Spindler, ed., *Education and Culture* (New York: Holt, Rinehart & Winston, 1963), p. 381. 'Personality is formed and education occurs as the growing child encounters cultural agents acting in the various roles and statuses provided by the social structure of his society.'

28 See M. Sahlins and E. Service, eds, *Evolution and Culture*, Ann Arbor: University of Michigan Press, pp. 28–29.

29 See Dobzhansky, *op. cit.*, p. 338: 'The adaptive value of forethought or foresight is too evident to need demonstration. It has raised man to the status of a lord of creation.'

30 See D. Elkind, *Children and Adolescents* (New York: Oxford University Press, 1970), p. 66: 'From the strictly cognitive point of view . . . the major task of early adolescence can be regarded as having to do with the conquest of thought.'

31 See C. Jung, 'The spiritual problem of modern man', in *Modern Man in Search of a Soul*, trans. W. S. Dell and C. F. Baynes (New York: Harper, 1933), pp. 198ff. In writing of 'modern man', in contrast to the contemporary mass, Jung says: 'he is completely modern only when he has come to the very edge of the world, leaving behind him all that has been discarded and outgrown, and acknowledging that he stands before a void out of which all things may grow'. But, before we consider this to be an acclamation of self-indulgence and solipsism, we should note that he must be sound and proficient in the best sense—a man who has achieved as much as other people, and even a little more. It is these qualities that enable him to gain the next highest level of consciousness'.

Aspects of Education
Edited by M. Braham
© 1982 John Wiley & Sons Ltd.

Chapter 5

Dialogue and Development

*John Newson**

The purpose of this paper is to outline a theoretical approach which puts communication at the centre of the stage in relation to the development of a human infant. The term 'communication' is not here being used as a synonym for language, but is intended to refer to a more general human facility upon which language itself seems to be founded. Thus this paper is concerned with the origins of our ability to empathize, to imitate and to share emotions with our fellow men, as well as with our ability to learn to speak any particular language. By talking about 'communication', then, I wish to make reference to our power to create shared understandings with other people via interactions which make use of mime and gesture as well as the overt display of emotions and feelings. Thus I shall take it as self-evident that in face-to-face communication we engage in reciprocally prompted actions which include non-vocal as well as vocal signals; while within the vocal mode itself, words are by no means the sole vehicle for our communication.

This approach is certainly not intended to deny the importance of language as a hugely powerful tool of communication so far as human co-operation and culture are concerned; but it does imply that it may be impossible to understand the evolution of formal verbal or written language systems, either in the personal history of the individual or in the evolutionary history of mankind, without recognizing that shared understandings between people predate the emergence of language systems. As a developmental psychologist, however, I intend to restrict the discussion that follows to the growth of communication competence at the individual level, by attempting to describe how shared under-standings begin to emerge during the first year of a child's life.

When we consider the question of communication between adults, we can usually take it for granted that they already share all sorts of mutual

* Co-director, Child Development Research Unit, University of Nottingham.

categories of thought and feeling. Between an adult and an infant, however, we have to try and comprehend the way in which a code of communication may be evolved *de novo*, as it were; and this poses a different problem from that in which one is merely concerned with the specification of some mechanism for translating from one established code into another. To understand how communication is first established, where none was before, is not easy. Problems arise at the conceptual level, perhaps because our conventional scientific language of description and explanation is shot through with all sorts of deterministic, mechanistic and behaviouristic assumptions. To illustrate this point, I will first try to tackle the issue of communication using a form of descriptive language which deliberately adopts the perspective of a neutral or non-participant observer, my aim being to push explanation within such an expository framework to its natural limit. Subsequently, however, a rather different account will be offered; and this strategy may enable the reader to judge for himself the relative merits of these two approaches. It may also help to explain why we ourselves have been driven to adopt the second one.

During the past decade, there has been a great resurgence of interest in psychological studies of human infants; and within this movement many researchers have been drawn towards the particular study of the complex and sophisticated social activity which all normal babies so obviously manifest when in the presence of their everyday caretakers. For the student whose knowledge of babies is drawn from psychological textbooks, and not from real life, the most striking effect of exposure to ordinary mothers and their infants is the revelation that, by the age of 10 or 11 months, normal babies are highly competent in the art of communication. By this age it is obvious that they deliberately make known their desires and dissatisfactions, join in games, share jokes, imitate all sorts of obviously meaningful actions and gestures, and can even tease their mothers. Furthermore, it is quite clear that they accomplish all this without the help of formal language and without even a passive understanding of words as such. Like researchers in many other centres, we ourselves have been concerned to develop ways of giving an accurate description of how pre-verbal infants typically develop such complicated social skills in interaction with their mothers. In the Child Development Research Unit at Nottingham, we now have on file a substantial number of video recordings illustrating mother–baby interaction in free-play settings obtained from regular weekly recording sessions with infants between 4 and 11 months of age. It is on the basis of a careful study of these and other similar records that the following propositions are offered as guidelines for further discussion.

1. It seems to be a necessary condition for the evolution of communication that the two individuals involved are capable of performing discrete and distinguishable actions which can serve the function of signals. Each of the two individuals must have a repertoire of 'displays' or potential signals, together with some independent capacity to exercise selective control over the performance of such actions.

2. Equally important, however, is the notion that each individual must be sensitive to the occurrence of similar 'displays' when these are offered by the other individual. Furthermore, both partners must apparently be impelled regularly to relinquish their own activity in order to be able to attend effectively to the activity of the other.

3. For communication to develop, it seems to be necessary for the discrete 'signals' of the two interdependent organisms to be repeatedly interwoven in familiar alternating sequences. This process, in time, gives rise to a recurrence of patterned sequences to which both partners are sensitive and to which both partners contribute.

The whole process may be summarized by saying that adults and infants actually engage in 'conversation-like' exchanges. These typically take the form of well-worn rituals of interaction to which the baby clearly makes a real and positive contribution. Even young infants play a highly active role in constructing dialogues of reciprocating activity, and apparently have little difficulty in sustaining that role even though responses are demanded at a rate which frequently exceeds 30 gestures per minute, or one every other second.

In a previous paper (Newson, 1974) I have stressed the debt which developmental psychology owes to Colwyn Trevarthen for highlighting the fact that human babies characteristically exhibit a variety of intrinsic activity patterns which serve as a basis for communication competence. Even at birth, it is possible to detect gesture-like actions which are complex co-ordinations of arm and hand movements, head and eye orientations, mouthings and vocalizations. This activity of the infant is not formless but highly integrated. It is patterned as a function of time, and displays a specific rhythm so that each separate action builds up to a clear climax followed by a subsequent decline. Typically, babies evince such patterned activity when faced with 'objects' which are themselves responsive in like fashion: exhibiting, that is, patterns of sound and movement with that particular climactic periodicity which is characteristic of the behaviour of most mammals.

In early infancy these temporally organized patterns may be obscured unless we search carefully for them. They tend to be interrupted by unco-ordinated 'jerky' limb movements, and are suppressed or masked by frequent discomfort reactions. Young babies also tire easily. Under optimal conditions of wakefulness and physical support, however, it is possible to demonstrate and record quite perfect gesture-like actions, remarkably similar in form and speed to those habitually used in gestural communication by adults. In practice these gesture-like actions are executed with such rapidity that it seems to be necessary to make use of slowed down video or film recordings to study them and demonstrate their occurrence with certainty. Trevarthen's evidence is, however, very compelling and suggests that babies are capable of emitting discrete 'pre-formed' actions which simulate adult communication gestures. Given that conversation-like gestures can occur in babies, it is obvious that we should ask what factors prompt and sustain them; and to begin with it seems clear that their occurrence is not at all random, but timed to accommodate to the reciprocal gestures offered by some person with whom a baby may be confronted. Typically, the infant and his regular adult caregiver come to operate according to an alternating or turn-taking sequence, in which each partner first acts and then attends to the activity of the other (Schaffer, 1974). There is controversy about whether this alternation of activity indicates some intrinsic predisposition for turn-taking in the baby, or is an artefact of a controlling influence exerted by the more sophisticated adult partner. Much neonatal-type activity follows a burst–pause cycle; if the adult merely filled in the infant's own pauses with his own bursts of activity, and inhibited his own gestures when the infant began to be active again, a semblance of deliberate alternation would obviously result.

There is, however, more to this. When an infant is faced with an 'object' which is responsive to his own activity, it is clear that he may easily become locked into a sustained sequence of actions; his movements give rise to effects which attract his visual or auditory attention, eliciting an 'orienting response': and as a result of this his previous movements are inhibited. Then, as his attention begins to falter, he starts to indulge once more in an active phase of bodily movement which again produces change, and this is likely to attract his attention once more. An easy way to demonstrate the persistent engagement which can take place between an infant and an 'environmentally responsive' object is to link the infant's limb with some device which responds variably at a suitable time delay. When, for example, a string attached to the child's wrist is linked to a mobile placed clearly within his view, thus causing it to be disturbed whenever he waves his arms, it may be observed that even a very young baby seems to be constrained to 'work' at operating the device, and his attentive involvement with it will characteristically be sustained over a long period of time (Papousek, 1967; Kalnins and Bruner, 1973).

The precise feedback characteristics which facilitate such 'self-rewarding' activity are still but little understood; but they obviously include an optimal time delay between action and consequent reaction, and a variable, but not entirely unpredictable, outcome in the form of some consequent effect to which the infant does in fact attend. This optimal time delay may be related to the natural rate of signal exchange already referred to.

A mobile is, however, only sensitive to the infant's actions to a very limited degree, in this case being merely responsive to gross arm movements above a certain minimum amplitude. As an 'environmentally responsive feedback system', a human caregiver is a lot more sophisticated than a mobile and a piece of string. In particular he or she can, and does, 'monitor' other aspects of the activity of the infant and hence is able to respond sensitively to all sorts of things the infant may do in addition to waving his arms. Such a caregiver will be guided by the nature of the infant's attention-paying gestures, including associated changes of facial expression, direction and intensity of gaze, etc. It should therefore not surprise us if the joint activity of adult and infant does soon begin to resemble a dialogue in which the partners take turns to act and to attend towards one another, thus producing a very adequate simulation of mature human discourse.

Let us now pause to take stock of the kind of account we have been attempting to give. So long as we restrict ourselves to the language of detached observation, we can only say that the infant makes 'gesture-like' signals, or that conversation is being 'simulated'. We cannot assert that the infant himself—or for that matter the adult—attaches *meaning* to his actions, and it is for this precise reason that we have been driven to describe the infant's actions as 'displays'. By such usage, attention is directed towards the outward form of certain actions which are classed as signals, perhaps because of the consistent effect they can be observed to have on other members of the same species (Smith, 1965). Such a description cannot, however, offer an explanation for the evolution of those shared understandings which constitute the *meaningful content* of whatever is being communicated. To give an account of the ontogenesis of communication in this deeper sense, it is obviously necessary to grapple with the more difficult conceptual problem of how signals first acquire their 'significance' within the mental experience of the infant. It should by now be clear, however, that no such account can be given while we restrict ourselves to a form of language which is only suitable for the description of what is outwardly observable. The language of the detached 'scientific' observer quite simply contains no terminology for describing the reality of intersubjectively shared experience. In other words, the language which physical scientists so successfully use to describe relationships or interactions between material objects—with whom we have no power to communicate directly—must be different from the form of language needed to describe how socially shared understandings can arise between people. A change is required both in the form of language and in the style of exposition before we can expect further insight. At this point in the argument, therefore, we need a change in standpoint: we must shift perspective, as it were, so as to look at the process of communication from the point of view of a *participant observer* (Newson and Newson, 1975).

Once we are permitted to project ourselves into the role of someone who is trying to communicate with the infant, it becomes clear that such a person is bound to respond selectively to precisely those actions, on the part of the baby, which one would normally respond to *given the assumption that the baby is like any other communicating person.* In other words, the caregiver, being already well practised in the art of communication, will not respond indiscriminately to all aspects of the infant's activity. Instead he or she will selectively attend to those actions to which one would habitually attach significance as gestures which are normally meaningful in ordinary human discourse. Changes in the infant's facial expression will, for example, be attended to closely, because these will be automatically interpreted as changes of state which the infant is assumed to be experiencing. If he begins to look 'pained' it will be assumed that he is suffering distress. Similarly with a young baby, one responds in different ways to unco-ordinated jerky movements of one limb and to directed hand-swipes apparently aimed with some degree of intention towards objects in the external world.

The response mechanism of another person is, however, so delicately tuned that it can respond *in anticipation* to what might be called actions-in-the-making. Thus, for example, when a mother sees the beginnings of a turned-down mouth in the facial expression of her child, she may immediately act to distract him *before* his lower lip begins to tremble, and thus may succeed in diverting him before his discomfort irrevocably engages his attention. In this instance the action is deliberately prevented from running its 'normal' course. It is in fact a taken-for-granted aspect of normal mothering that distress in an infant may be cut short by using such distraction strategies. Somewhat less obviously, perhaps, actions which the mother values may skilfully be drawn out of the infant. Thus, by judicious anticipation allied with angling for the baby's attention at the right moment, full-blown smiles may be got from a baby by building upon the first incipient smiling gestures which the mother thinks she is able to detect. What eventually leads her to distinguish between a mere grimace and a true social smile is probably that the latter can be reliably elicited in a ritual consisting of nodding and smiling at the infant. In this case it is the context and timing of the baby's gesture, in relation to the mother's attempt to bring it out during the course of a social exchange, which is critical in determining whether a smile is considered 'social'. It follows that the meaning of a smile, as a social gesture, is inseparably bound up with the infant's ability to use it in a socially appropriate manner, i.e. at precisely the right moment within a dialogue of social interaction.

What is being argued here is that, whenever he is in the presence of another human being, the actions of a baby are not just being automatically reflected back to him in terms of their physical consequences, but are instead being processed through a subjective filter of human interpretation, according to which some, *but only some*, of his actions are judged to have coherence and relevance in human terms—either as movements born of intentions, or as communications (or potential communications) addressed to another socially aware individual. It is thus only because mothers impute meaning to 'behaviours' elicited from infants that these eventually do come to constitute meaningful actions so far as the child himself is concerned. Actions achieve this status to the extent that they are capable of being used as communication gestures which he knows how to produce, on cue, in the context of a social exchange between himself and someone else. In a real sense, therefore, gestures only acquire their significance in so far as they can be utilized as currency within social dialogues.

The desire to establish a degree of shared understanding with her baby is normally a powerful motive for the mother. She treats him from birth as a person who can be credited with feelings, desires, intentions, etc., and looks for confirmation that he will relate to her in a person-like way. His social smiles in response to her approaches provide important confirmation of human-ness, and the fact that he can produce conversation-like vocalizations when she talks to him provides similar reassurance. By 3 months, many mothers also enjoy playing socially stimulating games with their babies; for instance, games of anticipation like 'threatening head', in which a warning signal is followed by a mock attack on his person with explosive lip noises and physical contact between the mother's mouth and the baby's face or body—a ritual in which mild alarm repeatedly ends in excited giggles. It is not only in games, however, that the dialogue form predominates. Thus in the serious matter of spoonfeeding, the child will soon know how to play his part in the ritual, accepting or rejecting each proffered spoonful by anticipatory mouth opening or by turning away. In a similar way the baby will now actively assist in the process of drinking from a cup, by such actions as clinging to the cup and pulling it towards his mouth, showing impatience for more, pausing and looking up between swallowing bouts, and so on.

In all these activities, the co-ordinated looking activities which the infant performs with his eyes are obviously of fundamental importance in maintaining and establishing rapport with any caregiver. In the situation of direct face-to-face interaction, the infant will be visually attracted to scrutinize his caregiver's face when she is talking to him: it has, after all, the fascinating qualities of being a moving, self-deforming, and noise-producing 'object' which is also precisely and delicately responsive to his own actions and changes of mood. As we have already noted, however, the infant may be almost equally preoccupied in paying visual attention to an inanimate mobile, especially if it is one over which he himself can exert some form of control. He may be similarly drawn to devote his full attention to the puppet-like actions of a single hand scrabbling about in front of him; and if this is made to approach and touch him in a game-like interaction ritual, a hand in play may hold him spellbound. The interesting thing about this is that at 3 months of age there is little evidence to suggest that the infant understands the relationship between the dancing hand and the person who is controlling it. For theorists of cognitive development, like Piaget, the emergence within the infant of a clear distinction between 'person objects' and 'thing objects' marks a momentous watershed in mental development; and while it is by no means clear what prompts this 'Copernical revolution' in human mental organization, the whole course of subsequent mental development is thought to be altered as a consequence.

From the caregiver standpoint, it is clear that mothers regard their infants' attention-paying gestures as immensely important within the dialogue of reciprocal actions which develops. The infant's tendency to pay them visual regard matters to them particularly, and direct eye-to-eye contact is seen as an especially rewarding and significant interpersonal event.

When between 3 and 4 months their babies begin to sit without support, and hence become rather fully involved in exploring and exploiting all sorts of inanimate objects, handling them themselves with full visual concentration, mothers often seem to suffer a period of relative deprivation as their babies' new-found interests now apparently exclude them. One may even observe mothers bending right down to seek eye-to-eye contact with their infants at this stage. Two important communication-maintaining strategies now emerge, however. One is the use by mothers of some reliable vocal gesture to call the baby's visual attention back towards themselves—the recurrent use of the name of the child is one example of this, although it is not always particularly successful. As an alternative, therefore, some mothers seem to develop an idiosyncratic and specialized auditory signal like tongue clicking or even blowing noisily on the child's face to make him look up and meet their eyes.

The second common communication-maintaining strategy is to provide the baby with a simultaneous vocal-intonational commentary, which serves to highlight interesting moments relating to what the infant may be simultaneously experiencing *vis-à-vis* the object he is involved with. Here, once again, it is important to appreciate that the mother has the power to *anticipate* effects which her baby may inadvertently be about to produce, not just to react to things *after* they have happened. This means that she is able to offer him a dramatic intonational 'marker' at athe precise moment when the effect will be registering on the child himself. Certainly it is highly characteristic of this stage of development that mothers do repeatedly offer their baby vocal markers which highlight the occurrence of specific events so as to enhance their salience for him. Frequently also, maternal vocal signals are used as 'pacers' to sensitize the child to the time-course of significant dynamic processes which he has inadvertently set in train. An example would be a mother's intonational commentary accompanying the occurrence of an interesting rotary movement set off by the child (for instance, when he begins to touch and explore a roundabout toy). Once again, however, it is in the mother's power to anticipate the likely outcome of the occurrence, before it is actually begun, which permits her intervention to be made with such delicate and precise timing that it coincides maximally with the child's visual attention-paying to the event in question.

The intuitive use of intonational marking and pacing signals by a baby's habitual caregiver provides him with a valuable running commentary on his own actions, even though this commentary cannot yet be effective by virtue of its verbal/semantic content, since the infant can be induced to experience shared states of feeling when a mother's voice-tone is associated with actions he is simultaneously performing. It seems likely, for instance, that in the course of repeated encounters an intonational commentary can begin to impart to the infant's actions a sense of coherence and goal-directedness which they would not otherwise have. Suppose, for example, that a baby is fumbling towards extracting a small object from within some kind of container. His mother's commentary—change of pace, tone of voice, dramatic interjections, etc.—will reflect the relative effort of his initial approach, will serve to sustain him to go on striving when success is judged by her to be imminent, and will express the drama of tension relief at the moment that a meaningful result is finally accomplished. In this way the tone of the maternal voice will convey to him both the need for continued activity and the sense of climax when his efforts are about to pay off. Certainly babies of a few months are highly sensitive to the tensions of audience expectation when they are battling with cognitive problems in the presence of an interested group of student onlookers. When one is demonstrating the abilities of babies, one is highly conscious of audience participation effects, of the kind which caused Von Eherenfeld's horse to continue tapping its hoof until it had counted out the correct number of raps to complete the sum which its audience could see on the blackboard. In a broad sense, therefore, it seems that the roots of cognition and of social empathy may be a good deal closer than has hitherto been recognized. After all, many mothers deliberately teach their infants the meaning of 'dirty' by registering dramatic disgust whenever the child starts to put some unclean object into his mouth; and if an unexpected happening occurs, they likewise reinforce the baby's sense of surprise, dismay, etc., by the whole quality of their own contagious emotional reaction, particularly through the tonal quality of their spontaneous vocal response.

The fact that marking and pacing signals, when offered in the auditory mode, do not distract the child from giving his full visual attention to whatever events he is himself controlling, implies a powerful and economic use of two independent channels of communication. One feels driven to speculate, therefore, about the peculiar disadvantages which must be suffered by the deaf child at this particular stage of development. After all, although it is possible to use marking and pacing signals which may be seen rather than heard, their use could be predicted to have a highly distracting effect upon the infant's visual attention-paying strategies, when used simultaneously.

Eventually, of course, even the child with intact hearing must learn to withdraw his visual attention from his own object-oriented activity in order to receive gestural—as opposed to auditory—confirmation about the reactions of his onlooking caregiver; and this clearly demands the operation of a memory-holding function within visual attention-giving, such that the activity may be interrupted, while the infant makes a visual check-back from object to person, and be smoothly resumed in the light of encouragement received or delight shared. In short, the infant must learn to make what we call a 'referential glance' towards the caretaking person, thus providing a potent and deliberate act of communication about the effect of his actions on things. One important reason for the emergence of the referential glance could be that child's play with objects often produces unexpected or mildly frightening outcomes. For instance, something may fall over and make an unexpected noise, or the child may accidentally bang an object into his own face. It may therefore be that reference-back-to-the-caretaker, for reassurance in states of alarm, represents an entrenched and primitive communication strategy which the child simply learns to carry forward from earlier days and put to new use. Perhaps, too, mothers deliberately tend to recruit their children's visual attention, particularly in 'emergencies', by using urgent auditory warning signals which the child will be rather unlikely to ignore. This sort of speculative discussion, however, is mainly useful in drawing attention to the general principle that it may be a mistake to look for the precursor of any particular communication gesture, without referring to what has happened previously in the communication interchanges of the two interacting partners. Thus in the development of communication competence the *historical dimension*, in terms of idiosyncratic strategies previously developed by a particular mother–infant pair, is likely to be of fundamental importance in understanding how new strategies develop.

None the less, the ability to refer from thing to person, and back to thing again, must be seen as a significant accomplishment in the communication history of any child. It clearly has a lot to do with the infant's developing ability to distinguish operationally between persons and objects, and probably with his capacity to operate in the light of the even more fundamental distinction between self and other.

Obviously much more could be said about the diverse strategies used by ordinary mothers to establish and sustain communication with their babies. Susan Pawlby, for instance, has devoted a whole project to documenting the development of imitative routines between mothers and babies in order to show how such gestures are routinely used to communicate to the baby similarities between his own actions and those performed by others (Pawlby, 1977). Another study by Hilary Gray (1978) has concentrated on the way giving and taking gestures develop within a communicative context. It is not possible to elaborate on all these issues in a single short paper.

To sum up: the dialogue between a human infant and his regular caregiver represents a 'cultural construction' of the utmost importance to the infant's whole future mental development. In attempting to describe the complexities of interaction during the first year of life, the very notion of dialogue is inescapable, and can most fruitfully be conceptualized as an alternating sequence of communication gestures. These are initially held together by a determination, on the part of the adult partner, to construe each and every act which is made by the infant as a meaningful signal in the light of the given situational context and of the immediately preceding signals which have been directed towards the baby. In many instances the relevant actions contributed by the baby himself will be indications that he has attended to the communication gestures offered to him or they will be spontaneous acts directed by the infant towards interesting objects or events which have monopolized his attention almost by chance. The caregiver, however, needs to operate within the format of an assumed ongoing dialogue, because as a communicating being this is the only way that it is possible for her to begin to make sense either of the baby's actions, or of her own in relationship to him.

Furthermore we, as observers, must use an effort of imagination so as to share with the baby's caregiver the general feeling of what it is to engage in an ongoing dialogue with him: otherwise we will not be in a position to describe the evolution of those shared understandings which subsequently begin to develop through this intricate process of interpersonal involvement and negotiation. From the baby's point of view it is only by being continually involved, as a participant actor, within an almost infinite number of such sequences that he is finally brought into the community of language. In short, it is only because he is treated as a communicator that he learns the essential human art of communication.

References

Gray, H., 1978, 'Learning to take an object from the mother', in A. Lock, ed., *Action, Gesture and Symbol* (London: Academic Press).

Kalnins, I., and Bruner, J. S., 1973, 'The co-ordination of visual observation and instrumental behaviour in early infancy', *Perception*, **2**, 307–314.

Newson, J, 1974, 'Towards a theory of infant understanding', *Bull. Br. Psychol. Soc.*, **27**, 251–257.

Newson, J., and Newson, E., 1975, 'Intersubjectivity and the transmission of culture', *Bull. Br. Psychol. Soc.*, **28**, 437–446.

Papousek, H., 1967, 'Experimental studies of appetitional behaviour in human newborns and infants', in H. W. Stevenson, ed., *Early Behaviour: Comparative and Developmental Approaches* (New York: J. Wiley & Sons).

Pawlby, S., 1977, 'A study of the nature and structure of imitative sequences observed in interaction between mothers and their infants', in H. R. Schaffer, ed., *Studies in Mother–Infant Interaction: The Loch Lomond Symposium* (London: Academic Press).

Schaffer, H. R., 1974, 'Behavioural synchrony in infancy', *New Scientist*, 4 April, 16–18.

Smith, W. J., 1965, 'Message, meaning and context in ethology', *Am. Naturalist*, **XCIX** (908), 405–409.

Aspects of Education
Edited by M. Braham
© 1982 John Wiley & Sons Ltd.

Chapter 6

Child and Parent, School and Culture: Issues in Identification

Elizabeth Newson*

> Man is not a naked ape but a culture-clothed human being, hopelessly ineffective without the prosthesis provided by culture.
>
> J. S. Bruner, 1972

Most of the general statements made in this paper[1] hold true for children at any stage in their development from 3 years to adolescence. The background to the paper is a longitudinal study of 700 children and their life-styles from birth to adulthood, mainly based on long interviews with their mothers at focal points in the child's life: 12 months, 4 years, 7 years, 11 years, 16 years, and so on (Newson and Newson, 1963, 1968, 1976). The actual data presented here come from the 7-year-old age stage of the research; the reader should therefore bear in mind a child who has been at school for 2 years, and who is generally supposed by both parents and teachers to be getting down to 'real work' after the halcyon days of the infants' or first school.

By the time he goes to school, the human child is already a product of his culture if only by virtue of the fact that he has been reared by adults who have themselves, for two, three or four decades, been exposed to cultural pressures. It is not possible to envisage a culture-free child: the 'child of nature' (whatever that may be) must reflect a culture in which 'nature' is tolerated, just as a test-tube child would reflect a culture that had produced laboratories.

* Co-director, Child Development Research Unit, University of Nottingham.

Children brought up in a nuclear family, in a commune, or by an unsupported mother, must subtly adjust to the way their adult care-takers see their position in a society which has views about the normality and acceptability of nuclear families, communes, and mothers on their own. In many other ways, long before he is necessarily aware of a world beyond his family, the child's notions and expectations are shaped by an enormous variety of manifestations of his culture, as mediated by his parents. His mother's choice of his first feeding medium, whether human nipple or rubber teat; the kinds of dirt (agricultural or industrial, say) that his skin is exposed to, and how or whether it is cleaned off; what is considered 'naughty'—*whether* any-thing is considered naughty—and how the notion of naughtiness is conveyed; the spoken language he hears around him—whether it reflects a technological society and closely approximates to written language, whether its roots are wholly oral, or whether his parents, though living in a culture which is dependent on written language, belong to a subculture which is comfortable only with the oral form: all these diverse experiences are only a few examples of the means by which the culture makes itself felt at a quite implicit level in child upbringing.

Parents cannot help being the carriers of implicit cultural messages; but they do have some choice in how far they explicitly offer the child experience of institutions and concepts which belong to the world beyond basic family subsistence. We cannot imagine a culture-free child, but there is such a thing as a culture-deprived child: we can discern many possible degrees of contact between children and those activities and ideas which are provided by the culture in the community but not immediately available in a closed family unit. The young child is de-pendent upon his parents to welcome and seek such experiences for him.

The experiences I have in mind are of various kinds. Some involve the formal coming together of groups within the wider culture for a specific purpose: for instance, theatres exist to put on plays, variety shows, and pantomimes, and audiences convene to watch these events; parents may or more not think it important that their children should take part in this kind of extra-familial cultural activity.

(At this point I may seem to be using the word 'culture' in a different way: 'improvement or refinement of mind, manners etc. by education or training', as one of the Oxford dictionaries has it. However, the dictionary itself combines these two uses under one head—'particular form or type of intellectual development or civilization'—and I would regard them as so closely interwoven in origin that I deliberately choose to confuse them here. I certainly have no intention of entering on value-judgements as to what activities are 'cultural' in the sense of refinement or intellectualism.)

Religious services, the screening of films, dog shows, trade exhibitions, Nottingham's Goose Fair, football matches, race meetings—all these are examples of cultural events which cannot be fully simulated within the family, and through which parents can therefore choose to widen the horizons of their children or not. Other formal manifestations of the culture include those permanent shrines of our values, interests, or beliefs which can be visited by members of the culture without reference to specific events: museums, art galleries, stately homes, cathedrals, monuments, zoos, and places of sentimental or historic association such as Big Ben, Banbury Cross, Gretna Green or Carnaby Street.

These experiences are necessarily formal for the child in the sense that a deliberate effort has to be made by an adult in order to seek them out—and indeed they take on the status of 'outings' and 'treats'. But there are also day-to-day ways in which parents can welcome the outside culture into their child's home life. One is by the provision of books and comics, which offer the child a different view of the world, whether through the eyes of David Copperfield or Desperate Dan. A less obvious way of opening up the family culture is by answering children's questions. The mother who takes the child's questions seriously—listens to them, thinks about them, and tries to furnish him with a satisfying answer—not only gives him further information about the world but, by treating his inquisitiveness as natural and sensible, and his questions as interesting to her, expresses to him her own involvement with the culture.

This is perhaps the crux of what parents are doing when they take an active role in introducing the culture to the child. By taking him on visits to places of interest, making sure that he has access to the written media, answering his questions and searching for the answers elsewhere when her own knowledge is inadequate, the mother repeatedly characterizes cultural interests as relevant to herself and, by identification, to the child as well. Values which are both taken for granted (rather than stated) and demonstrated in action are likely to have a special potency for a child during his formative years. Consider the difference in the hidden messages reaching the child in these two families: both quotations are in answer to the inquiry, 'Can you always answer his questions? What do you do if you can't?' The first shows lively minds through three generations.

Building foreman's wife:

Well, I explain it as far as I can, and then I say, 'Now look, I don't understand'—I *tell* him I don't understand it. Well, me Dad's pretty up on them sort of, you know, as I'd term it, general knowledge, you see. Well, he'll praps be able to answer them. Or what we can't answer, we try and find out. [Where from?] Well, books, or praps verbal if we can find an explanation about it. I mean . . . you know . . . when you're going to Birmingham, there's a big gravel pit. Now it's full of water. Well then, when we went by one time it was all grass all over it, you see, so I says to me Dad, 'Weren't that full of water?' So he said, 'Yes'. So Barry said, 'Well *why*, Grandpa?—cause you said gravel pits are very deep, well why isn't it deep now, cause what have they done with the water?' So me Dad says, 'I don't know, me duck, but I'll see what I can do'. And do you know what they'd done? You know from the power station, they'd had the ashes blown in, you know, instead of taking them with the lorries—it had saved them, oh, he did tell Barry how many pounds it had saved them—they'd done this pipeline across and filled it. Now you see, he went and found out for him.

[Where did he find out from?] I don't know, but I know when I was a child, he . . . you know, even now we'll be going along and I'll say, 'What's that?' Me Dad'll say, 'Do you think I'm a walking encyclopaedia?' But he always seems as though he can find it out, such things as that. But my kiddies have never gone to sleep in the car, you can go from here to Kingdom Come, and they'd never sleep; and me Dad says no, you don't expect them to, and we've always tried to make the ride interesting. Me Dad's a van-driver, and on Saturday morning Barry will go with me Dad, and the things he sits down after and he'll be telling you! They'll pass something, a building, you see, and me Dad can tell him. Ever so interesting, and me Dad's as interested as Barry is.

Unemployed labourer's wife:

Not always—I've lost my schooling now! I mean you don't keep it up, do you, what you learn in your own schooldays, I mean I'm 46, and I think you don't sort of keep that interest. He was on about Nelson or something the other day, wanted to know if it were all true, but I can't remember all that. I just said, 'I don't know owt about it, duck, you'll have to ask your teacher.'

It was because the active participation that spells out relevance seemed to us the vital factor, that we did not include television as a way in which parents involve children with their culture. Television is almost universally provided, and therefore does not readily distinguish attitudes; and simply witnessing a programme together may or may not convey parental values to the child. The mother who has tears in her eyes as she watches news reporting of some human disaster expresses without words her involvement in life beyond her own street; the mother who chats gaily through the same news sequence identifies the suffering of others as removed from and irrelevant to her own conception of reality. Recognizing these subtle differences as important, we yet did not feel competent to gauge them adequately within the limitations of this study.

Taking as a starting point the unquestioned fact that middle-class children are more academically successful than working-class children, the factors that bring this about in terms of direct influence from home and family on to the child are still not clearly delineated. One line of explanation that we should keep in mind derives from our own findings on child-centredness at both 4 and 7 (Newson and Newson, 1968). Child-centredness increases markedly as one ascends the social scale; and it may be that middle-class children acquire a firmer confidence in their own worth, their own capabilities, and their own rights to the attention of adults: which may add up to a powerful motivation towards active learning and the discovery of concepts and ideas for their own sake. And this brings us close to the thorny question of the improvability of the child's 'intelligence'. Bruner has quoted P. M. Greenfield as questioning, in a conference paper: 'If a mother believes her fate is controlled by external forces, that she does not control the means necessary to achieve her goals, what does this mean for her children?' (Greenfield, 1972). We would extend her question: if a child does not believe in his own intrinsic worth, in his own basic *considerability*, how can he be motivated to achieve his goals, or indeed to set himself goals at all?

'We go out together . . . we got toffed up . . .

We asked a number of questions about whether the child had experi- enced, *with his parents*, various outside events or visits to places of cultural interest; in addition, we included a question about extra-curricular lessons, which usually entail attendance at a dancing studio, music teacher's house, gymnasium or swimming bath, and which meet our criterion of involvement with the outside culture organized, and therefore endorsed, by parents. Schools themselves, of course, try to provide all children with a basic common denominator of such experiences by arranging not only school assemblies and formal concerts, but also trips to museums and theatres, visits to factories and fire stations, and so on; but we are not here attempting to measure the child's *total* experience of such things, but rather how far the limited school provision of them is actively affirmed and backed up at home. Thus Saturday morning children's film shows, which children attend unaccompanied, would not rate positively as 'being taken to the pictures'.

Table 1 shows the class differences[2] that emerge from parents' answers to these questions. The only difference that does not reach

Table 1   Cultural contacts provided by parents for 7-year-olds

	I&II %	IIIwc %	IIIman %	IV %	V %	Middle Class %	Working Class %	Overall popn %	Class trend
Extra-curricular lessons	22	8	6	5	4	15	5	8	****
Cinema with parent	90	85	70	59	48	87	66	71	****
Concert (not school) with parent	10	9	7	6	7	10	6	7	n.s.
Theatre with parent	77	59	41	35	27	68	39	47	****
Museum/art gallery with parent	89	88	69	70	52	88	67	73	****
Zoo or circus with parent	89	88	81	67	64	88	76	80	****
Other exhibitions/shows with parent	31	30	15	14	7	31	14	18	****
Sporting event with parent	37	31	25	20	14	34	23	26	****
Religious service with parent	57	40	28	23	19	49	26	32	
High scorers (5 or more) on index based on above activities	66	48	28	15	8	57	23	32	****
Low scorers (2 or less) on index based on above activities	4	9	28	37	51	6	32	25	****

Sex differences reach significance for lessons (girls more ****), sporting events (boys more ***), and religious services (girls more ****). Girls are slightly more likely to attend the theatre than boys (*). No other sex differences, and none found for overall index scores.
Significance convention: **** $p<0.001$; *** $p<0.01$; ** $p<0.02$; * $p<0.05$.

significance level is in concert going, and this because concerts are simply not popular with 7-year-olds and their parents. The museum data may seem surprising. During the short period when a Conservative government imposed museum charges, it was frequently argued that families who were interested enough to visit museums would also be prepared to pay an entrance fee. These figures are of interest in comparison with those for theatre attendance, when one looks at the economically deprived end of the class scale. Half the Class V children have been to a museum with their parents, compared with only a quarter of this group who have been to the theatre. It is clear that many of these already educationally deprived children would be still further deprived by a charge on museums, which for a family in poverty may be the only family outing feasible.

Looking at the lower part of the table, where these activities are brought together to form an index of the child's general cultural experience from the home base, we can see how powerful the accident of social class can be. The strength and consistency of the social class trend, particularly steep in this case, is remarkable. When one reflects that the child only needs *one* experience of being taken to a museum, football match and so on in order to score in each of the contributory categories, the deprivation of the low-scoring children can be seen as very great indeed: that this should be true for half the Class V population, and for a third of working-class children generally, is disquieting. It is particularly so because it cannot adequately be compensated for by direct educational provision; that is to say, while the school can provide the actual cultural experience as part of its curriculum, it cannot so easily make good the parental involvement which conveys to the child the family's identification with the cultural and educational aims which the school explicitly represents.

Mothers and fathers are faced with both choices and constraints in relation to the wider culture. Living willy-nilly within a cultural web, they may none the less choose whether to exploit it, or partially to isolate their children from it by not becoming involved as a family with any of the cultural events that are offered; though this choice may, of course, be somewhat determined by the difficulties of lack of money and lack of energy experienced by parents of large families. On the other hand, parents are very heavily constrained to hand over their children to the culture-bound institution of school; this is a powerful repository of cultural values, which it is made extremely difficult to opt out of. In so far as school is concerned with cultural activities generally, as well as with literacy and numeracy in particular, the child will, in truth, feel more 'at home' at school if his parents make it clear that they regard such activities as relevant to themselves as well as to him. For this reason alone it seemed apposite to consider in this context parent/child involvement in general cultural events.

But parents also exert choices within the home, in that they can choose to build a 'nurturant environment' for their child's interests simply by taking his questions and activities seriously and making him a present of some part of their time and attention, without going further afield than their own neighbourhood. This, too, backs up the child's school experience, even leaving aside ways in which parents directly try to involve themselves in any formal teaching of the 'three Rs'.

The 'index of home–school concordance' shown in Table 2 is based on items which we saw as evidence of such a nurturant environment. It will be seen that both child and parent behaviour are drawn on to provide this evidence; for instance, children need permission and encouragement from their parents if they are to make a habit of taking things along from home to show their teacher and enrich the school experience.

Miner's wife:

He's got two fossils that he's very proud of, which his Daddy brought them up out of the pit. And he's very fond of taking them to show his teacher. They've got leaves, branches of leaves. And he's got a very, very old newspaper, about eighteen-ninety something, which he likes to take. I'll tell you what he's very interested in—museums, castles, anything old he really likes. He will take an interest.

Again, children are more likely to bring school back into the home, in the form of either questions or activities, if the home environment welcomes this.

The results given in Table 2 very clearly confirm marked social class trends of both low scorers and high scorers on home–school concordance. In the working-class group as a whole, families are rather evenly spread across the score range, with just under a third appearing in each of the high and low categories and just over a third in the middle category; the unskilled group, however, is notably unlikely to score high (13 per cent), and unskilled-class boys in particular score low (42 per cent). In the middle class, families are not at all evenly spread through the score range: only 12 per cent show a low degree of concordance. Professional-class girls stand out as especially likely to score high (55 per cent).

The clear-cut sex difference on the total index deserves comment; it might not have been expected, since only one of the individual items (taking things to school) produced a sex difference of a similar magnitude. This is an example of how an overall index measure of this kind

Table 2   An index of home–school concordance at 7 years

	I&II %	IIIwc %	IIIman %	IV %	V %	Middle Class %	Working Class %	Overall popn %	Class trend
Child often takes things to show teacher	57	52	46	50	39	55	46	49	**
Asks parents questions about topics arising at school	73	64	57	59	49	69	56	60	****
Mother takes responsibility for finding answers to questions if doesn't know (see Table 3)[1]	71	60	47	40	23	65	48	49	****
Parents often help with school work (not reading)	34	26	21	17	11	30	19	22	****
Index is based on above items, plus child's continuance of school activities at home and drawing at home, which show no class differences on our rather low criteria:									
High scorers on home–school concordance (7–9)	47	37	32	27	13	42	29	33	****
Low scorers (0–4)	12	12	29	31	36	12	30	25	****

Sex differences: 'showing teacher', girls more ***; high scorers on index, girls more ***; low scorers, boys more **.
[1] Made up of first two items in Table 3, p. 82.

can in fact tell us something over and above what we can learn from the individual items that make up the scale. In other words, the index allows us to draw conclusions about the *degree* of home–school concordance which is experienced by boys or girls; whereas the individual items strictly only allow us to make statements about the proportions of girls, as compared with boys, who behave in a certain way.

'He's so insistent . . . it seems a shame they shouldn't get to know . . .'

I have already touched on children's questions and mothers' responses to them, and these are of particular interest; it is worth looking at this topic in more detail. To some extent it is a circular matter: the child is likely to ask questions about what he perceives as relevant, and his mother's encouraging response not only rewards this question and stimulates additional ones, but also confirms his perception of the relevance of investigation generally; conversely, a mother who fobs off questions not only reacts aversely to the act of questioning but also devalues the spirit of inquiry that prompted the act. Thus we must expect, and we do in fact find, some correlation between child's and mother's behaviour.

Insurance inspector's wife:

Oh yes, always [asks questions]. This teacher—I think all primary teachers are marvellous!—she gets their interest. Wollaton Park, for instance, was a topic, they were drawing it and painting it. And he has to know all the details you know yourself, if you know any. We do eventually hear about all the topics they've been discussing, and if he hasn't heard enough or heard correctly, we have to tell him.

Administrative assistant's wife:

He does, usually because he doesn't quite know what the teacher's said; and then I've had to try and work out what she's thinking and what he's heard from his tale, and go on from there! Because he'll come out and ask a direct question, 'What do you know, do you believe so-and-so, Mummy?' And I'll say either yes or no, according to what. . . . 'Well, my teacher says . . . '—the opposite, as a rule. And then I have to put her in the right as well, and I have to get a bit further just to see what she *has* said, and work it out from there! [Would he tend to trust you rather than the teacher, or the teacher rather than you?] Well, when it was Mrs Lester, his first, it was the teacher all the time, I just didn't stand a chance! But now it's often 50/50, according to what he thinks I'm capable of knowing!

Lorry driver's wife:

Oh yes, he likes to know the ins and outs of everything. He came home one day and said, 'Mam, you know that man that had his head cut off when he . . . this woman was dancing with him . . . he lost his head . . . there was a chapter in the Bible all about it . . . there's a very sad ending in the chapter, do you know it?'—he was going on in a garbled way. I said, 'Do you mean John the Baptist who had his head cut off?'—'But Mr. Field said there's a very sad ending to it—the chapter—do you know it?' So I read through this chapter and I thought, well, *I* can't find a sad ending to it, and the doves came down from Heaven and everything; and I thought, oh well, I can't go through the whole Bible, it'll take weeks. So in the end he nagged me about this, he wanted to know the sad ending; and I put my coat on and I went down to see the Headmaster, and apparently it was just that he'd had his head cut off; well I *knew* that, but I was looking for the sad ending. But they come home from school and expect you to know everything about everything.

Lorry driver's wife:

They'd been talking about London; and I've got a set of encyclopaedias which are for him when he's old enough, but of course I fetched them down. When was the Tower Bridge built and who lives at Buckingham Palace and who built St Paul's, and all sorts like that. I filled a great sheet of paper.

Jointer's wife:

I'm too busy really—I don't always listen. She jabbers on—I don't always know *what* she's on about.

We asked mothers whether they could always answer the child's questions, and what they would do if they couldn't. Table 3 gives some idea of the strategies which they gave as typical for themselves. Some examples of responses in the four categories give the flavour:

Consults book, newspapers, etc.

Teacher's wife:

We've got an encyclopaedia and we'd look it up in that, or in a book in the library. But usually between us we've got the book or the knowledge. We go on to the end to satisfy him—if only because *we* become interested. He might perhaps have lost interest, you know, on the way, but we still go on!

Tobacco worker's wife:

I would tell him I didn't know about it and we'll try and find out, and a lot of things he does want to know . . . my sister's got a terrible lot of encyclopaedias. I don't tell him that *he* should ask his Aunty, I tell him that *we* will find out.

Student teacher's wife (herself a teacher):

We can't always, but we know where to go to find the answers. [And do you do

Table 3 Mothers' strategies when unable to answer their children's questions[1]

	I&II %	IIwc %	IIIman %	IV %	V %	Middle Class %	Working Class %	Overall popn %	Class trend
Consults books[2]	38	21	11	9	3	30	10	15	****
Asks someone[2]	33	39	36	31	20	35	33	34	*
Nothing: admits ignorance	23	29	37	40	62	27	41	37	****
Conceals ignorance	6	11	16	20	15	8	16	14	***

Sex differences not significant.
[1] 'Unable' denotes that she does not *know* the answer. There are of course questions which parents do not *wish* to answer; these are excluded here.
[2] The item in Table 2, p. 79, 'Mother takes responsibility for answering questions', is made up of the first two items in Table 3.

that?] Yes we do. The other day she was asking about music and we'd no idea, and I'd got an old book there which has one or two things, and we looked and found what we wanted. [Father:] Yes, that was another thing—we were informed only a few weeks after they went back to school that we were not as clever as Miss Machin, she *knew* the answers to everything—*we* kept having to have a look in a book!

Asks someone

Miner's wife:

Sometimes I can, other times I don't know how to word it, sort of; sometimes I manage quite well. [What do you do if you can't?] Say, 'Tell you what, darling—I'll ask somebody and tell you tomorrow.' [And do you?] Yes, quite often—maybe have a word with one of the teachers at her school.

Machine operator's wife:

Well, the parents round here are pretty good. What we don't know, they do. The boy next door comes here for certain things—English and Maths—and Edgar goes down the street to a chap who's a Jehovah's Witness for religion, and we sort of . . . I mean, this chap down the street, what he doesn't know about the Bible isn't worth knowing, and it's very handy. And the lady next door, she's very good as well, she'll answer pretty well everything that we can't, and we do the same for her children.

Does nothing, but admits ignorance

Driver's wife:

I've always said, 'When I find out the answer, I'll let you know'—and they've been satisfied with that. [Do you find out?] No.

Miner's wife:

I mostly find out how to [answer], I have to think it over carefully first. I say, 'Oh well, wait a minute, Barbara, I'll tell you in a minute when I've done this', and I'll think about it first, which way I'm going to answer. [What do you do if you *don't* know the answer?] I say, 'Well, I don't know the answer, Barbara.'

Tries to conceal ignorance

Metal polisher's wife:

I put him off. It's a funny thing, that . . . you try to put 'em off, don't you?

Railwayman's wife:

I pretend I haven't heard her then. Say if she asks me if I can spell such-and-such a word, and I can't; then I say, 'Oh, ask me a bit later, I'm busy'. I'll put her off if I can.

Structural cleaner's wife:

I tell him his brain isn't big enough now to hold it all.

Middle-class mothers, by virtue of their own educational advantages, are better equipped to answer their children's questions; this is likely to encourage their children to turn to them with questions more frequently, and no doubt contributes to the class difference in the actual asking of questions arising out of school which we have already seen in Table 2. The mother's attitude when her knowledge is not enough for the child takes the situation a step further, however. It can be assumed that the first two categories given are educationally supportive, since an effort is made to acquire the information asked for; that the third is neither supportive nor discouraging; and that the fourth, concealing ignorance, is clearly unsupportive, since the child is usually deliberately discouraged from persisting with his questions, which diminish the mother's self-image.

Consulting books obviously comes more easily to middle-class mothers: more likely to have books at hand, to know their way around a library, to be able to pursue a topic through an index and to cope with formal and elaborated prose, their whole white-collar or professional life-style imbues them with the expectation that the most authoritative information is obtainable from this source, and, moreover, that it is there to be used. The mother who consults books with her child, however, does more than induct him into an important subcultural expectation; she also immediately involves herself in the inquiring role in a particularly active way. This is much more marked in consulting books than in asking other people; although a mother may 'get him to ask his Daddy while I'm there, so we both know about it', her role tends to be active only in the initial stages, soon becoming passive as the informant takes over. The use of books, on the other hand, is likely to remain a co-operative effort throughout, since 7-year-olds are not yet very skilled at winkling the knowledge they need from a book without help in scanning and actual reading. Additionally, because of this personal involvement, she thereby identifies his questions as being of interest to *her*, and worth giving *her* time and trouble to answer; whereas referral on to some other person is rather variable in how far the mother continues to be involved in any way at all. Thus, while we can hardly be surprised at the very clear class difference in turning to books to satisfy children's questions, the most significant feature of the act is its implication: in that it defines to the child *the pursuit of knowledge via reading* as relevant for mothers as well as school-children.

Looking at the second half of the table, we find ourselves with a rather large group (57 per cent) in the working class who are not educationally supportive of their children when they do not know the answers to their questions. Of some interest among these, although a small group, are those mothers who attempt to conceal their ignorance from the child by various 'fobbing-off' methods: twice as many in the working class as in the middle class. We can understand this divergence by looking at other attitudes which make up class styles (Newson and Newson, 1968, 1976). For instance, the more authoritarian stance adopted further down the social scale depends upon the premise that mother knows best by virtue of her status; a demonstration of her ignorance is more difficult for her to tolerate and incorporate into her image than it would be for the more democratically oriented mother, who has already conceded to the child that she can be wrong (a parallel to this is the class difference in mothers' willingness to apologize to the child). If middle-class mothers do feel that they have lost face by not knowing the answer to a question, they can easily regain it by showing their expertise in using resources; this course is less open to the lower working-class mother, who may indeed feel it safer not to embark on a search which may still end in failure. Further up the social scale, educationally oriented mothers may even welcome a situation which gives them the excuse to introduce the child to the use of dictionaries and encyclopaedias; further down the scale, mothers are less well equipped with such aids. Over and above material aids, however, this is in fact just one of a number of ways in which the lower working-class mother may try to maintain her *authority* at the expense of truthful dealing with the child.

Thus far, I have been exploring the ways in which the school is or is not backed up at home by the parents' willingness to enlarge the child's cultural horizons and to provide an environment stimulating of and responsive to his ideas. The rather dismal findings which I have presented can be summed up briefly by saying that, as we move down the social class scale,

1. the range of cultural interests experienced by children as members of their family group becomes more narrow and restricted;
2. children become less inquiring at home on school-inspired topics;

3. parents become less inclined to take up and expand children's questions, of whatever source, by whatever means;
4. parents are, in particular, less likely to use books or newspapers to further the child's knowledge, and are more likely to attempt to conceal their own ignorance;
5. children are less likely to receive help, whether direct or in the form of the encouragement of a 'hospitable environment', with school work other than reading.

It is, of course, also the concern of the school itself to provide such an environment; but, as I have tried to show, there is no way of compensating the child for the loss of that voluntary involvement of the parents which identifies his educational and cultural interests as theirs also. A feeling of relevance—home to school, school to home—seems irreplaceable. In the light of these findings, to involve parents, not just as visitors to the school, but as *contributive* members with their own funds of skills and expertise to offer, must be recognized as an essential factor in any compensatory programme.

Biographies and victims

Finally, however, I want to open up the subject just a little further, both in terms of child-rearing patterns generally and in terms of the child's future prospects.

Parents act and talk on the assumption that the child is indeed father of the man; we particularly saw this to be true when we were looking at problems of discipline, where mothers are continually exercised by the problem, 'If I let this go now, what will be the effect in time to come?' In the same way, parents are often anxious about the child's progress at school at 7 and this anxiety is entirely derived from the belief that school progress is both prognostic and causative. That is to say, they believe that if their child *is not* doing well at 7, this *predicts* that he will not do well later and also *causes* him not to do well later. If parents felt that time lost now could be easily retrieved, nothing would matter beyond the child's happiness. Parents on the whole work on a Kellyan basis: 'There is a continuing movement toward the anticipation of events, rather than a series of barters for temporal satisfactions, and this movement is the essence of life itself'; at the same time they find it difficult to accept Kelly's reassurance that 'No one needs to be the victim of his biography' (Kelly, 1955). It is precisely because they fear that their children *will* become victims of their biographies that they try to write the early chapters to a pattern which they hope will build up to a successful dénouement.

We ourselves as developmental psychologists must also admit to a long-term orientation: indeed, it is hardly likely that we would have undertaken longitudinal research with all its logistic inconveniences if we had not had a rather certain notion of a developmental pattern which would make it important to look at the same children throughout their childhoods rather than take separate groups at different points in childhood. I suspect, too, that both we and others would be astonished if we did not eventually find some consistent and cumulative pattern in individual children's progress towards adulthood, or if our data forced us to talk entirely in terms of 'a series of barters for temporal satisfactions' rather than (as we think it does) compelling us to look at child rearing as a long-term process.

Four years after the period that I have been talking about, when these children reached 11, they were subjected to the 11-plus selection procedure. The major component of this consisted of two NFER tests of verbal reasoning administered on separate days, and we were fortunate enough to be given access to our children's verbal reasoning scores for research purposes. The test scores in fact correlated at 0.95, and we therefore were able to use the child's average score between the two tests (see Table 4).

The differences in terms of social class are extraordinarily dramatic, particularly between middle class and working class: once again, the blunt instrument that we originally assumed the Registrar-General's classification must be turns out to be surprisingly well sharpened.

None the less, to say 'verbal reasoning scores are associated with social class' and leave it at that will hardly do; although we may have started out by defining social class, for simplicity and ease of replication, in terms of the Registrar-General's classification, we have seen that the life-styles which characterize different social classes, of which father's occupation is only one part, are far more complex, even where we only look at them from the vantage-point of child rearing. In the end, the life-style defines the social class: father's occupation is merely a short-hand index to it which happens to be more reliable than most other indices that one might choose.

Of more interest, then, is to look at the relationship between the verbal reasoning scores obtained at 11 and the indices which we had devised to describe child's or mother's behaviour or style, or both, at 7. Table 5 shows a number of these indices. Each of them shows a close association with social class except the last. Now obviously if the indices are associated with social class and so is verbal reasoning performance, one will expect to find an association between verbal reasoning scores and these indices; and so one does, to a very marked degree. Much

Table 4   Children who score high and low on verbal reasoning at age 11 years

| | Social class | | | | | Summary | | Overall popn |
	I&II %	IIIwc %	IIIman %	IV %	V %	M. Class %	W. Class %	%
High scores (110+)								
boys	48	29	9	7	0	39	8	16
girls	67	39	10	6	3	54	8	21
both	58	34	10	6	2	46	8	18
	Significance: trend ****			boys/girls n.s.		middle class/working class ****		
Low scores (under 85)								
boys	2	8	32	36	56	5	34	26
girls	2	16	17	22	55	9	22	19
both	2	12	24	29	56	7	28	23
	Significance: trend ****			boys/girls n.s.		middle class/working class ****		

Table 5   Indices which maintain a correlation with verbal reasoning scores (significant at 0.001) when analysed within middle-class or working-class categories (i.e. which operate in relation to verbal reasoning over and above the occupational class factor)

Index	Correlation with v.r. Q.	M. class/W. class
Child-centredness	positive	w. class only
Bamboozlement	negative	both
Temperamental aggression in child	negative	both
Home literacy	positive	both
Reading/writing competence	positive	both
General cultural interests	positive	both
Home–school concordance	positive	both
Child's liking for school	positive	m. class only

more enlightening is to hold occupational class constant and look *within* classes at whether these indices at 7 are correlated with verbal reasoning scores at 11; in this way, the effect of occupational class *per se* is allowed for, and we are now considering separately as factors some of the attitudes and behaviours that go to make up *social class styles*. Table 5 in fact lists only those indices which are highly significantly related to verbal reasoning scores (at 0.001) *when middle-class or working-class affiliation is held constant.*

Among these findings, perhaps the presence of the first three indices is the most striking. The rest are, after all, more or less directly connected with school and how school activities are backed up at home. But in the first three correlations, we have evidence that children whose parents are child-centred (as defined in terms of behaviour in a number of different situations) are at an advantage in verbal reasoning, while children who are themselves aggressive in various ways, and children whose parents are prepared in the name of socialization to 'bamboozle' them—to 'deceive by trickery, hoax, cozen; to mystify' (*Shorter Oxford English Dictionary*)—are at a disadvantage in that respect.

The concepts of advantage and disadvantage thus take on a wider dimension. At this point we are explicitly moving beyond poverty, poor resources and poor understanding of citizens' rights, and saying something about child rearing as it affects children's competence. Within a working-class milieu, perhaps the child whose parents are child-centred, and who therefore can give him that sense of personal worth and considerability which is (we suggest) the core of being 'advantaged', is compensated further than we have yet fully realized. Within a middle-class environment, perhaps children are more diminished than their mothers intend by the 'bamboozling' technique. Children who have no sense of worth are defeated children; children whose parents attempt to rule them by trickery are defeated in the act of starting a dialogue with those who care for them most, let alone in their transactions with the outside world; aggression, too, may perhaps be regarded as the tactic of the defeated. Social class is of interest in child development and education, to the extent that it is associated with attitudes and practices which produce such effects.

. . . insofar as a subculture represents a reaction to defeat and insofar as it is caught by a sense of powerlessness, it suppresses the potential of those who grow up under its sway *by discouraging problem-solving*. The source of powerlessness that such a subculture generates, no matter how moving its by-products, produces instability in the society and unfulfilled promise in human beings.
(Jerome S. Bruner   My Italics.)

Notes

1 The material in this paper appears in more diffuse form in John and Elizabeth Newson, *Perspectives on School at Seven Years Old* (London: Allen & Unwin, 1977).

2 The data that are presented in this paper are based upon a sample of 700 7-year-olds in Nottingham. Percentages given in each social class are based on a minimum of 100 children in any class. Overall population figures are for a random population, in which the class breakdown is: I & II combined, 14 per cent; III white-collar, 13 per cent; III manual, 50 per cent; IV, 15 per cent; V, 8 per cent.

Registrar-General's social class groups are:

Middle class	I & II	Professional/managerial—doctors, solicitors, teachers, nurses, shopkeepers, business executives, administrative officers, clergy, social workers, etc.
	III	White-collar—shop workers (not own business), clerical, police rank and file, salesmen, etc.
Working class	III	Manual: skilled tradesmen—plumbers, painters and decorators, bricklayers, electricians, mining face workers, lathe operators, drivers, etc.
	IV	Semi-skilled—stokers, loaders, machine operatives, 'mates' of skilled men, packers, bus conductors, ticket collectors, porters, etc.
	V	Unskilled—labourers, cleaners.

References

Bruner, Jerome S., 1972, 'The psychology of pedagogy', in *The Relevance of Education* (London: Allen & Unwin).

Greenfield, P. M., 1972, 'Goal as environmental variable in the development of intelligence' (Conference on 'Contributions to intelligence', University of Illinois); quoted in 'Poverty and childhood', essay in Bruner, 1972.

Kelly, G. A., 1955, *The Psychology of Personal Constructs*, Vol. 1: *A Theory of Personality* (New York: Norton).

Newson, John and Newson, Elizabeth, 1963, *Infant Care in an Urban Community* (London: Allen & Unwin).

Newson, John and Newson, Elizabeth, 1968, *Four Years Old in an Urban Community* (London: Allen & Unwin).

Newson, John and Newson, Elizabeth, 1976, *Seven Years Old in the Home Environment* (London: Allen & Unwin).

Aspects of Education
Edited by M. Braham
© 1982 John Wiley & Sons Ltd.

Chapter 7

Growth to Autonomy Within a System of Conventions

*John Shotter**

My task in this paper is not just that of outlining a framework of thought for understanding how a new member of a society, a child, comes to be socialized and to act as those already in his society require him to act; it is to outline how he may, while still making sense to all those with whom he shares his life, come to act as he *himself* requires. In other words, I am interested in how men may develop a degree of autonomy while living within a system of conventions, with how they may become masters of their ways of life rather than being slaves to them—and surprisingly, perhaps, I shall argue that this kind of freedom *is only* possible for us within a community, that only through others can we ever come to know and learn how to control ourselves.

The child does not appear in the world as the effect of a chain of causes. He appears, I shall suggest, as an active agent who, from the moment of his birth, in the course of interchanges with others, is engaged in the task of making himself into a being able to take his own 'place' amongst them, as a personality, a human being with a self and a persona, who is able to choose different ways of being and acting.

A 'new theme' in social studies: the 'social world'

Now the 'new theme' that I would like to contribute to our discussions draws upon the recent clarifications of the nature of the *social world* and our conduct within it provided by such philosophers as Wittgenstein (1953) and Winch (1958), and such social scientists as Schutz (1972) and Garfinkel (1967). Their accounts of the social world differ markedly from the accounts of the natural world (of atoms and molecules, billiard balls

* Lecturer, Department of Psychology, University of Nottingham.

and planets) in terms of which we have tried to explain human conduct in the past. As is quite clear, collections of atoms and molecules do not (we assume) regulate their interactions with one another in terms of the meanings they assign to each other's behaviour; while equally clearly, people do so act. It is in their account of 'meaning' that the writers mentioned above depart so much from the natural scientific view: for they take 'meaning' to be a human activity, a practical activity; it is something that people *do*. They do not take meanings as things which, as the products of processes, could exist independently and in isolation from the processes in which they are produced.

They are thus saying two important things: one is that people must be treated as *agents*; that is, no matter what metaphysical notions one may believe about universal determinism, etc., people can—without quite knowing how it is that they can do it—cause at least some of their own motions. The other thing is that one cannot find the sense in a person's action just by looking at the logical structure of the movements in which it consists; one must study how these movements are put to use in a social context. And thus what one must learn if one is to become a member of a society is, among other things, 'how to mean' (and I take that expression from the title of Halliday's (1975) recent book in which he explores the development of language in much the same terms as I shall here).

Now learning to-make-sense-to-others is not just a matter of learning to make well-defined patterns of responses—that is, learning something *objective*—it is a matter of learning how to adapt and modify one's actions in the face of continually changing circumstances in their relation to an ideal or standard—that is, one must learn a *practical skill*. In fact, one must learn many different practical skills if one is to relate one's behaviour intelligibly to the behaviour of others in one's social life (whether others happen to be present at the time or not), for one must learn, for instance, how to agree, to request, to name, to describe, to command, to promise, to negotiate, to love, to hate, to rationalize, to carry out, in fact, a whole host of different practical accomplishments. And the whole point about the nature of such activities is that they are all only differentiated from one another in terms of the language, or at least in the different ways of meaning, that one must use in conducting them. Thus 'our idea of reality', says Winch (1958, p. 15), 'is given for us in the language that we use. [And] it may be worth reminding ourselves of the truism that when we speak of the world we are in fact speaking of what we mean by the expression "the world" . . .'. It is in acquiring mastery of the concepts embodied in our everyday ways of talking that a child acquires mastery of his society's ways of life; and indeed, that is the only way, for it is in the ways that we talk that we conduct the distinctive patterns of social exchange constituting our particular society.

Given this it is clear that a man cannot learn how to act in his world merely from the position of an uninvolved observer. Actions in a social world do not present themselves to mere observers as being already structured; observers of people's movements in unfamiliar societies may make very little sense of them at first. Only with a degree of active involvement in activities of that kind at some point or other can one come to understand what-is-going-on. But if one is to learn how, precisely, to involve oneself, then one must learn the appropriate practical skills. And it is that process—the process in which in the course of dialogical exchanges one moves from a crude, undifferentiated grasp of a social process to a more detailed and refined knowledge of how to involve oneself in it and to understand what is going on—that I want to discuss below. But before I do, I want to discuss what is 'always already there', so to speak, for those engaged in this developmental process to draw upon: what is 'there' in the child innately and what is 'there' in our social institutions.

What is 'always already there'?

In the study of child development recently, we have all been surprised by findings (Fantz, 1961; Bower, 1966, 1974) which seem to suggest that infants may show characteristic human responses to their environment much earlier than ever before expected. But what, exactly, do these brilliant researches show? While they may certainly be revealing of what is 'already there' in advance of experience for the child himself to call on, the task of understanding how the child learns to use what is 'already there' still remains. To see the nature of the task the child faces here, let me consider him just for a while as an organism rather than as a personal being.

Now undoubtedly, as an organism, an infant is an extremely sensitive differential reactor to his circumstances. Thus with ingenuity and care (and perhaps with the help of the appropriate laboratory apparatus and recording techniques) one could presumably detect and identify the characteristics of his differential responding to many different situations. But no matter how clear, distinct, and characteristic the results of such investigations may be in such a situation, the characteristics would be ones which you as an outsider had elicited, detected, and identified in his differential responding: nothing in one's results would indicate that the infant *himself* had directed, detected, and distinguished his own differential responding in the same way; and even less would they indicate that he knew its significance, i.e. what is implied for how he *himself* might go on to deal with the situation (in contrast to merely reacting to it). If one is going to be a person, acting in the knowledge of who and what one is and what one is trying to do in relation to the others with whom one is sharing one's life, then something more than merely behaviour in ways that others can recognize is involved—one must be able to recognize what one is doing oneself.

In other words, genuine human action is essentially 'reflexive' in a way organic activity is not. If one is to act with understanding, one must act back to influence oneself *in the same way*, suggests George Mead (1934), as one influences others. Human action is necessarily referred to a *self*, a self that is both agent *and* patient in action, and subject *and* object in thought. And the development of the self is, of course, as Mead points out, something which has a development of quite a different kind from the development of the physiological organism proper.

Now while the child as an organism may seem to be provided innately with the capacities to act in many different ways, 'where' might the potential source of knowledge be located about the different particular uses to which these, otherwise rather indeterminate, capacities may be put? Well, the way in which a new member of a social world finds the structure of it already 'pre-established' seems to me to be rather well put by Berger and Luckman (1971, pp. 77–78) who, following Schutz, say:

An institutional world . . . is experienced as an objective reality. It has a history that antedates the individual's birth and is not accessible to his biographical recollection. It was there before he was born, and it will be there after his death. This history itself, as the tradition of the existing institutions, has the character of objectivity. The individual's biography is apprehended as an episode located within the objective history of the society. The institutions, as historical and objective facticities, confront the individual as undeniable facts. The institutions are there, whether he likes it or not. He cannot wish them away . . . .. Since institutions exist as external reality, the individual cannot understand them by introspection. He must 'go out' and learn about them, just as he must to learn about nature. This remains true even though the human world, as a humanly produced reality, is potentially understandable in a way not possible in the case of the natural world.

In other words, the knowledge which the child must acquire if he is to learn how to put his innate capacities to use, intelligibly and responsibly, is 'out there', in his society, encoded, not as ideas in people's heads, but in the *practical activities of everyday life*.

And this is a really most important point: the classical image of man that we seem to have inherited from the Greeks is of man as a thinking subject, set over against the world as an object. In our new approach, man is primarily a doer, immersed in the world as an agent who has the power to act on the world and to change it to accord more with his own needs and interests (Shotter, 1975). Reflective thought is a secondary activity, occurring if at all only when man is withdrawn from practical activities; and his thinking then may or may not serve to inform his subsequent doings. Thus, in the view I am taking, practice precedes the theory of it.

Institutions

Ryle (1949, p. 31) takes a similar view. In discussing the relation between theory and practice, he maintains:

Efficient practice precedes the theory of it; methodologies presuppose the application of the methods, of the critical investigation of which they are the products. It was because Aristotle found himself and others reasoning now intelligently and now stupidly, and it was because Izaak Walton found himself and others angling sometimes effectively and sometimes ineffectively that both were able to give to their pupils the maxims and prescriptions of their art.

If we are to establish institutions which are appropriate to the circumstances in which they must operate, then efficient practice must precede the theory of it. But there is a point in the attempt to formulate, once practices do prove effective, the theory of them. Ryle's comments suggest two reasons: (1) theoretical accounts may, if their application is understood, serve to indicate intelligent rather than stupid, effective rather than ineffective conduct, and thus function to institute standards of correct and incorrect conduct enabling one to evaluate actions; and (2) as such, they may also be used as aids in the instruction of others into the practice, making clear what it is that one must learn to do. But there is another even more important reason: (3) by using one's theoretical account to formulate a plan, one may extend one's practices, deliberately, into areas other than those in which they were initially developed. And this is most important. For if men are ever to be self-determining, and to act as they require rather than as their circumstances require, and to project themselves into the future, they must develop the ability to deliberate before they act; that is, they must develop the ability to decide courses of action in theory before executing their choice in action (Macmurray, 1957; Taylor, 1966). And to do this they require neither merely 'subjective', idiosyncratic knowledge, known only to them alone, nor solely 'objective', impersonal knowledge, known in the same way by everybody; they require 'inter-subjectively shared' knowledge of how they, personally and individually, may satisfy their own desires in ways which others find intelligible and morally acceptable. It is the growth of this ability to act not only intelligently but also intelligibly and responsibly, deliberately in anticipation of the future, that I want to discuss in a moment below.

But before I do let me draw your attention to some comments of O'Neill (1970, p. xv) in introducing Merleau-Ponty's account of human institutions. 'We do not invent our language', says O'Neill,

any more than we invent our history. Rather, we find ourselves in history just as we do in our language. We owe to language the assurance of the exchange of thoughts and values and thereby our notions of a common mankind and a universal history. The foundations of the human sciences do not rest upon any object, properly speaking, or on any theoretical construction, but in the institution between ourselves and others which each of us undertakes according to his situation, and yet by which we are drawn into the drama of a universal culture.

And O'Neill then goes on to quote Merleau-Ponty's (1970, pp. 40–41) phenomenological account of institutions. 'Thus what we understand by the concept of *institution*', he says,

are those events in experience which endow it with durable dimensions, in relation to which a whole series of other experiences will require meaning, will form an intelligible series or a history—or again those events which sediment in me a meaning, not just as survivals or residues, but as the invitation to a sequel, the necessity of a future.

Thus activity within an institution unfolds within a field of meaning, in which my act now is meaningfully connected to what I have just done, and a range of possible next acts, meaningfully connected to what I am doing now, lies open to me. It is to the way in which the child is inducted into human institutions that I now wish to turn.

Mothers, meanings, and motivations

I want now to begin to focus my discussion upon the relationship between a mother and her child in that period of life leading up to the child learning, as we say, language. In this pre-verbal period, both face the task of constructing between them a matrix of mutual understandings, their own personal institution, from scratch; an institution within which both may carry out significant projects in relation to one another—within which, for instance, they may 'request' certain actions of one another but, most importantly, within which a mother may begin to present her child with the nature of the social reality encoded within her practical activities. As a 'teacher', then, in these early exchanges, one part of the mother's task is plain: her child is reliant upon her to give what he does *meaning*. That is, it is up to her to reflect back to her child the socially significant consequences of his actions. For, while she may be self-determining to a high degree, able to evaluate the social significance of her own acts as she performs them, able to act at one moment in terms of the meaning she had assigned to her acts of the previous moment, her child is not so self-reliant. He has no idea of how to project himself into the future and to regulate his actions in terms of their relation to an imagined goal. While his actions may seem to have an intentional structure to them, he clearly has no skill, as yet, at formulating intentions and holding them in mind while attempting to execute them. As he is unable at this stage to bring off any sensible projects at all, his mother has to show him to what—in the social world into which he happens to have been born—his actions can lead.

But there is another part to her task: besides showing him the socially intelligible uses of his actions, a mother may also, by intelligently interlacing her activities with his, involve him in sustained and organized projects—as simple as, for instance, paying sustained visual attention to an object, or as complex, perhaps, as building toy brick towers or doing jigsaws—projects that he would never otherwise undertake if left to his own devices.

Thus the child is learning in his exchanges with his mother a number of different things about his social world: he is learning about the *goals* that may legitimately be pursued in his society, that is, what constitutes the 'done things'; he is also learning about the guidelines, rules, and conventions that he must observe in his actions, for only if he acts in certain *ways* does his mother find his actions acceptable and respond to them; but futher, in learning about how to conduct sustained courses of action, he is learning about the *occasions* upon which one action rather than another is appropriate; the ways in which different actions may be related to one another as parts of an overall project. He is thus learning about what, how, and where things are done—why they are done, at least in one sense, becomes his problem only later, when he turns to a study of the social sciences.

Early social exchanges

Now while mothers may treat their babies in a personal manner from birth (Macfarlane, 1974), the assumption that they should be treated as persons from birth for the purposes of science has not yet found much favour. Many scientists have assumed that the child is at first *asocial* (Schaffer, 1971, p. 13) *animal matter* (Richards, 1974, p. 51), that develops as an aspect of *embryogenesis* (Piaget and Inhelder, 1969, p. vii) only later into a person. Macmurray is one of the few writers to insist that infants must be treated both practically and theoretically as personal beings right from the start. He says (Macmurray, 1961, pp. 49–50),

> In general, to represent the process of human development, even at its earliest stage, as an organic process, is to represent it in terms which are equally applicable to the development of animals, and therefore to exclude reference to any form of behaviour which is exclusively human; to exclude reference to rationality in any of its expressions, practical or theoretical; reference to action or to knowledge, to deliberate purpose or reflective thought. If this were correct, no infant could ever survive. For its existence and its development depend from the beginning on rational activities, upon thought and action. The baby cannot yet think or act. Consequently he must depend for his life upon the thought and action of others. The conclusion is not that the infant is still an animal which will become rational through some curious organic process of development. It is that he cannot, even theoretically, live an isolated existence; that he is not an independent individual. He lives a common life as one term in a personal relation.

And a part of what it is for the infant to be in a personal relationship right from the start is for his mother to treat his activity, not in organic terms as merely reaction to a stimulus, but in personal terms.

Thus, on the one hand, mothers may act to elicit from their children certain forms of no doubt innately organized activity, but activity which makes sense to them and which, without their intelligent adjustment of the eliciting circumstances (as I shall make clear using an example from Newson and Newson (1976) below), would undoubtedly remain unexpressed. In other words, a mother acts to motivate certain types of activity in her child—Schutz (1953) would say, she provides a *because-motive*; he acts because of what she does. On the other hand, having motivated some characteristically human activity, she now acts to interpret it as having a *meaning*: 'Oh look,' she says, after having got her infant to look at her by cooing and smiling at him, having placed her face in his line of regard, 'he's looking at me.' So she replies to his look with a 'Hello, hello, you cheeky thing'. The point here being that whatever she does, she interprets her baby's activity as something which he himself does, not merely as something she has succeeded in eliciting from him; it is thus activity worthy of being treated as an expression in a dialogue, an expression requiring a meaningful reply. She thus supplies him with what Schutz (1953) would call an *in-order-to motive* as well; for here he learns what he can bring about by his actions.

As an example of the way in which the intelligent adjustment of the adult to the child's own activity may function to elicit complex human action from him that he might not otherwise express, Newson and Newson (in press) have described well, I think, the task of getting a supine 4-week-old infant to follow visually a dangling ring:

In this superficially simple task, the test demonstrator will carefully attend, not just to the general state of arousal of the infant, but to his precise focus and line of regard. Having 'hooked' the attention of the infant upon the ring, one then begins gingerly to move it across his field of vision in such a way that the infant's eyes continue to hold the object with successive fixations until eventually the head follows the eyes in that co-ordinated overall movement pattern which denotes successful tracking. If the test object is moved too suddenly, or is left static too long, the visual attention of the infant will flag and the attempt will have to begin all over again from scratch. In this instance, what is in fact happening is a highly skilled monitoring by the adult and a consequent adjustment of the dangling object, moment by moment, depending on the feedback which is being obtained from the spontaneous actions of the infant.

Thus, as they go on to say, 'the resulting action sequence of the infant is therefore a combination of his own activity and an intelligent manipulation of that activity by the much more sophisticated adult partner'. It is in the sense, then, that the child can be a competent participant in interactive exchanges such as these that he may properly be counted as 'one term in a personal relation'.

The institution of 'pointing'; gestures

Let me move on now to discuss something more akin to language: Vygotsky's (1966) account of the genesis of the pointing gesture fits in well here. He suggests that the process is best conceptualized as taking place in three stages; first there is the occurrence of a gesture *in itself*, which becomes as a result of the way others treat it a gesture *for others*, but which later, once mastered, may become a gesture *for oneself*.

He suggests that first something like a pointing gesture may occur in the course of an unsuccessful grasping movement. But whether the origins of the movement are always to be found in such circumstances is not crucial. All that is required for the next stage is that the child do something to which the mother can respond *as if* he were in some way 'pointing'—and by that I do not just mean making appropriate finger and hand movements, but also manifesting a general orientation to and concentration upon an object. To the extent that there is nothing in the child's behaviour to suggest that he expects any social consequences to follow from his 'gesture', we may say that what he does, initially, means nothing in itself. But his mother may take it as an indication of his interest in an object and respond accordingly. Others, then, provide the whole structured context within which it becomes possible for the child to realize that just an aspect of his expression of interest in an object may be taken by others as an indicator, a stage he only attains at 9 months to a year or so.

Upon the internal processes responsible for such a realization, we need not speculate. The fact seems to be that, with the mother's help, the character of the child's movement changes: it changes, Vygotsky points out, from a movement directed towards an object to a movement directed towards another person; it becomes a means of communication, a grasping (if that is what it was, for it hardly matters) becomes a 'pointing'. But, as Vygotsky says about this stage in the process, while the child may seem to have learnt how to point *for others*, it is only later that it becomes a pointing gesture *for the child himself*. That is, it is only later that the child realizes what it is for him to point, such that he can respond, say, to a request to point at something, or respond to others pointing as they respond to him. The child thus comes to participate in the institution of pointing, without, I might add, ever receiving any theoretical instruction whatsoever; for him it is merely a practical skill.

In case the process described above may seem like reinforcement learning, *à la* Skinner—because it entails the mother responding contingently upon what the child does—let me make clear why it is not. If each time the child pointed he was given a reward, a sweet, say, or anything other than his mother attending to that at which he was pointing, one may still succeed in increasing the frequency of pointing-like movements. But the child could never possibly learn that such movements were something which could be used, not for getting reward, but for directing someone else's attention.

Now there are plenty of other actions of children in daily life which, through the interpretative intervention of adults, come to function as meaningful gestures. Lock (1975a) points out how the way in which a child raises his arms just before being picked up, comes to be used by him as a gesture meaning 'I want to be picked up', just because his mother treats it as such. But all kinds of movements may be institutionalized between people as gestures. In another paper, Lock (1975b) describes how he chose to respond to the arm flapping that was manifested as a part of an infant's excited reaction before an out-of-reach object as if it meant 'I want it'. Acting as if that was its meaning, Lock induced the child to address him with an arm-flapping gesture whenever there was something he wanted Lock to fetch for him. Such examples may surely be multiplied; but whereas these gestures are rather idiosyncratic micro-institutions, existing between just two individuals, other forms of gesture—like pointing—that the child may learn at an early age are already a part of the institution existing between us all in our society. And in learning it, the child is learning not just to communicate with his mother, but with us all; he is learning to be one of us.

Mothers as investigators and negotiators

Let me move on now to discuss more extensive enterprises involving connected sequences of acts; and in particular, I want to describe how mothers investigate their children's actions for their meanings, and how they *negotiate* possible meanings with them.

In an incident Shotter and Gregory (1976) describe, a mother is attempting to show her young child (Samantha, aged 11 months) how to place shaped pieces on a form-board. Having just physically helped her little girl to place one of the pieces correctly, Samantha's mother then said, 'Oh, clever girl.' But Samantha did not pause in her activity and signal by eye contact and smiling that she *knew* that she had just done something of significance, she just went straight away on to manipulate another piece. So her mother leant forward, caught her eye, and repeated her 'marker' more emphatically: 'AREN'T YOU CLEVER?' Samantha then stopped, and smiled at her mother for a moment, and then her mother continued to try to help her once more.

Now the point I want to make in describing this episode is that mothers are not satisfied with their children just doing the tasks that they require of them. The children must lso give indications in their actions that they did what they did as a result of trying to do it, that they knew what was required of them, that their actions were based in some knowledge of the socially defined requirements of the situation. They must come to show in their actions, not just an awareness of their physical circumstances, but a *self*-awareness; that is, an awareness of the nature of their relations to others. And thus mothers 'analyse' the knowledge in their actions by testing it for its implications: 'If she [Samantha] knows that what she's just done is significant then she should expect or at least accept acknowledgement from me . . . . I will give it . . . .. She doesn't accept it . . . . Therefore she does not, perhaps, yet know,' says Samantha's mother in effect. And as she does not yet seem to know about these things, her mother provides her with yet another occasion on which she may learn. Mothers can be seen then to be actively investigating their child's activities to see if they have put the correct interpretation upon them.

So far, in discussing the interpretations that mothers put upon their child's activities, I have tended to present it as if it were a 'one-pass' affair; as if a mother just arrives at an interpretation and then acts upon the basis of it. But the example presented above tends to suggest a more complex process. Quite often it must be a matter of an initially wrong or inadequate interpretation being modified in the light of subsequent 'investigations', until a result acceptable to both parties is achieved. In other words, there is a social process of *negotiation* involved. And the point about the negotiation of interpretations here is really quite general: the meaning of an action (or utterance) is not just a matter of the intention it expresses, it is also a matter of how it is taken. The character of people's activities is something to be negotiated amongst those who are concerned with the meanings being communicated and the projects to which they relate—the same activity being seen as having any one of a number of different interpretations according to the overarching project in which it is included.

Now in acting like this, as an investigator and negotiator of her child's activities and their interpretation, the mother might be said to be acting as a 'double-agent': for she is acting both on her own behalf and also her infant's behalf in what goes on.

At first, an infant clearly has little power to satisfy his own needs. But to the extent that a mother can interpret her infant's behaviour as having an intention behind it (no matter how vague and indefinite it may be on his part), she can help him to complete or fulfil it, and in the process 'negotiate' a satisfaction of his needs with him. The child's action is thus made to eventuate in a consequence that is at least intelligible to her; and she does it by rendering herself available to him as an 'instrument' or 'mechanism' acting to produce a result which she feels may be one 'intended' in his activity—whether it is the actual, precise intention in his activity, no one can say, least of all the child, for his activity is so diffuse and uninformed that any intention there may be in it at all must be presumed to be, at this stage, really indeterminate.

As a result of her help, as a result of the way in which a mother completes the realization of what might possibly be her child's intention, his actions may become incorporated into the circle of reciprocal exchange between them both. Thus he learns to act, both in expressing himself and in manipulating the things about him, in such a way that *at least makes sense to her*—the child himself not understanding till later the nature of *what* it is that he is actually doing, it being enough at first that he understands *how* to do it. And thus the process continues, with the child being 'helped' by his mother in this way to retrospectively evaluate his states of feeling and the consequences of his actions. Now it is not so much in this process that he experiences new states of feeling or performs new patterns of action that have never ever occurred to him before, that would otherwise be biologically unavailable to him, but that he learns *meanings* or *socially significant uses* for feelings that he may have or movements that he might make any time. He comes to learn the way other people fulfil the meaning in his movements, so that later he may fulfil their meaning himself—as Mead (1934, p. 46) puts it, 'the . . . gesture becomes a significant symbol . . . when it has the same effect on the individual making it that it has upon the individual to whom it is addressed . . . and thus involves a reference to the self of the individual making it'. In acquiring knowledge of how to order his activities in relation to others, the child *himself* learns how to act; he learns, gradually, how not to act like a child, reliant upon others to complete and giving meaning to his behaviour, but to relate what he does and what he feels to his own knowledge of his own momentary 'position' in his culture; he relates his own activity to his *self*.

The non-causal process of child development

This is what a child may learn, then, in his exchanges with others; but then again he may not. The work of Bernstein (1971, 1972) and Hess and Shipman (1965) suggests some reasons for this. For Bernstein, too, takes it that practice precedes theory. And that in learning language, in learning how to mean, one is not learning to grasp a general *idea* of language which, once grasped, may be put to use to inform any utterance, for any use, at any time. One is learning simply to participate in a great rag-bag of different linguistic institutions. And what particular linguistic practices one learns depends upon one's particular, everyday life linguistic exchanges: one may learn to joke and to commiserate, for instance, but fail to learn to describe or to command others—at least, in some contexts. Thus if one is going to learn theorizing as a practical skill, especially theorizing about the nature of one's own social life in order to deliberate upon and to plan one's future courses of action, one must engage oneself in exchanges with those in whom this is already an everyday life activity; being instructed in the theory of a practice is of little use if one is not being instructed at the same time in the practice itself. Thus it is that children may fail to learn things if they miss the opportunity to engage in certain kinds of social exchange.

But even with such opportunities, the child may still fail to learn. For the child is not just a passive recipient of all the ministrations of others, inevitably shaped one way or another by what is done to it—as some purveyors of educational theories seem to suggest (and hope). The child seems to be an active agent in the process of his own development. A mother cannot *cause* him to do anything (like one may cause one billiard ball to strike another if one hits it appropriately with the cue); she can only intelligently interlace her actions with his in an attempt merely to help his development. How he responds to what she does is up to him and the extent to which he has learnt to use what he can do in ways which make sense to her. So, although we might hope that one day we will know *for certain* how to educate our children, know in fact how to *cause* their development, if children really are agents in their own development, then that will be impossible. The best we can hope for is a realistic understanding of what will actually help. And this is surely better than the illusory hope that we can find certain ways of causing their development, thus misleading ourselves and them in all kinds of quite irrelevant and positively unhelpful ways.

Reference

Berger, P. L., and Luckman, T., 1971, *The Social Construction of Reality* (Harmondsworth, Middx: Penguin Books).

Bernstein, B., 1971, *Class, Codes and Control*, vol. 1. (London: Routledge & Kegan Paul).

Bernstein, B., 1972, *Class, Codes and Control*, vol. 2. (London: Routledge & Kegan Paul).

Bower, T. R. G., 1966, 'The visual world of infants', *Scientific American*, **215**, 80–92.

Bower, T. R. G., 1974, *Development in Infancy* (San Francisco: Freeman).

Fantz, R. L., 1961, 'The origin of form perception', *Scientific American*, **204**, 66–72.

Garfinkel, H., 1967, *Studies in Ethnomethodology* (Englewood Cliffs, NJ: Prentice-Hall).

Halliday, M. A. K., 1975, *Learning How to Mean* (London: Arnold).

Hess, R. D., and Shipman, V. C., 1965, 'Early experience and the socialisation of cognitive modes in children', *Child Development*, **36**, 869–886.

Lock, A., 1975a, 'On being picked up', paper read at the Association for the Study of Animal Behaviour Symposium 'Mother–Child interaction in man and the higher mammals', London, December.

Lock, A., 1975b, 'Acts not sentences', in W. von Raffler-Engel and Y. Lebrun, eds, *Baby Talk and Infant Speech* (Lisse, Netherlands: Swets & Zeitlinger).

Macfarlane, A., 1974, 'If a smile is so important', *New Scientist*, 25 April.

Macmurray, J., 1957, *The Self as Agent*, (London: Faber & Faber).

Macmurray, J., 1961, *Persons in Relation* (London: Faber & Faber).

Mead, G. H., 1934, *Mind, Self and Society* (Chicago: University of Chicago Press).

Merleau-Ponty, M., 1970, *Theme from the Lectures at the College de France*, trans. John O'Neill (Evanston, Ill.: Northwestern University Press).

Newson, J., and Newson, E., 1976, 'On the social origins of symbolic functioning', in V. P. Varma and P. Williams, eds, *Advances in Educational Psychology 3*, (London: Hodder & Stoughton Educational).

O'Neill, J., 1970, Translator's Preface, in Merleau-Ponty, 1970.

Piaget, J., and Inhelder, B., 1969, *The Psychology of the Child* (London: Routledge & Kegan Paul).

Richards, M. P. M., 1974, 'First steps in becoming social', in M. P. M. Richards, ed., *The Integration of a Child into a Social World* (Cambridge: Cambridge University Press).

Ryle, G., 1949, *The Concept of Mind* (London: Hutchinson).

Schaffer, H. R., 1971, *The Growth of Sociability* (Harmondsworth, Middx: Penguin).

Schutz, A., 1953, 'Common-sense and scientific interpretation of human action', *Philosophy and Phenomenological Research,* **14,** 1–38.

Schutz, A., 1972, *The Phenomenology of the Social World* (London: Heinemann).

Shotter, J., 1975, *Images of Man in Psychological Research* (London- Methuen).

Shotter, J., and Gregory, S., 1976, 'On First Gaining the idea of Oneself as a Person', in R. Harré, ed., *Life Sentences* (Chichester, England: Wiley).

Taylor, R., 1966, *Action and Purpose* (Englewood Cliffs, NJ: Prentice-Hall).

Vygotsky, L. S., 1966, 'Development of the higher mental functions', in *Psychological Research in the USSR* (Moscow: Progress Publishers).

Winch, P., 1957, *The Idea of a Social Science and its Relations to Philosophy* (London: Routledge & Kegan Paul).

Wittgenstein, L., 1953, *Philosophical Investigations* (Oxford: Blackwell).

Chapter 8

Things for Use and Things for Meaning: Reflections on Play and Discovery

*R. A. Hodgkin**

> Even in Leonardo's time there were certain obscure needs and patterns of the spirit, which could discover themselves only through . . . the analogies provided by stains on walls or the embers of a fire. Now, I think that in this inward-looking age, when we have become so much more aware of the vagaries of the spirit, so respectful of the workings of the unconscious, the artist is more likely to find his point of departure in analogies of this kind. Theya are more exciting because they . . . take us by surprise, like forgotten smells: and they seem to be more profound because the memories they awaken have been deeply buried in our minds.
>
> Sir Kenneth Clark, 'The blot and the diagram'

In this paper I shall reflect on the experience that we all have, especially as children, that sometimes things are ordinary and 'mine', and at other times they are extraordinary and 'other', pointing to unfamiliar worlds of meaning. We shall consider how toys and play may be the source of skilled thought and action on the one hand and of exploration and the creation of new forms on the other. The second aspect, which relates to symbols, is the more difficult, so we may as well grasp the symbolic core of the problem at once: why do artists, especially painters and poets, cultivate ambiguity? We may then be led to wonder why teachers, who

---

* Formerly of the Department of Educational Studies, University of Oxford.

are also artists of a kind, do not recognize ambiguity and the study of it as a more central concern.

The ambiguous smile

I am not sure whether a smile is a *thing:* like many of the products of art and of human intercourse it is both evanescent and enigmatic. John Shotter (1973) has stressed the importance of a smile as a marker in the early establishment of interpersonal relations. The first smile indicates, according to him, the start of the critical phase when the mother and child live in a kind of psychic unity or symbiosis, and within this the essentially social potential of the infant has its first flowering. The phase lasts until about the time when the child first becomes mobile and begins to explore the world 'on his own'. During this period it learns, from a prelinguistic sign system, which includes smiles, when it can use its mother as an instrument of play or gratification and when her autonomy or absence must be accepted. All these non-verbal communications are more ambiguous and more charged with feeling than is usual in developed language. Their domain is evocative, conditional, and sub-junctive for they call up what might be, what is latent in the other: humanity in the child, motherliness in the adult.

But how is it that ambiguities evoke meaning? This can be well illustrated by another famous smile, the Mona Lisa's. This certainly is a material thing, fixed particles of paint on wood; yet it acts by making us act. Professor Gombrich points out that Leonardo da Vinci was the first conscious master of pictorial ambiguity. The strange, two-level back-ground of the *Mona Lisa*, for example, plays calculated tricks with our perception, making us see her at one moment as more exalted and at the next warm and earthbound. More cunning even than the background are the famous smudges round the eyes and mouth—what painters came to call *sfumato*. 'These blurred outlines and mellow colours', writes Gombrich, 'allow one form to merge into another and always leave something to the imagination' (Gombrich, 1950, p. 219). The controlled and calculated vagueness of Leonardo forces us to work, to project alternate meanings on to those smudges which say so much by saying nothing clearly. Henri Nathan makes a somewhat similar point in regard to the evocative powers of smell. It may be that just because we do not have a complex analytical system for describing smells these are more readily associable to those feelings of childhood which have also escaped the net of verbal categorizing.

That is not how it works in life; for a smile is not a smudge but rather it seems to *play* over a man's or a woman's face and by using the word 'play' we recognize its ambiguity. It comes and goes, keeping you, the lover or the learner, guessing and only rarely, mercifully rarely, does a real face congeal to a cheesy grin. Leonardo achieves this trick with a blurr. He makes us pause (though we are scarcely conscious of it) and consider alternative hypotheses. He not only simulates something of the mobility of a living face but in so doing he heightens the quality of feeling in his picture. As soon as we receive an unambiguous message from a face or from a work of art our feelings cool or take on a cruder form; head takes over from heart. This is one rather striking example of what must be a general aesthetic principle though I have not seen it enunciated in explicit form: artists use symbols and symbolic techniques in which ambiguity is intended so that more complex thoughts and more appropriate feelings may be evoked in the perceiver; they are concerned to delay logical, sequential thought partly in order that this may be enriched by feeling. Comparable ideas could be expressed in regard to the brain's two hemispheres or to binocular vision; indeed we all make much better sense of the world if there is some contradiction and complementarity in the data we receive, than if it is all clear and simple. Even in politics we are right to value dissonant voices and to suspect unanimity.

Artists, from earliest times and in all cultures, have used the power of symbolic forms to make us pause, draw breath and feel emotion as we project *our* meanings on *their* smudges. Leonardo was the first Western artist to comment on this phenomenon and thus precipitated the development of modern consciousness of these two aspects (Clark, 1963; Gombrich, 1960). Two hundred years later, at the beginning of the eighteenth century, Vico in his *New Science* was exploring similar ideas in regard to language (Berlin, 1976, pp. 45–46). Ernst Cassirer, Susanne Langer, and others have clarified our understanding about how symbols work. But the central idea that symbols act through their ambiguity is still not adequately grasped by some psychologists: Professor Inhelder, for example, uses 'symbol' to denote any arbitrary sign. This linguistic confusion is not quite as serious as it might appear, for no one disputes that symbols are a kind of sign. Some of the more hard-headed psychologists and philosophers, however, are unwilling to admit what sounds like a magical notion, that some signs have power. Yet the process of projecting meaning on to slightly contradictory stimuli is now a commonplace among psychologists who study perception (R. L. Gregory, 1966).

In language a similar process will be familiar to teachers and writers. If a poet takes a word (sign) and uses it in such a way as to heighten feeling and to introduce complex, overlapping fields of reference, he is creating and recreating that word's symbolic possibilities. He is no witch to be ducked in some positivist pool, for almost all words and signs have symbolic potential. Conversely, however, much art and literature can easily be reduced to the unambiguous commonplace, to the 'mere' or plain fact. Not that there is anything wrong with plain signs; if we are legal draftsmen or scientists, communicating our findings, then we seek out and prize this unsymbolic, unambiguous quality of language. Carrying this further one could, perhaps, suggest that the invention of currency was an early move to project on to things a cold and unambiguous value; but that is another subject.

In order to stress the ambiguity which is essential to the concept of symbol it is worth reflecting briefly on the origin of the word itself— 'sym-bol'; it is to do with things 'thrown together'. Those things were apparently, in pre-literate Greek communities, two halves of a broken sherd. When a rendez-vous had been arranged between strangers, each would carry a broken bit of sherd and test the identity of the stranger by fitting these together. The symbol brought about, as true symbols always do, a change of level, in this case from potential enmity to friendship (Stein, 1957).

Winnicott's potential space and the frontier of discovery

Is it not strange that an infant should be heir to the whole world, and see those mysteries which the books of the learned never unfold? The corn was orient and immortal wheat which never should be reaped and never was sown. I thought it had stood from everlasting to everlasting.

Thomas Traherne, 'Centuries of Meditation'

An adequate educational theory should be interested, at least marginally, in wholeness, even in holiness, as well as in particular efficiencies. David Winnicott in *Playing and Reality* (1971) provides us not only with a deep sense of the worth and value of the children whom he helped but he also offers the rudiments of a conceptual model which can relate to toys and play, tools and skill, symbol and discovery. He developed this in considering very young and disturbed children and their need to discover themselves, and the world, through play. But if we take this, basically psychological, model and extend it we find that it is capacious enough to resolve a number of difficulties in educational philosophy and it opens up new interesting lines for both our thought and action. Indeed, I think Winnicott's model has powerful political implications, too, in regard to freedom and diversity in society.. His approach requires that we accept the idea, known to the ancients, that play is a universal concept, a divine activity, which in human experience runs right up to the frontiers of human endeavour and down to the routines of practice and relaxation.

If we consider our own experience, as we acquire competence within any open, generative system, such as language or music or mountain climbing, we will notice that we learn to sharpen and then to integrate a number of sub-skills; but we can only do this in a relatively unstressed and protected context. Psychologists have established that the more complex the task to be learnt, the more inappropriate is pressure for learning it. Even in learning a skill where danger is an inherent and perhaps desirable aspect of the task, an initial domain of safety must be sustained by the teacher. So the function of education can always be seen as being made up of two parts—making or protecting the space in which learning happens, and introducing new structure by the indication of appropriate problems or challenges. Only the latter function can correctly be termed 'instruction'. In varying degrees, however, both functions must be present, and unless they are, what we do is not education.

Let us consider for a moment an instance which is not, in this sense, educational. You are on your own. You have pushed out your musical or literary play to the limit; no Tortelier at your elbow, though you may remember former mentors. You are at the frontier where occasionally you press back the limits of your art. The words of your poem seem to 'strain, crack and sometimes break under the burden'. The music or the language racks you, a willing victim. This is your frontier or mine. For each child, man or woman, the frontier is always different, and for everyone it is a place of possible achievement *and* of danger. It is an existential reality which circumscribes your or my 'potential space'.

For everyone of us there is such a patch of freedom, rather like a back garden in an unfinished suburb. The homely back door basis of it is our own unique mixture of skills and constructs, how we cope and make sense of our view. This is our competence, and here our own little patch stretches away from us, with our neighbours' expectations, requirements, and rights more or less clearly known on either side. But down at the bottom there is some wild ground, no fence, willow herb, tangled country where we sometimes go and where the children go whenever we let them. Education begins whenever another person touches any of this space with the intention of protecting it or in order to enrich it.

Our competence exists on the threshold of the present, even when we are asleep. Its roots lie in our experience and it is cumulative. It creates a field of potential action for us and, had there been time, I would have presented the case for moving the concept of motivation away from its central place in educational psychology and for adopting a more dynamic view of human energies (see Bannister and Fransella, 1971, or Hodgkin, 1976). Our frontier, like our competence, is also existential and its appearance is more fleeting. We apprehend it through symbols and fantasies and we speak of it in the subjunctive and conditional tense and we perceive it branching, ambiguously, into the future.

The teacher or the parent needs both to recognize and to respect the learner's unique frontier. He can know it by a kind of empathy and, in unpressured moments, he can enter the space of play which it encircles.

Two Ends of a Garden: Two Ends of a Stick

We may hold these ideas together in the form of a diagram (Figure 1)—a schematic version of 'the garden'. Each of us has some existential freedom. The hither end of this is strongly characterized by our individual competence, which consists of inherited patterns enriched by subsequent experience (Bruner, 1969). The 'lateral' limits are socially

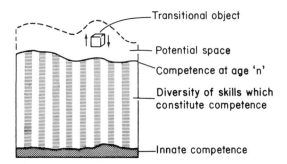

Figure 1   This diagram sums up the relationship between competence—the system of innate and acquired skills relevant to a task—and freedom. The vertical boundaries, or 'walls of the garden', are all those social and environmental constraints within which competence is exercised. The frontier is the existential limit at which a person grows, mentally and physically, and within this is Winnicott's 'potential space', where play and practice happen. 'Transitional objects' are all those things we play with—tools, probes, words, hypotheses—first in a protected context and then, as competence increases, we reach out with them to make new works of art or meaning and explore new ground

and politically modifiable, but even in the most unfavourable situations there is a frontier at the outer end. Examples come crowding in, from Helen Keller in her garden to Solzhenitsyn or Bunyan in their prisons. All teachers and parents are readily aware of their custodial task— looking after the normative boundaries and, if they are 'progressives', they will also be much concerned with enlarging these. As instructors we have a subtler task. From time to time we throw a new item into the potential space, a not very large doll, for example, or a non-lethal knife. We ask questions about these and suggest tasks. This questioning is the point at which the structure of knowledge begins to be manifest to the learner. Almost always the early stages of such educational process should be playful and protected. Then, as play turns into skill, so toys become tools and the learner's competence is increased. Gradually these things become, psychologically, extensions of the person using them and emotional bonds are established which would not be in evidence towards more trivial property. Toys develop in the other direction, as symbols. The knife may be a focus of fantasy about the future, about self-sufficiency, power, and manhood. It becomes a symbol, not in the restricted, phallic sense of popularized Freud, but in pointing towards many forms of potency, including sex. Tools, writes Joseph Weizen-baum (1976), are

pregnant symbols in themselves. They symbolize the activities they enable . . . . An oar is a tool for rowing and it represents the skill of rowing in its whole complexity. No one who has not rowed can see an oar as truly an oar . . . .. The tool as a symbol transcends its role as a practical means towards practical ends.

One notices this ambivalence—things for use and things for mean-ing—particularly strongly with adolescents. I must stress in passing that it is always those activities in which there is a strong symbolic element that offer opportunities for moral and religious education. Whether we are teachers or learners it is where our competence is stretched, where commonplace skills and mastery are taxed, that our feelings and attitudes are made manifest. Even more, when two or three people, or a group, encounter a frontier experience together, shared symbols and shared myths sustain them and common attitudes are forged and sharpened.

Part of the contemporary failure in education derives from our sentimental attitude towards play. We have failed to see that the concept should include markedly contrasted elements and, unless play is seen essentially as a means for leading a learner into more serious activities which may be demanding and even disturbing or dangerous, then our educational and recreational practices will remain too safe and feeble.

Consider the two opposite directions in which play may become serious: firstly, towards increasing competence; secondly, towards exploration. So-called 'progressive' teachers have tended to belittle the value of repetitive practice, of exercising a new skill until it is mastered. Of course drill can be overdone. But if you watch children's own spontaneous, rhythmical beatings, drummings, and repeatings or if you consider, at a more sophisticated level, the graduations of playful practice enjoyed by small Japanese children as they consolidate musical skills in the Suzuki method, it is hard not to reflect that we may be impoverishing our children by not helping them to learn thoroughly by hand and heart. This is the assimilating aspect of play on which Piaget lays stress.

Then there is the other direction—exploration. This requires lengthy discussion but, put briefly, we need to reassess those qualities of openness and ambiguity which sustain the learner's interest in that curricular and cultural world which we create around our children. Far too often what children and adolescents perceive in school is blocked-off vistas, black boxes (both metaphorically and in actuality), where the limits of doubt and exploration are clearly marked, where ambiguity is suppressed and paradox trivialized. The television set is a central symptom and symbol of this. You cannot answer it back. You cannot explore its inside without being electrocuted or breaking the guarantee seal. The principles on which it functions are undoubtedly difficult to comprehend, and even the creative techniques of television art are inaccessible, for very few children ever visit a studio or have the chance to work or play with television cameras. Children and adults may sometimes discuss programmes, and there perhaps lies some salvation, but to do this is never easy in the normal atmosphere of family viewing.

Or take another example from our boxed-up world of education. Teenagers from a Midland education authority visit North Wales for 'adventure training' and yet they are not allowed to go above the 1500-feet contour unless they are accompanied by a teacher with a Mountain Leadership Certificate. Of course it is of great importance that in such mildly challenging terrain a sense of skill, responsibility, and judgement should be in the air; what is disturbing, however, is a widespread bureaucratic blindness to the fact that artificial regulations and certifications are gradually blocking the child's vision of freedom and sense of adventure which up to now have drawn people to the mountains.

Play is the beginning of all education but a play-pen mentality can be its ruin. Unless teachers are determined to accept almost all questions as serious ones and to open, wherever possible, vistas towards the frontier, where inevitably some danger and conflict lurk, and to call on the qualities of discernment and responsibility which doubt and challenge can evoke in children; unless the characteristic attitude of teachers is to welcome problems and uncertainties as well as to cultivate competence, then our education will continue to be but a grey affair.

One more mental diagram neatly summarizes the complementary polarity of precise skill and groping exploration and it is one which carries the philosophical issue beyond education into cosmology; I refer to the probe or to the blind man's stick. The philosophical implications of the probe have attracted many thinkers—Einstein and Neils Bohr, for example. The idea is central to Polanyi's philosophy of discovery, for he sees a probe as exemplifying in practice what Gödel showed in mathematics—that a logical system is either consistent and incomplete *or* it is complete but contains inconsistency (Polanyi, 1959; Torrance, 1974). I do not understand much of Gödel but I do understand what it feels like to probe my way along a pavement with my eyes shut or over a snow bridge with an unseen crevasse below. It is then essential that I hold this end of my probe or my ice axe firmly; the handle must be as if it were a part of me. But it is equally important that I move the other end about and the tip keeps tapping things, bumping into them, asking questions: is it kerb or tarmac, is it space or solid snow? This is how we make sense of the outer end of our probe, by allowing it to generate useful ambiguities. So we see the origins of symbolism even here; the near end is solidly part of me, like a tool or a limb, but the distal end equivocates. Nevertheless, the probe *is* only a probe because it transcends both aspects, the loose end which produces manageable doubts and the firm end which enables me to construe them.

When we, teachers, just occasionally, succeed, it is usually because of some uncovenanted space or freedom that falls in our way and we grab it, open it up. We pass the time of day with someone in a corridor and find—forgoing coffee, perhaps, if we are of such stuff as martyrs are made—that there *is* time to discuss a burning issue, of human rights and hair length, of fruit juice and Linus Pauling, or of a plan for a journey. All the creative things in school require, first, that we have wit and will to make elbow room and, second, that somehow we see the bundle of ideas, the probe, whose hither end we are grasping here in the noisy corridor, has a distal end out there where Socrates asked too many questions and Hitler asked too few. And because questions are only beginnings we may also succeed a little as teachers if we show that there *is* a direction to be followed, a pattern to be discovered, a principle to be sustained, even when we do not see clearly where the Way leads.

References

Bannister, D. and Fransella, F. 1971, *Inquiring Man* (Harmondsworth, Middx: Penguin Books).
Berlin, Sir Isiah, 1976, *Vico and Herder* (London: Hogarth Press).
Bruner, J. S., 1969, (On Voluntary Action', in A. Koestler and J. R. Smythies, eds, *Beyond Reductionism* (London: Hutchinson).
Bruner, J. S., Jolly, A., and Sylva, K., 1976, *Play—its Role in Development and Evolution* (Harmondsworth, Middx: Penguin Books).
Clark, Sir Kenneth, 1963, 'The blot and the diagram', *Encounter*, January.
Gombrich, Sir E. H., 1950, *The Story of Art* (London: Phaidon Press).
Gombrich, Sir E. H., 1960, *Art and Illusion* (London: Phaidon Press).
Gregory, R. L., 1966, *Eye and Brain* (London: Weidenfeld & Nicolson).
Hodgkin, R. A., 1970, *Reconnaissance on an Educational Frontier* (Oxford University Press).
Hodgkin, R. A., 1976, *Born Curious* (Chichester: Wiley).
Inhelder, Barbel and Piaget, Jean, 1969, 'The gaps in empiricism', in A. Koestler and J. R. Smythies, eds. *Beyond Reductionism* (London: Hutchinson).
Polanyi, Michael, 1959, *Personal Knowledge* (London: Routledge & Kegan Paul).
Shotter, John, 1973, 'Prolegomena to a study of play', *Journal for the Explanation of Social Behaviour*, **3**, (1). Also in M. P. M. Richards, ed., *The Integration of a Child into a Social World* (Cambridge: Cambridge University Press, 1974).
Stein, Leopold, 1957, 'What is a symbol supposed to be?' *Journal of Analytical Psychology*, **II**, (1).
Torrance, T. F., 1974, 'The place of Polanyi in the modern philosophy of science', unpublished paper.
Traherne, Thomas, 1950, '*Centuries of Meditation*', in V. Gollancz, ed., *A Year of Grace* (London: Gollancz), p. 75.
Weizenbaum, Joseph, 1976, *Computer Power and Human Reason* (San Francisco: Freeman), p. 18.
Winnicott, D. W., 1971, *Playing and Reality* (London: Tavistock).

Aspects of Education
Edited by M. Braham
© 1982 John Wiley & Sons Ltd.

Chapter 9

The Unawakened Mind

*James Hemming**

Man's ideas about himself impose strictures on his being and upon the education of children. We are imprisoned by our concepts of what we are. When men thought of themselves as fallen angels and born in sin, it was logical that they should suspect their natural impulses and set about beating the devil out of their children—and learning into them. Later models—Locke's *tabula rasa*, for example—were also limiting; being was held to be a mostly passive business of receiving impressions, and teaching a matter of filling an empty mind with useful knowledge. To come to our own times, the Piagetian model of serving the process of growth and learning from appropriate experience is a good deal more comfortable to live with but does not, perhaps, quite capture the energy and excitement of individual development within the context of a socially and materially dynamic world and universe. So all the models to date have, to some extent, fallen short of the actual human situation, and many have reinforced distorted images of the human reality.

As we see him today, man is a creative being in a creative universe; a dynamic system within a dynamic system, and in symbiotic relationship with it. Everywhere energy throbs and moves, taking on endless forms of being and activity. The human individual, compounded of that energy, and controlling some of it, looks out on the incomprehensible scene with curiosity and wonder. Bit by bit he pieces together patterns out of the chaos of sensory input; little by little he comes to understand more. The purpose of education, obviously, is to help children to feel at home in this strange universe and to interact with it so that they gradually grow in consciousness of what they are, and where they are, and move towards competence, confidence, and fulfilment in their

---

* Educational psychologist, author of *Democracy and School Life, Individual Morality, You and Your Adolescent*, consultant to the World Education Fellowship and member of the UK Commission for UNESCO.

transactions with life. And that growth and movement are not just for the years of schooling but for a lifetime.

Just to state the situation puts us on the threshold of such a vast array of possibilities—the outer mystery of the universe, the inner mystery of the self, and consciousness linking the two—that a congress of the wisest could spend months of discussion and touch only on the fringe of it. One, therefore, has to make drastic selections.

You have probably heard the story of the man who went to visit his friend, a learned astronomer. He found him late at night in a hut on the top of a hill. He had two candles for light and was working assiduously with pencil, rulers, and dividers on a large piece of paper on the table. 'What are you doing?' asked the friend. 'I am studying the night sky,' said the astronomer. 'Then why don't you take the roof off and look up?' 'Oh,'' said the astronomer, 'that would be too much at once.' I shall, therefore, limit myself to a brief glance at three dimensions of the educational scene and of man's view of himself, which seem to me to be receiving insufficient attention at present.

One area of misinterpretation is the neglect of the great genetical potential inherited by every normal individual. The potentiality embedded in life is one of the astounding features of the universe. It has two aspects. Within the genetical store are great reserves of change and development so that, for example, clever husbandry can, by selecting from that store, produce the tasty, luscious dessert apple from the bitter, woody crab. The farmer does not *add* anything; he merely draws out what is there and gives it the opportunity to thrive. It takes him several generations to do that. But any individual has an infinite number of potentialities waiting to be developed here and now. Americans are teaching chimpanzees to communicate, and the Russians are teaching bears to ride motorcycles. Biologists are even finding that a single cell has a remarkable capacity to change in response to a changed environment, by drawing on capacities from within itself.

Such is the creative dynamism around us. Given energy and chance and environmental selection, all the rest of the universe follows, including the infinite variety of living forms, because within all things is this exuberant potential for the emergence of the new, a potential in which we all share.

At present, I suggest, our attitudes to ourselves and to our children seriously underestimate the powers within us. Sir Julian Huxley used to say that we are rather like motor cars that never get out of bottom gear. 'We are beginning to realise', wrote Sir Julian in his essay on 'Transhumanism', 'that even the most fortunate people are living far below capacity, and that most human beings develop not more than a small fraction of their potential mental and spiritual efficiency. The human race, in fact, is surrounded by a large area of unrealised possibilities'.

Unawakened lives are not only a sad loss of possibility in themselves but it seems likely that the problems of our human future can only be solved in a human way by an extension of consciousness and purpose to measure up to the recent, rapid expansion of our powers and responsibilities on planet Earth. In both personal and evolutionary terms we need to try to tap more of our human potential. And the start of that is to accept its presence in every child and to work to actualize it.

For many children today the educational process does the exact opposite. The lively, curious, keen 10-year-old turns into the bored, uninterested, apathetic 14-year-old and, all too often, stays unnecessarily limited as a person. Coming out at the top of the process are a minority of splendid, self-actualizing personalities, but the wastage underneath is appalling. And none of it is necessary. The facts of human potentiality are such that we can state with confidence that if normal children fail to respond it is because we, as educators, have failed to stimulate and nourish the actual powers of the children. As Mencius put it: 'If the mind of man gets its nourishment, there is nothing which will not grow. If it loses its nourishment, there is nothing which will not perish.'

Someone who works in music with abnormal children tells me that the breakthrough to a constructive relationship comes with a particular child when she finds 'the tune for him'. Education is about tapping potentialities. This is the antithesis of labelling children as dull, bored, not interested in careers, or anything else. I always think that teacher was on the right lines who wrote on an end-of-term report: 'I have again failed to interest Albert in Arithmetic, but at least I do try.' I hope he went on trying. Faced with the reality of unreached potential in the individual child, we experiment too little and give up too soon. We also give up too soon with ourselves. It is a myth that once you are adult you cannot learn. The Open University has proved that wrong in many impressive cases.

This brings me to my second area of comparative neglect. If we are to awaken the powers and perceptions of people we must, it seems to me, pay much closer attention to the education of the brain itself as the organ of life and the instrument of personality. The brain is the most complex and creative thing in the whole of the known universe and yet educators proceed, for the most part, as though it was not there. They think in such abstractions as learning, intelligence, pertinacity—useful words in their way but imprecise—and forget about the actual functions of the brain which need training and co-ordination if they are to work smoothly and effectively. It is like talking about 'time' and 'accuracy' and 'interval' without bothering about the workings of the clock.

To talk of the brain as the organ of experience disturbs some people. They feel it turns man into nothing but a biochemical machine. Such fears miss the point. What we actually *are*, we do not know in any complete sense. There are unplumbed areas all around us, and our existence and nature are two of them. This, surely, is all the more reason to educate the brain to function well in order to search better into human experience. All human activity, from the elusive ideas of a poet's vision to the right hook of a prize-fighter, have their neural equivalent in brain function. The converse is also true: if the functions of the brain are undeveloped, then the personality is denied the equivalent mode of action. If, from birth, a child had one leg immobilized while the other was exercised, the capacity ever to become a dancer would diminish with the years, not just because the muscles of one leg would be wasted but because the appropriate motor areas in the brain would be unused. The yogi has a greater control and awareness of his body because he has trained all its muscles, joints, and neural pathways to operate in a refined, differentiated way. In the last analysis, all learning is brain training and all being is brain function in action. We expand consciousness by tapping more of our brain potential.

There would be no need to spell this out were it not that models of education and of development have, for the most part, ignored the dynamics of the brain. Because we continue to do so, people run the risk of having their capacities and awareness blunted by the very process that exists to educate them.

The brain is a unity, since every nerve is joined by one network or another to every other nerve. It is also a palace of a thousand rooms with special treasures locked in each. In living, we unlock the doors or leave them for ever closed. The awakening of mind is the unlocking of the doors. What exactly we mean by mind, as distinct from brain, is still unclear. Perhaps we may say that mind is the name for the totality of brain functioning; the experience of one's own being.

Where does this get us in educational—that is to say, in developmental—terms? The starting point is an appropriate appreciation of the brain. I menton this because the bludgeoning and battering of young brains in the service of questionable stereotypes of what being educated means would just not be possible if each individual brain was respected as it should be. Furthermore, and incredibly, most young people leave school not knowing how their brains work and often with a profound sense of inferiority about the capacity of their brains. I would even suggest, on the basis of a limited personal experience, that the best way to control rash experimentation with alcohol and drugs is by developing a proper respect for the brain. Young people will undertake heroic self-control out of regard for their bodies while sometimes the same people will subject their brains to ruthless maltreatment.

So respect first, and after that careful concern to ensure that the brain is educated to function well in all its many parts. The brain will either be orchestrated as a whole or else it will become divided against itself and produce jangling disharmonies which, incidentally, is one way of describing a neurosis. When people say, 'We're all neurotics these days, aren't we?', what they mean is that they are aware of blatant disharmonies in their functioning. For example, a common disharmony in our society is fear of feeling. Many highly successful academics and businessmen are terrified of feeling. This is not, I suggest, because they have no potentiality for feeling but because they pursued other activities so avidly that feeling atrophied while non-feeling functions were constantly reinforced. Some people are awkward feelers because they were reared in emotionally cold homes, but that is the same process in another form; both show the undernourishment of the capacity to feel. And yet the non-feelers often long for the ability to show and receive feeling. They are aware of something missing within themselves.

Or the missing capacity may be that of social skill. People caught in this trap will run away from the exposure of social encounter by any stratagem they can use. One common strategy is to drink inhibitions away. I once knew a man who could only be sociable when drunk; he then often went on to drink so much that he remembered nothing the next morning. He thus cut himself off from the formative experience he needed to escape from his social isolation. Thus his incapacity reinforced itself. The recent arrival of social therapy is showing that social capacity can be educated. That, too, will have its neural correlate somewhere in the brain.

When a stimulus from the environment touches off the reticular arousal system deep within the brain, a scatter of neural impulses alerts the whole brain. If the stimulus has a well-tuned function waiting to marry with it, the psyche swings into positive response; if the stimulus instead comes up against an untrained function, the response will be feeble and negative. In the case of an inhibited personality, with its accompanying range of unexercised brain functions, almost every stimulus excites defence rather than a positive response. It is in this way that minds stay narrow and personalities become crippled.

The relationship between brain function and completeness of personality has been sharpened during the last few years by the study of the differential functioning of the two hemispheres of the brain, about which Dr Alvin Lishman gave us an interesting paper at this conference last year. Research continues, notably in the USA and the USSR, and the outcome gets ever more intriguing. I would remind you that the two hemispheres of the cortex were at one time regarded as more or less duplicates of each other, apart from the Broca area which mediates the motor elements of language. The Broca area is in one hemisphere only—the left hemisphere usually. Thus, the left hemisphere was regarded as dominant with the right hemisphere designated as an inferior organ, a mere supplement to the dominant hemisphere.

Now we know that things are nothing like as simple as that. After an initial period of high plasticity—thought to be the first six years of life—the two hemispheres, as well as having functions in common, settle down to specialize in certain particular functions. Even this is not simple—nature loves experimenting—because one cannot be certain that a special function, the speech centre, for instance, is always in the same hemisphere. For example, it looks as if the speech centre is in the right, instead of the left, hemisphere in about 10 per cent of right-handed people and in about 35 per cent of left-handed people. Nevertheless there are well-defined functions that are characteristically to be found in one hemisphere rather than the other. So we can, with a considerable degree of accuracy, talk about left-mode functions and right-mode functions, according to whether the functions are especially characteristic of one hemisphere or the other. The sources of information for the differential contribution to life of the two hemispheres include the follow-up of brain injury and surgery, the investigation of localized brain activity by the use of electrodes on the outside of the scalp, and the study of each hemisphere's function when electric shock therapy is applied to one hemisphere only, a treatment which puts the hemisphere temporarily out of action. The differences in specialization of function that show up are now well known. They can be summarized:

Left-mode functions	Right-mode functions
Logical thinking	Intuitional thinking
Analysis	Synthesis
Preference for symbols	Preference for patterns
Categorization	Collating data
Unit apprehension	Holistic apprehension
Awareness of separateness	Awareness of relationships
Pragmatic response	Creativity
Linguistic skill	Musical skill
Abstract thought	Imaginative thought
Linear awareness	Spatial awareness

It is important to notice that in listing the different functions of the two modes we are not dealing with an either/or situation but with a pattern of reciprocal function. The ideal is that all the functions of each mode should be educated and reinforced so that the brain will respond in an appropriate way—almost always a mixture of functions—to whatever situations the brain's owner is faced with. Language is a case in point. The hemisphere containing the speech centre is quite capable of producing words and stringing them together into sentences. But, if speech is to be pleasant and human, words are not enough. We need intonation, emphasis, and rhythm also and these are mediated by the other hemisphere.

Or again, the Polish composer, Andrzej Panufnik, starts with a mathematical design, then composes by working with both the piano and the design, mathematics and music testing each other, until the composition expresses his feelings with full power and precision. Thus, he brings the two modes of mind to the creative task, just as a poet must do, or an architect, or anyone else who wishes to marry beauty and function, impulse and design. In aesthetic creation both hemispheres are needed. The trials of completing the Sydney Opera House are, perhaps, an example of what can happen if the left-mode functions are not sufficiently in action during the process of creation. As Dr Vadim Lvovich Deglin, the Russian neuro-physiologist, puts it, 'In order to use one's mental faculties to the full the smoothly equilibrated operation of both hemispheres is required.' There is some evidence to show that this may even be true of emotions: the left mode, some research shows, tends towards extroverted optimism and the right towards introverted pessimism. We should notice that, at times, the two sets of functions can be antagonistic to one another, and that, if one set is consistently strengthened at the expense of the other, the neglected function may be reduced to impotence and the vital reciprocity lost.

Now that the two hemispheres have been given equal status in life roles, we are led on to consider whether individuals can be differentiated as 'left-mode dominant types' and 'right-mode dominant types'. It would seem that they can. When William James split mankind into the tough-minded and the tender-minded he was, it would seem, differentiating between left-mode dominants and right-mode dominants. Pavlov's division of mankind into thinkers and artists tells the same story. Several other such dichotomies are to be found in the literature of psychology; convergent/divergent, linear/lateral, and so forth. It obviously does not matter which category an individual falls into; but what does matter is that the functions of the non-dominant mode shall be exercised and developed at least as carefully and consistently as the functions of the dominant mode. Failing that, the individual will end up with great gaps in his or her capacity for interaction and response. He will be only half aware, only half responsive. When we draw a blank in our relations with one another it may sometimes be because, to a right-mode type of person, an exclusively left-mode style of mind seems totally out of reach, and vice versa.

The fully awakened mind, therefore, needs a brain that is educated in all its functions. Unfortunately, traditional secondary education consistently overvalues left-mode functions and consistently undervalues right-mode functions so that its products have a poor chance of ending up well-balanced, unless they make the gaps in their development good in their own time. This leads to the vicious circle that much of secondary and higher education has been designed by left-moders for left-moders. This imbalance is multiplied because, in addition to the initial design of courses, left-mode functions are consistently reinforced and right-mode functions consistently neglected. This is what progressive educators have been on about from the start, although they did not then know what a good case they had. Being right-mode types themselves— Herbert Read is an excellent example—they responded intuitively to what they felt to be the needs of children.

It follows that if a child or adolescent who is right-mode dominant finds himself in a school directed by left-mode educational values, he will feel lost and alien, if not cripplingly inferior. The so-called late developers may be children caught in this trap. In passing we may notice that Winston Churchill, one of our more famous late developers, was, among other things, an artist.

As brain research continues and we learn more and more about the specific functions of the various areas of the brain, we shall find ourselves increasingly challenged to educate people through the development and reinforcement of brain functions with the objective of helping them to discover themselves in the round. An individual needs a well-tuned brain as essential equipment for living. The quality of life is governed by a capacity for *appropriate* response. All high-order functioning is delicate and sensitive. The exquisite control of a top-class gymnast is the outcome of antagonistic groups of muscles working in reciprocal attunement with each other, involving trained neural pathways, a well-practised cerebellum and motor areas, a right-mode mastery of pattern and cortical will and judgement over all. The full response to a lover, or a friend, or a scene, or an event, is a similar creative balance between the capacities of awareness, feeling, knowledge, perception, intuition, judgement, and will. This is becoming increasingly true in all fields of life.

For example, the good manager in industry today is the well-rounded human being who responds sensitively and sympathetically, with all his perceptions awake, to the multiform problems, human and material, that face him. Or again, not all bureaucrats are boneheads, but some of them do the most extraordinarily insensitive things. They seem blanked out in certain ranges of awareness that are essential to their appropriate responses. So we get half-baked decisions that immediately backfire and have to be hurriedly reversed. 'Gobbledegook' is a terrifying example of unembellished left-mode communication in action. The same message can be conveyed with or without humanity. If it lacks feeling and sympathy it will arouse suspicion and resentment; if it shows feeling and sympathy it will arouse trust and co-operation. Hence, a more complete awareness and a better balance of response is coming to be a survival value for our species, whether seen personally or socially.

The full awakening of the mind needs something further besides a recognition of unused human potential and the acceptance and nourishment of the reciprocal functions of the brain. This is a coherent psychic environment, that is to say, a valid perspective. Both society and education are today seriously failing to give any sort of coherent perspective on the contemporary environment of man. Young people growing up in small communities and a simpler world had reference points and knew where they were; young people growing up in modern mass society lack reference points and do not know where they are. And we do not seem to have the time to do anything much about this debilitating lack. A few schools, a minority of teachers, one or two hard-working, under-supported institutions are doing what they can to give young people a context for their lives. For the most part, the young are left to find out for themselves—or to flounder.

The development of perspective is not an expendable frill but a pragmatic necessity. The result of not knowing where you are is undermining in several ways. It disrupts the integration of personality, as Jung pointed out; it leads to listlessness and a sense of hopelessness—or, alternatively, to resentment and hostility; and it undermines a capacity for responsibility. This, because it produces the orientation, 'Nothing adds up, so why should I care?' which, in its turn, leads to apathy or solipsism. Furthermore, it is in the context of a well-developed sense of relationship with the whole—what Adler calls social interest—that the high-order human qualities find their milieu of growth—such qualities as vision, imagination, commitment, concern, high purpose. 'Great things are done', said Blake, 'when men and mountains meet. These are not done by jostling in the street.' Nor are they done by a routine of unloved work and desperate escape within a climate of perpetual confusion. Without perspective, education becomes a processing for inept living.

But what perspective? There can be only one answer to this: 'A credible perspective of reality as we see it.' That, of course, leads us straight into difficulties, because reality as we see it today is unrecognizably different from the accepted reality of only 50 years ago. The snug, homely Christian cosmology has turned into the impersonal immensity of the modern universe. Another certainty has gone in that only a shrinking minority of people any longer believe in an intervening God. Or again, the economic system that seemed rock-solid 50 years ago, with reliable money, now looks as though it is on the verge of collapse. We have all these and other revolutionary changes, and yet the schools are expected to proclaim as certainties ideas that are no longer certain. The young sense that some sort of pretence is going on and withdraw their trust in the wisdom of their elders.

Yet the ideas are available to offer to the young a significant contemporary perspective: that life is about search, not about certainty; that man is a rising animal, not a fallen angel; that we are together inescapably responsible for the future of life on this planet; that a higher quality of life is attainable if we struggle for it individually and in co-operation; that man has the capacity to deal with his problems and to bring into being a better future; that everyone's thinking, involvement, and decisions are needed to help our species to surmount the problems facing it; that we can become fully ourselves only by relating to others with love, warmth, and concern. At present, in Great Britain, we are expecting young people to become civilized on the basis of one period of Religious Education a week—often founded on outmoded theology— and a thorough pasting with commercial values for the rest of the time. In other countries, also, philosophical confusion surrounds the young. We are presenting them with an inadequate, if not dishonest, picture of the world and are expecting them to grow into responsible, co-operative young people regardless. The confidence-building curriculum (and no other sort of curriculum, as Pestalozzi pointed out, is worth a button) needs a context of significant ideas to sustain and direct it. Today these ideas are missing. In place of the shapeless muddle of outmoded ideas by which we are surrounded, we need a quite new approach to man, to life, and to the responsibilities of living.

What is true for the young is also true for everyone. People are lost and confused, often depressed, because they can find no centre, or sense of direction, for their lives. We await an upsurge of energy and vision and action to transform despondency into hope. If that is to happen, we have to take the brake off our creative powers, and the powers of our children. The human mind is a system of creative energy which, unless blocked or discouraged, will, from its inherent drive, search into and interact formatively and feelingly with the creative universe of which it is the conscious aspect. Man's incredible brain is the instrument of this activity. The marrying of genetical potential with attuned brain functioning, in the context of a valid perspective, is the means to a fuller awakening of the mind, which is the *sine qua non* of both personal fulfilment and the further advance of our species along the evolutionary road.

Aspects of Education
Edited by M. Braham
© 1982 John Wiley & Sons Ltd.

Chapter 10

Education in a Plural Society

*Frank Musgrove**

I conceive education as liminality, the threshold state; it is movement across boundaries, intrinsically ambiguous, always potentially danger- ous—sometimes a journey into forbidden regions of the mind. My current interest is in lifelong education, and this paper will have a bearing on that. But I do not conceive 'recurrent education' or *l'éducation permanente* as a system for processing retreads for new fields of indust- rial employment. I conceive education as exploit. It is not tidily cumula- tive, progressive, and incremental: it consists of threshold experiences, periodic forays into marginal worlds.

I shall take it as self-evident that for a variety of economic, psycho- logical, and plain commonsense reasons we shall rephase educational provision over the whole of life. I am not a deschooler, and I think there is no doubt that certain abilities are never properly acquired if they are not learned by a certain age or during a particular critical period (Bloom, 1966). But the focus of our educational effort and the deployment of our resources must surely shift significantly from the adolescent years. The present phasing of educational opportunity made sense in pre-industrial Europe, when we could all expect with confidence to be dead by 50; when the average duration of a marriage was 15 years and few men would live to see their first-born child reach maturity (Stub, 1969). But the average duration of marriage has increased by a factor of three: it extends over more than forty years. The generations are getting longer (Berger, 1960), and social change can no longer be handled through the leisurely process of generational succession (Schon, 1971). Change is now too rapid to be handled inter-generationally: a generation must periodically transform itself as it moves through life. A generation-based system of schooling no longer makes sense.

* Sarah Fielden Professor of Education, University of Manchester, and author of *Ecstasy and Holiness.*

But it is the sheer human waste and desolation of contemporary mass schooling that must surely bring about its decline. We have constructed a vast national network of bear-pits called classrooms; and our job in teacher training is to give patience and endurance to baited bears. Teachers learn to cope with hatred and cumulative fatigue—often despair (Webb, 1962); pupils transform the reality of a hideous boredom by 'having a laugh', 'making trouble', and ingeniously and resourcefully 'doing nothing'. Perhaps it is all exquisitely functional—an appropriate training for meaningless lives. It is the hidden curriculum required by a deeply alienated society. On those grounds alone it is time we abandoned it.

My concern is with the conditions in which we can become and remain human: men and not things. And I am concerned with the problem of renewing our humanity throughout the whole of life. Neither psychologists nor sociologists can give us much help: we are quite incredibly ignorant about the nature and needs, the possibilities and capacities, of adult men and women. We have finely delineated phases and 'stages' for the first two decades of life; and thereafter a blank. Erik Erikson gave us eight ages of man: the first five relate to the first twenty years; thereafter, apparently, there is a stage when we resolve the conflict of intimacy and isolation; and throughout our maturity there is only ego integrity versus despair (Erikson, 1965).

My concern for the conditions in which we can remain or become human, and even as adults transform our identities, has taken me recently into marginal worlds. It is there that we see liminality most clearly at work, as it were; and it is there, I believe, that reality lies. I have tried to understand how men in the gaps and lacunae of complex societies refashion themselves: how they reconstruct realities in the margins of the world. It is often in margins that we experience not separateness, but wholeness: even, perhaps, holiness. The basic ingredients of reality—like time—may be profoundly transformed; time may go into reverse, and fragmented lives find an overarching pattern of significance. It is to the margins of the world that I wish to turn your attention.

I did in fact spend five years, from 1965 to 1970, studying the sandwich course in technological universities. I actually know quite a lot about curricular relevance. I am not going to tell you about sandwich courses for mechanical engineers. But I have no tidy curriculum model to put in its place. My paper is an exploration of the circumstances in which we might, perhaps, unscramble the conceptual categories which we habitually use to hold the world in place, and construct a new symbolic order to give meaning to the world. This, quite simply, is the process of artistic creation. I am interested in education, and life, as art.

The notion of liminality was first developed in 1909 by van Gennep in his classic study of rites of passage (A. van Gennep, 1960); it has recently been further elaborated by a contemporary anthropologist, Victor Turner (1974), who conceives of society as an alternation between 'structure' and 'communitas'. Structure is sharp definition, hierarchy, formality, constraint, and rationality; communitas is fluid and intuitive, with all the ambiguity of the threshold state. This idea is very close to the idea of marginality, and, indeed, Victor Turner says: 'In closed or structured societies, it is the marginal or 'inferior' person or the 'outsider' who often comes to symbolize what David Hume has called "the sentiment of humanity", which in turn relates to the model we have termed communitas.'

Liminality, communitas, marginality—these concern me as an educationist. There is, of course, a vast literature on marginality and so-called 'marginal men', beginning perhaps with Durkheim's social distinction between the sacred and the profane. Recently renewed claims have been made for the potency of marginality and its transfiguring potentialities. In England it is the anthropologist, Mary Douglas, who has been making these claims; in America the sociologist, Peter Berger. The new conception of marginality is highly melodramatic: for Mary Douglas it is the inaccessible and unstructured margins of society which are full of energy and danger and to enter them gives power (Douglas, 1970); for Berger the taken-for-grantedness of everyday life is apparently more precarious than we had thought, and marginality surrounds the middle ground of everyday normality, always threatening, encroaching, presenting new and often terrifying versions of reality (Berger and Luckmann, 1971). The threat of death is marginality *par excellence*. But marginality is not simply terrifying: it is liberating and transforming, the basis of deviant and detached definitions of reality, in which counter identities are born; it is ecstasy, literally *ek-stasis*, 'any experience of stepping outside the taken-for-granted reality of everyday life, any openness to the mystery that surrounds us on all sides' (Berger, 1971).

I have been trying to put these notions to some sort of empirical test (Musgrove, 1974, 1975a, 1975b, 1976) and in particular to distinguish between the outcomes of various forms of marginality. For it seems to me that it might make all the difference if marginality were voluntary or involuntary, and if it were high-status or stigmatized. And so I have studied seven marginal groups: four groups were 'voluntary and high status'—self-employed artists in a northern industrial town; late entrants to the Anglican ministry; a Sufi commune of Islamic mystics in the Cotswolds; and Hare Krishna devotees in a commune near London. (The devotees in both communes were young, mainly upper-class, English men and women.) Three contrasted groups where 'low-status and stigmatized'—men and women who had gone blind as adults; the incurably handicapped residents in a Cheshire Home; and homosexuals who had decided to 'come out'. They were studied through very lightly structured interviews and participant observation. I have tried to understand the processes of resocialization that occur when adults move dramatically 'off-centre' into ambiguous realms, and the way reality is reformulated.

In the main, as one might expect, the stigmatized construct a kind of supernormality. This was especially true of the blind, who worked hard and ingeniously to keep an open boundary with the sighted world. They became competitive and ambitious; and their dogs were an unfailing passport to the world of the sighted.

In the Cheshire Home the picture is more complicated. Many of the categories which we use to give meaning to our lives—like the categories of age and sex—held firm, even under sustained assault and the constant presence of death; but temporal categories were distorted, and time lost its linearity. A circular present of recurrent routines sat precariously on a deep past which contained everything of real importance. Life in the Cheshire Home was lived in the pluperfect tense.

But in all the *voluntarily* marginal worlds there were new realities and strong intimations of 'communitas'. Although they had apparently cut themselves off from mainstream society—by becoming parsons or artists, for instance, in a secular and industrialized world—there was a sense in which they had rejoined not only society, but humanity. This was not just a group 'togetherness' effect: the parsons almost never saw other parsons, and the artists seldom saw other artists. In the Sufi commune everyone was clear that they were not there for personal consolation and group therapy: quite the contrary, they were there for 'vertical alignment' and 'oneness' with the Essence. No one talked about his personal life and problems. But after our long periods of meditation in a cold stone barn, and a protracted exhalation of 'Hu', comparative strangers fell into each other's arms. As one young man explained to me:

Trying to solve personal problems at the personal relations level can't work: you can only keep going round and round. Solutions are vertical. We let go of ourselves. But this is not a negative thing, it is a way to completeness. Sufism doesn't cut you off from society. Quite the contrary—it unites you with it through oneness with the Essence.

Victor Turner cites both Sufism and the cult of Krishna as examples of 'communitas'; and a Hare Krishna commune is to be found in a well-to-do suburb of London. It is the temple of an Eastern Religion and its 50 to 60 members are young English men and women. The devotees shave their heads (except for a tuft of hair which is a hand-hold for God), wear saffron robes, take new, Sanskrit, names, and live a regulated life of austerity. Their music has strange rhythms. The God Krishna dances on their tongues and his footprint, the 'tilak', shaped like a tuning fork, is stamped on their foreheads in clay. They have an unvarying vegetarian diet of boiled rice, curried vegetables, fruit, yoghurt, and milk. For the devotees, the local suburbanites are 'demons' and the whole world beyond the temple is 'stool' and 'nonsense'. The temple appeared to be sufficiently 'off-centre' in modern Britain to be included in my study of the other side of social reality.

Of course, there were many social and conceptual continuities with the outside world: the boundaries are by no means impermeable. In some ways it was strikingly 'continuous' with a very traditional Victorian morality, and one young ex-public schoolboy was there with the blessing—and perhaps heartfelt relief—of his grandparents because of the commune's Spartan regime. The young man was formerly 'into the drug scene', but this was now firmly behind him. There were theological continuities, too: whereas the God of the Sufis is highly impersonal, abstract, and the Sufi himself becomes God, Krishna remains quite other than his devotees and, like the Christian God, is personal, even idiosyncratic: the food he prefers is butter, his favourite bird is the peacock, and the musical instrument that gives him most delight is the flute.

But conceptual discontinuities were striking, especially in relation to purity and pollution, and to causality and time. Time is an eternal present, enclosed in the tight boundary of daily routine and 'regulative practices', which begin at 4.00 a.m. Krishna Consciousness is detachment from 'Karma', the futile search for satisfaction through sense gratification; it is purification through chanting and dancing, through austerity and a scripturally regulated life. Devotees briefly and lightly dismissed their previous biographical selves and generally de-emphasized the past (*their* lives were certainly not lived in the pluperfect tense); and the future is depersonalized, merely a succession of spiritual platforms. Krishna is an escape both from Karma and time: from birth, death, and rebirth. As one devotee said: 'Krishna is time; he is before and after time; he transcends time.' But a recent recruit to the commune pointed to the detailed timetable of chanting: 'It seems like a job of work, all that clock-watching. I mean, that's what I came to the Temple to get away from: all that nine-to-five routine—'Do this by such-and-such-a-time, or else. . . .' He was firmly reproved: 'That is what the Vedic life is like: a routine. After all, Krishna is time, the controller of time. Krishna is time itself.'

The temple is sharply marked off from the world, in which people are uptight, anxious, frantic, unclean; it has a strong sense of its superiority and its separateness; and the body's boundaries are scrupulously cleansed and its orifices controlled. There are careful rituals for conveying food to the mouth without using the left hand or the index (or poking) finger; 'stool' is passed only once every day (at the same time); and only a narrow spiritual passage, the 'jiva', leads outwards, from the heart to the spiritual platforms. The body's exits and entrances are elaborately protected, and shaving the head is one means of cleaning up the body's boundaries. And the devotees are encircled in Krishna's protective embrace: those in the outer world who mock and despise them have a way of ending up mutilated or dead under lorries and buses.

Their world is 'bliss', described usually as 'pure nectar', and their previous lives in the outside world were 'heavy'. Their acceptance of Krishna had usually been remarkably rapid (unlike my parsons who, on average, had spent 18 agonized years deciding to enter the ministry). A young art school graduate from Blackburn, who had worked in graphic design and has now been in the commune two years, explained the change in his life. He wore National Health spectacles and his pigtail was curly.

My life changed completely. Before this my life was very unhappy, I felt very dissatisfied with myself. I went to art college and after that worked in graphic design; but I really wanted to be an artist, you know . . . . I got this design job, but was never really into it. Nothing gave me any satisfaction at all. I sort of drank a lot with friends, smoked a bit of pot, and had affairs with girls . . . . I did actually go to a sort of Buddhist commune in Scotland for about a week, but you had to leave when your money ran out. And then one day I was sitting in Piccadilly Gardens in Manchester, opposite Woolworth's you know . . . . It was a sunny day but I felt very low and not knowing what to do with myself. And I heard this music, so I just crossed over into the gardens, and there they were, with their shaved heads and yellow robes. I didn't know what to make of it, but they all looked so happy. I went back with them to the temple; I ate some 'prasadam' and heard them preach, and I began to feel really great, for the first time in years. Anyway, within a week I shaved up and became a devotee myself. I was sure I'd have to surrender sooner or later, so I thought it might as well be straight away. It was just the happiness, really . . . . You become purified, you see . . . . I no longer look beyond this moment, 'bhakti-yoga', the instant happiness of Krishna's service . . . . If we chant his name he is with us directly, in fact he is dancing on our tongues.

In a different way my parsons had also left 'structure' and discovered communitas': instead of an alienated world of restricted marginality, they had somehow transcended their formerly fragmented lives and discovered a more embracing unity. As they left the centre for the margin they found not a narrower but a wider social sphere, and their conceptual categories seemed correspondingly subverted: hard and rigid distinctions that had seemed important dissolved. (In particular they enjoyed funerals, unless they had been bureaucratized by cremationtoria. There was no satisfaction in burying people you did not know. But ordinarily it was in funerals that they found a sense of significance. By burying the dead they found unity with the living.) There seemed to be similar changes among homosexuals who decided to 'come out': they, too, described their new world as 'nectar', and found an apparent freedom in role without status, in society as process. There was also in these different voluntarily marginal worlds a notion of 'openness': of offering oneself up to events and experiences in an unprogrammed way. There was a sense of gaps and spaces in life and in time to which we should surrender ourselves.

I will quote in conclusion one of our interviews with a lesbian, an art school graduate in her mid-20s. It illustrates the paradox of integrity and wholeness through separation and marginality; and it also presents a 'separate reality', in which our conventional symbolic categories—of time and causality—are transformed. I shall call her 'Petula' and let her tell her own story—which is of a profoundly disturbing journey through liminality to 'communitas'.

She was interviewed in her flat, sparsely furnished with a few rugs, trunks, and benches. There were enormous, brightly coloured paintings on the walls, and easels with half-finished paintings. She wore faded blue-denim jeans and a shirt, and sat on a mattress on the floor. She told me how she first came to realize her true sexual nature when she had a passionate but unconsummated affair with a woman teacher at art school. The affair ended, and then, said Petula,

I died. I just deteriorated slowly. And eventually I got taken into hospital because I was smoking and didn't want to know anybody. I stopped talking for about two weeks. And I felt dead. You know, I was really dead inside. I just died. And all I could draw was a nose, an eye and a mouth. Lots of strange things happened during that time in hospital. I don't know what it was, but I died. And slowly I tried to get back. I was still in love with this woman. And I started to become her, to be her, I started to become that person. And then I started to be anybody I wanted. Just anybody but me. I didn't know who I was. I was utterly confused, frightened and alone: way out somewhere. I couldn't reach anybody.

She recovered slowly, began to face the nature of her sexuality, and when she finally did so was overcome with joy. This was her rebirth:

I zoomed off to Canada, just on a moment's notice, with no money . . . landed in Toronto, hitch-hiked across Canada to Vancouver, and just knew thousands of people.

In Vancouver she held a few exhibitions and sold her paintings on the streets. She moved on to California and was tempted to stay there— 'seeing so much beauty, I mean, it was so incredibly beautiful'. But she concluded that her work was 'about people' and decided to return to England and work with subnormals—'people that society's frightened of'. She paints and writes poetry and works at a centre for subnormal children. She enjoys her work at the centre:

Those kids are supposed to be cabbages. But I'm getting through to them, and I'm just learning from them every day. Their experience is so different from ours, they don't see life as we do. I mean, if you can through all the snot and shit, and get through all that—you have to allow yourself to switch on, be open to them—then you reach them, you know.

She has climbed out of the abyss and been reborn. 'I feel I have such an important life, and yet I know I'm nobody.' Petula has rejoined humanity:

I went to a Gay Liberation meeting. I'd still never really met lesbians, and it just blew my mind to find there were lesbians who look just like me and not like dykes. I felt just wonderful. There was someone else! Because all though this time I'd had the idea that I was the only one in the world. It was like being born. That was three years ago. I could be myself, for the first time in my life. And I did a drawing and I wrote a poem. I'm not trying to be anything any more. And since that time three years ago I've felt so good. And I've been through different experiences of being gay: sleeping with people. That was the main thing—being able to sleep with another body the same as yours. And suddenly I've come to this stage where I'm not lesbian, not heterosexual, or whatever. I'm just me. And I've experienced so many wonderful things.

Petula has emerged from the ambiguities of liminality to communitas, and she feels no more restricted social bonds, but a wider kinship, a generic bond. But during her period of liminality time went into reverse:

There's another thing where I thought I was the only one in the world. I was lying in bed reading Laing's *Bird of Paradise*. And I read this book, and it's an account of a guy feeling he was going back in time—'ten-day voyage'. And I jumped out of bed and said, 'Wow! There's someone else experienced it. This is another minority group I'm in. It's marvellous that there's someone else experienced this thing.'

Petula is deeply conscious of time as non-linear, non-continuous, with spaces in it, into which one should stray, opening oneself up to what is predestined:

I mean, what is time? We created time. This is something else. All my work deals with reality and fantasy, the whole thing. When we go to sleep, where do we go to? You know, this is what I'm trying to get at. I try to live for today. Well, it's not exactly that. If I'm walking along a road to work, some intuition tells me to go down another road that I've never been down' . . .. I feel there's some reason for everything that happens. On a bus you might start a conversation, and you might learn so much. I sort of make time for that sort of thing. But a lot of people jump out of bed, go to work, and don't see anything around them. I set off an hour earlier so I can walk and look, at things and see things. I'm no freak and I don't believe in religion, yet things have happened, I've been sent into people's lives. Why did I just leave and go to Canada like that? I didn't know anybody. I was protected right across that journey—I was looked after, I know it. There's a reason for everything that happens.

Time began again after her rebirth and stretches forward from this baseline into the future, marked by her drawings: 'It's like some people keep a diary, I keep drawings. I can look back over them, right from starting up as a lesbian.' Her pictures stretch into an infinite future but relate her to life:

I got so much from that particular picture that I could go out and was ready to talk to people. I wasn't working for a diploma or to sell it to someone. Therefore I had all the time in the world to do this picture. It has become very detailed. It could go on until I die.

I have given you a glimpse—perhaps a rather bewildering glimpse— of my marginal worlds. You are entitled to some sort of hard-headed conclusion. My conclusion is simply this: that if we are thinking of lifelong education as the opportunity for periodically remaking ourselves, we must forget crass notions of curricular relevance and think instead of alternating phases of structure and communitas. It is in this dialectic that the possibility of being human lies.

There is no automatic pay-off from plunging people into off-centre worlds. The blind and the disabled in my study did not unscramble the conceptual framework which had always held the world in place: they constructed a supernormality. But the Sufis, the Krishna devotees, the artists, and the homosexuals all experienced a state of limbo and ambiguity; and many constructed new worlds. But the homosexuals and the Krishna devotees were the extreme cases. For a long time they had felt utterly lost.

Many of the Krishna devotees had been hippies: the great pop festivals were their liminality. And the homosexual remained always a stranger in his 'own' homosexual world, without reliable recipe knowledge, and without established social roles in which he could find a comfortable anonymity. But homosexuals and Krishna devotees used strinkingly similar terms to describe their experience of transfiguration: it was all 'bliss' and 'pure nectar'.

But I am not talking about a cosy togetherness. My search has been for clues which will enable us to think about strategies and contexts for remaining human. Of course, I am not suggesting that we all become homosexuals or join Krishna communes. I *am* proposing the deliberate staging of 'communitas' as an educational plan throughout life, geared, however loosely, to inevitable and perhaps natural periods of transition and crisis: available (in a wide variety of forms) perhaps soon after starting work, marriage, the birth of one's children, a major job change or promotion, the experience of divorce or bereavement, and any large change of fortune. But this is not psychotherapy. My subject is not consolation; it is confrontation. I am not talking about group dynamics; I am talking about cognitive change and expansion. I am talking about lifelong education as episodes and exploits which provide a context for personal re-alignment with reality.

I am not quite sure what the role of the teacher can be in mediating marginal, liminal, literally 'ecstatic' experiences. The business of teaching is ecstasy; and the process of teaching—or anyway, of schooling—makes the extraordinary and the terrifying orderly, tame, and routine. In the Sufi commune we reflected at length on the role of intermediaries—teachers, professionals, and priests, who stand between us and reality. We pondered the significance of the silken thread which tied the novice to the sheik, a thread which must be neither too taut not too slack. And we pondered Ibn Arabi's *Treatise on Unity* which tells us that:

It is necessary that thou know him after this fashion, not by knowledge, nor by intellect, nor by understanding, nor by imagination, nor by sense, nor by the outward eye, nor by the inward eye . . .. He sent himself with himself to himself. There was no mediator nor any means other than he. There is no difference between the Sender and the thing sent, and the person sent and the person to whom he is sent. The very existence of the prophetic message is His existence.

There seemed to be no place in this knowing for intermediaries, for teachers, for the bewildering clutter of audio-visual aids and curriculum kits. We were struggling with a new kind of conceptual apparatus to grasp the world.

I am impressed by the search that many young people are making today to gain access to such experiences, through which they can re-order and reformulate the world. I mean their communes and their journeys to the East; I mean their attempts to enter the worlds of people labelled 'insane'. I mean their deep and proper contempt for education as domestication. I mean their willingness to 'go native'.

These are the counter-cultural generation. They are only a minority of (mainly gifted and highly intelligent) young people in their twenties and early thirties, but they are the authentic 'curriculum developers' of our day and should claim our attention no less than the Schools Council. I will focus for a moment on their willingness to 'go native', because this reflects not only a profound social change of our times, but an even profounder reorientation to knowing and experience.

It is partly an aspect of a post-imperial age. In the days of imperial splendour one must never, of course, lose caste. One could go native— like Sir Richard Burton— only to spy. It was as an intelligence officer for General Napier that Burton, his face stained with henna, haunted native bazaars. Burton, too, became a Sufi—but only to gain access to forbidden cities. John Buchan's heroes were heroic precisely because they went native for a similar purpose: there could be no possible doubt that beneath their outlandish disguises they held firm to the purity of social categories and the staunch values of upper-class Englishmen.

Today it is, perhaps, easier to go native. We are a highly plural society, which means we encompass diverse systems of honour. There is no single and exclusive chivalric code. Light-skinned negroes no longer try to pass as white, northern accents are carefully preserved in the metropolis, and homosexuals (often) courageously 'come out'. But our contemporary willingness to go native reflects something of even deeper significance: it reflects a shift in our conception of knowing, in our mode of apprehending reality. Reality is only imperfectly grasped from outside. Detachment is falsification. Reality must be known, lived, and experienced from within. There are signs that even professional anthropologists will go native soon. Their methodology was part of the coherence of an imperial cosmos which has now fallen apart.

The counter-cultural young have rejected conventional education and its mode of knowing, as a form of pollution: it is a thick pall of smog hiding reality. Books, from their sheer quantity and the way they percolate into every corner of our lives, are now defilement. We have a glut, a veritable bombardment of information, of so-called 'data'—of things given; and we have a veritable famine of experience. Anyone today can readily lay his hands on facts, and even on theories and ideas; we can practically never lay our hands on an authentic experience. Any idea, D. H. Lawrence once said, can be pigeon-holed; but the world cannot pigeon-hole a new experience. Actually, he was wrong. Education has made even experience 'safe': every group that organizes itself around an experience constitutes a pigeon-hole. It is the destruction of pigeon-holes, whether ideational or experiential, that my paper is about.

It is not only facts that are nowadays ubiquitous: even high culture is everywhere, seeping into our lives. And it, too, has been defused and made safe. It is no longer scarce and undistributed; it is pervasive: it saturates the environment. The terror and mystery of Dionysiac impulse, which lies behind most modern art, has been tamed and domesticated, converted to piped Wagner in Tesco—Valkyries earthbound among the tinned soups and asparagus tips.

The real problem of education (and justice), at all stages of life, is not the distribution of 'objective' knowledge, which is readily available in superabundance (the difficulty is not to obtain it, but to avoid it); but the distribution of experience, which is terribly scarce. Experience is the scarce commodity which we must try to expand. This is difficult, because it is visibly shrinking, and even in the form of paid employment is likely to diminish as human beings become too expensive for modern economies to use.

The new-style anthropology has been pioneered by Carlos Castaneda, a young American student at University of California, Los Angeles and perhaps it is his new-style anthropology that offers the educational model I am seeking. Castaneda apprenticed himself for five terrifying years in the mid-1960s to a Yaqui Indian, and found, for a time, a separate reality (Castaneda, 1973). But to be fair I think we must point to Joseph Conrad's *Heart of Darkness*, which first suggested the significance, for modern man, of going native. (T. S. Eliot saw Conrad's story as somehow symbolic of our modern predicament.) Conrad's Mr Kurtz was an eloquent and civilized European who engaged in unspeakable African rites and allowed his unlawful soul to transgress permitted bounds. He began by writing a treatise on the suppression of savage customs and ended by embracing them.

Carlos Castaneda similarly began with a (doctoral) thesis and ended as a sorcerer's apprentice. He struggled to become a man of knowledge, and discovered how thinking, talking, and doing are shields against reality. 'You think and talk too much,' said his mentor, Don Juan. 'You must stop talking to yourself . . .. We maintain our world without internal talk . . .. A warrier is aware of that and listens to the world; he listens to the sounds of the world.' Castaneda had to learn how to 'see', and 'When a man learns to see, not a single thing he knows prevails. Not a single one . . ..'

Castaneda was chilled by Don Juan's idea of detachment. 'You must be joking,' replied Don Juan,

the thing which should give you the chills is not having anything to look forward to but a lifetime of doing what you have always done. Think of the man who plants corn year after year until he's too old and tired to get up, so he lies around like an old dog. His thoughts and feelings, the best of him, ramble aimlessly to other things he has ever done, to plant corn. For me that is the most frightening waste there is.

We are men and our lot is to learn and to be hurled into inconceivable new worlds.

Seeing is for impeccable men. Temper your spirit now, learn to see, and then you will know that there is no end to the new worlds for our vision.

Acknowledgement

The author is indebted to his former assistants, Roger Middleton and Pat Hawes, for help with the fieldwork on which this paper is based.

References

Berger, B. M., 1960, 'How long is a generation?' *British Journal of Sociology*, **II**.

Berger, P. L., 1971, *A Rumour of Angels* (Harmondsworth, Middx: Penguin Books).

Berger, P. L. and Luckmann, T., 1971, *The Social Construction of Reality* (Harmondsworth, Middx: Penguin Books).

Bloom, B., 1966, *Stability and Change in Human Characteristics* (New York: Wiley).

Castaneda, C., 1973, *A Separate Reality* (Harmondsworth, Middx: Penguin Books).

Douglas, M., 1970, *Purity and Danger* (Harmondsworth, Middx: Penguin Books).

Erikson, E., 1965, *Childhood and Society* (Harmondsworth, Middx: Penguin Books).

Gennep, A. van, 1960, *The Rites of Passage* (London: Routledge & Kegan Paul).

Musgrove, F., 1974, *Ecstasy and Holiness* (London: Methuen).

Musgrove, F., 1975a, 'Dervishes in Dorsetshire: an English commune', *Youth and Society*, **6**.

Musgrove, F., 1975b, 'Late entrants to the Anglican ministry: a move into marginality?', *Sociological Review*, **23**.

Musgrove, F., 1976, 'A home for the disabled: marginality and reality', *British Journal of Sociology*, **26**.

Schon, D. A., 1971, *Beyond the Stable State* (London: Temple Smith).

Stub, H. R., 1969, 'Education, the professions, and long life', *British Journal of Sociology*, **20**.

Turner, V. W., 1974, *The Ritual Process* (Harmondsworth, Middx: Penguin Books).

Webb, J., 1962, 'Sociology of a school', *British Journal of Sociology*, **13**.

Chapter 11

The Dustbin Men

*Spencer Millham**

Just before Christmas 1975 I was at a concert at a maximum security Borstal. It was built in 1860, is modelled on Dartmoor prison, and houses 350 teen-age lads who all live in cells. The concert started with a marvellous chorus:

> We are the dustbin men,
> Born in 'em,
> Kept in 'em,
> And when we get out
> We are going to empty 'em.

Sociological truths come by strange paths and it is these 'dustbin men' about whom I wish to tell you in this paper.

How big are the problems posed by these young people and how relevant are today's schools to their needs? In the sylvan glades of Dartington you do not see many of them about. In fact, our idea of youthful deviance tends to be a noisy jazz band on the school roof, and our definition of poverty: faggots from the deep freeze for lunch. But away from Torbay things are rather different and I shall first sketch out to you the levels of poverty found in our society.

The Child Poverty Action Group talks of two and a half to three million people in Britain who are living in poverty while Peter Townsend and Brian Abel Smith have put forward an even higher figure. Ken Coates, who gave these figures to his Nottingham evening class, was ridiculed by his incredulous students so he told them to go and undertake a survey in the St Anne's district of the city. The students discovered, of course, that the rates were a distinct underestimate for that part of town.

---

* Director, Dartington Social Research Unit, Dartington Hall.

A more recent inquiry is found in the report of the Finer Committee (HMSO, 1974) on one-parent families, which published findings just over a year ago that two thirds of a million parents were looking after one million children single-handed. What is more, a third of these one-parent families were receiving Supplementary Benefit[1] as their main source of income. Most of them were fatherless families with all that this implies for the care of children, particularly for the upbringing of boys.

These figures for levels of poverty are, I suggest, appalling and the implications of this situation are particularly serious. As the poor and the problems that bedevil them are so concentrated, schools, which are the main agencies for supporting children in poor localities, have to work under terrific pressures, as do all the other social support services in these areas. All sorts of problems seem to cluster among the same group. For example, 40 per cent of our national housing was built before 1919 but in London and Liverpool the figure rises to some 50 per cent and in some central areas of our large cities is sometimes as high as 80 per cent. Liverpool City Planning Department undertook a very interesting study in 1970, in which it compared the extent of social malaise in the inner suburbs with that found in outer districts. On 29 criteria of social malaise, such as levels of maladjustment among children or rates of suicide and unemployment, the researchers found that the inner areas displayed much greater problems than elsewhere.

The implications of all this for education are very important; the studies of Douglas (1964), National Children's Bureau (Fogelman, 1976), Plowden (HMSO, 1967), and Halsey (1972) all suggest that by the age of 7, poverty is strongly correlated with poor academic progress and maladjustment. Recently, junior school teachers in South Glamorgan undertook a study of their own classes and found that something like 15 per cent of the children were considered to be educationally and socially at risk. Also relevant to the theme of my paper is West's study of maladjustment and delinquency among adolescent boys which shows that these problems are clearly related to poverty in the family and all the accompanying stresses associated with it.

Even the criminal statistics point a moral here. In 1975, 186 000 juveniles under the age of 18 were convicted or officially cautioned. It seems likely that at least three times that figure, that is over half a million, will have actually committed an offence and almost all of them will come from the bottom end of our class system. I suggest, again, that these numbers are very high indeed and even if we ignore the stress and the suffering that these imply, the sheer size of the problem would suggest that it is useful to take a closer look at these 'dustbin children'.

My concern for the past seven years has been with those children who opt for a delinquent solution to their problem. I would not claim that this group is any more important than any other, but governments unfortunately are more keen to commission research into delinquents than they are to pay for studies of other deprived groups. However, the problems presented by the 1200 boys involved in my research study do mirror, perhaps in a slightly more exaggerated and dramatic form, the problems of some million of their contemporaries. Whether this group represents the elite of trouble makers in our society I very much doubt.

Those who work with middle-class adolescents may question what I am saying. We all know that middle-class children have their share of family disruption and can be highly delinquent, but the fact is that they are better protected from the consequences. You certainly seem more likely to come to the attention of the control systems in our society if you are poor than if you are better off. We can hardly conceive of our own 'dustbin' child getting himself a reservation in the 'nick', but for many children such a fate has more favourable odds than being fully employed or living to three score years and ten.

Let us look more closely at the career of a child who is persistently delinquent. In my illustration, I shall not be using the ideas of labelling theorists such as Becker and Lemert, or Matza's ideas of the drift to crime, because I think that their explanations start too late and are too much concerned with the supposed traumas of going to court and being apprehended by the police. They tend to forget that the careers of deprived children start long before they ever reach a court. I wish, therefore, to steal Hargreaves's concept, developed in his book on classroom behaviour, and to look at 'routine deviance'. This will enable me to chart the career that deprived and delinquent children build up.

Let me describe a persistent offender. He is usually born into a large family after insufficient pre-natal care. There are more boys in his family than girls, and this has a very important influence on his role. He is usually the second or third child to be born and this again has important implications for the care he receives. Dad will be absent for long periods, either due to work, disappearance, or being 'inside', Mum is therefore hard-presssed and will certainly have been hospitalized during the past few years, often because of mental illness, such as severe depression. They will be poor with all that this means—poor housing, poor food, and many to a bed. Much of the boy's early rearing will be in the hands of a slightly older sister or a 'Gran' and, as soon as he can practically move, he wanders out into the street to join a hectic, rumbustious community life. Control in home and street is by proscription, by a smack or lift under the ear, and this is quite different from middle-class practice. We, of course, control our children by explanation and the withdrawal of love. So, we plead with our awkward offspring, 'Please, Jeremy don't spit in Mummy's yoghurt, otherwise she gets so tense'!

It comes as little surprise, therefore, that our 'dustbin child' finds much of what happens in school completely baffling. The lack of communication makes almost meaningless most of what is purveyed. If we agree with Bernstein's hypotheses, then the implications for secondary education should be obvious. But, with a bit of luck, our deprived youngster might go to a nursery school or be accepted for an 'educational priority area' experiment where, to the splashing of paint and clay, he is introduced to creative play. There, as he experiments with Galt toys, he will probably notice that some children and some mothers look, dress, and smell a good deal nicer than he does. But he remains contented and people continue to make an effort. The 'dustbin child', also seems to make some progress and he probably does not notice that Jeremy—our sort of child—is going home with Ladybird books and is already beginning to coil his first pot. If you feel that these observations are a bit cynical, I suggest that you look at Barnes's evaluation of an educational priority area in London and examine the research done in North America on compensatory education and poverty programmes in the United States. Both of these studies show that the needy children, for whom the projects were originally set up, tend to get the least benefit from them.

Let us follow our difficult lad into the the primary school, where high priority is given to a number of alien mysteries, such as reading and writing, little of which he ever sees used outside. Certain moral expectations also come as something of a surprise. He is exhorted not to tell lies and not to run away, both pieces of behaviour which he has already effectively fashioned into a strategy for getting out of difficulty, and one that he will use again in truanting from school and absconding from residential institutions.

Before the week is out, his classmates will be defining his position: his runny nose, dirty shirt, and too big trousers will make sure that he does not get a place in the leading crowd. Whatever the system of dividing children whether it is 'A' and 'B' streams or 'Monkeys' and 'Alligators', the school's formal pecking order will begin to reflect the informal friendships of the children.

But our deprived child is happy, or at least, he says he is. Indeed, these children make a very clear distinction between the experience of the primary school, which is child-centred, and that of the secondary school, which is large and academic. It seems that transfer to the secondary school for many of these children often initiates a period of truancy and conflict with the system. Much of the research in educational priority areas would suggest that deprived children find the child-centred atmosphere of the primary school particularly rewarding. Mums cluster at the gate and siblings take them home. It is much more local and, of course, there is only one teacher looking after them. But the 'dustbin group' certainly do not like their secondary schools. From the group of 1200 children we studied, some 80 per cent said that nobody in their secondary schools cared for them. I can remember one boy scrawling on my questionnaire which sought to inquire about his feelings for secondary school—'I only went for the dinner'. Having had dinner at that place, I can assure you he *must* have been deprived!

The 'dustbin men' find the size of their new school baffling and are frustrated by the subject-based rather than teacher-based curriculum. Lessons end on the bell and children trek along psychedelic corridors beckoned by one-way Tannoy systems to distant faces in alien rooms, yakking on about integrated studies. Thus, our deprived child slides into the residual group of early leavers in the bottom forms. He truants because he sees the curriculum as irrelevant and the structure as inhibiting care on the part of the teachers.

With young offenders, the group with which I am particularly concerned, problems have started to show a good deal earlier than the age of 11. Remedial efforts in primary school do not seem to have had much lasting effect and their attendance has become somewhat fitful. In fact, when I looked at the 10- and 11-year-olds in my group, something like 80 per cent of them were already four years retarded. Some even seemed to be going backwards! But, despite these early signs, we have to wait until early adolescence for our 'dustbin child' to become a serious problem. So, at 13 he is writing 'bum' on the lavatory wall and is even bullying our Jeremy. No wonder we are all rapidly getting fed up with him.

Outside school, our awkward lad is going around with friends and brothers who are slightly older than himself. Together, they embark on a round of petty vandalism starting with an empty house, and then moving by means of open windows to more serious crime. Everybody in the neighbourhood knows about this and his family express concern, alternating good hidings with threats of being sent away. But, the ethos of the twilight area, the example and encouragement of his peers, and the growing resentment to the system, all combine to keep him going. Naturally, he gets caught. The police visit, first to warn but later to demand his presence at an official admonition at the police station. Thereafter, he reaches a court, an experience which proves to be terribly exciting, with more policemen than he has ever seen in his life and with people standing up talking legal jargon. Everyone is concerned for him.

Mum weeps and the social worker with a 'violin face' says, 'For God's sake, wear a collar and tie and a blazer. Say you didn't mean it, Say you're sorry. Tell him you're going in the Army at 16, and with a bit of luck you'll get a conditional discharge.'

Naturally, his school puts the spoke in. Clearly they cannot take him back. A long period of suspension forces the hands of the social workers, and thus, off he goes to a series of residential placements associated in his eyes with either the mad, bad or destitute. The day school has now passed the buck to social workers, whose success rate is going to be equally dismal. Something like three-quarters of my approved school population were back in serious trouble within two years of leaving their institution, and for the younger Borstal population reconviction rates are even higher with four-fifths of them in serious trouble within a year. I was looking at one maximum security Borstal not so long ago, where a boy still under 16 had just arrived for his third spell inside.

What do our 'dustbin men' think about all this? Here are some of their answers transcribed from a video-tape.

Boy 1

I got on all right with teachers. They do just look on you as a bit mischievous when you do something wrong at primary school, most of the teachers did but I don't think headmaster did because he used to tell us in assembly and get us out the front, when we'd done something wrong, and tell rest of school to look at us because we'd be the ones who'd be smashing telephone boxes up and things like that and that we'd end up as delinquents and end up in prison.

When you're at primary school, you've just got one teacher what takes you for every subject, writing and reading, but when you go to Northcliffe, they're all different teachers. You hear all that many stories about it, they cane you and everything—I was frightened at first.

I was in Mr Jones' class for two years—he was deputy HM and deputy HM before him went on to be Head at Station Road. I forgotten what they call him but he used to slipper 'em and be dead strict, but Mr Jones used to be all right, you could have a joke with him and things, he used to let us call him Pete, we used to make models and things, we'd go out and do gardening, keep budgies and try to breed 'em. You know, let us do all sorts of things we wanted to do, he tried to get us interested in things rather than reading, writing and what all of rest of class does. If we didn't like it, he'd try and interest us in something else.

Q.   Could Northcliffe have done more?

They could have been a bit stricter. It's worst you could get expelled, well not expelled, suspended; they'll just suspend you for a couple of weeks and then you'll come back and do same again and get suspended again. Some say because they get suspended, everyone talks about them. They like it.

I used to play truant. I didn't go much. In 3rd and 4th years, we used to go swimming in river. I got fed up with school and wanted to do something different. Only certain lessons I'd truant—I used to go to fieldcraft and football, but I didn't like maths, and humanities and sports days and things like that. I used to wag it then and when I thought I was going to get into trouble for something, I'd wag it for a couple of weeks until I thought they'd forgotten about it.

It just depends what you've done. If you've done something what's not too bad like, he'd just talk it over with you to see if he could stop you doing it. You could tell him all your problems because he used to take sociology and you could tell him all your problems in sociology because it were only a small class. You could go to his office in dinner or breaks and he'd sort it out with you, but he could be strict if that didn't do no good and that's what I liked about him.

Boy 2

What it is with them at senior school is they just teach, do their job. Don't look after you like at primary school. They just seem to be there to do a job: some are O.K. People who came from a posher, better background, parents treated them better and they got better things; teachers thought more of them; they seemed to get on better. I'm not saying I came from a bad background but I never used to get on well at home—still don't—and that makes a difference: if you don't get on well at home, you don't seem to do well at school. Some people do, but it just happened with me.

They're not bothered about teaching people like me. All they bothered about is, 'They're brainy enough to teach and they do a job.'

Q.   Was anyone bothered about you?

No, I don't think so, not in school, only my Mom at home.

Boy 3

There was a teacher in one primary school who used to let me sit on her lap and all this shit. You get mothered. In some instances it works the opposite from what you expect, for the guy who hasn't got anything—you know, the waif.

It's the good boy with the good family who wears his nice white shirt and his tied up shoes and who comes in with his pressed trousers who gets the best education in primary schools.

Boy 4

I passed the 11+ and went to a local grammar school. My father went there. It was a very well thought of school. Very straight, white or grey shirts, grey socks. Anything colourful was taboo. It was always thrashed in us—you've passed the 11+, you are in the top 25 per cent of your age group and you're very privileged.

I was put into the 'A' stream and from the minute I got there, I almost opted out. I could stick it for a year of pretence.

Q   What pretence?

A pretence that this is what I wanted, that this is how it should be. Perhaps two terms of the first year I was O.K.—although I resented the school. I resented the teachers and I resented the way it was run. I resented the prefect system where lads of 17 and 18 used to walk round like demigods, kick you in the pants, knock you about. Although it was an ordinary day school, the fagging system was still in operation; the teachers used to watch it happen, it was accepted that the first years were used by the second, third, and so on.

I was very interested in football. Football was my life at about 11. I could not play football, all it was was rugby—if you played football in the playground, the ball was taken away and you were put in detention.

I went down from the 'A' stream to the 'B' stream in the second year and I think it was then that I really started knocking about with the guys who were bucking the school in a very minor way. We opted out of rugby, just little things at first, and they would try to knock us back into line. This is when the big confrontation with the prefects came, and they were so unfair—it was unbelievable. I think it was something to do with the school trying to create a class, they could say you are middle class, if you don't go to university, then you're going to a very good job. You are going to be the managers and this is what we want you to be. You couldn't run it like this. It's a very old school, fee-paying at one time, but it was still run on those lines. The area is a big mining area and you get miners' sons going to this school, and then you try to knock it into them that they should be this, that, and the other. With some it works, while others just reject it. You cannot run a school on such false lines.

The teachers all wore cloaks, mortar boards. You had to call them 'Sir'. You could never question a teacher or anything. This progressed until the 4th or 5th year. I continued to go, I didn't start opting out of school until the 4th year and then only in a very minor way. I didn't have weeks off at a time. My way of opting out was to act out at school—do no work. By the 4th year I was being as disruptive as I could. It was my only amusement. I got no kicks out of the lessons. First, the teachers banged down then they condoned and expected it, and just waited for an opportunity to get me out. By the 4th year I think they had given up completely.

The 4D, as it was called, the last class in the school, they put all the delinquents and all the people who didn't want to work in that class and that was it, and left us to our devices and waited for an opportunity to get us out.

I do not really need to say very much more as they describe their feelings a good deal better than I can. But, there are just one or two points that I would like to make in closing.

First of all, I would raise an old theme in education, the tendency for our educational and social services to create the problems which we face. Few schools, in my view, have changed to meet the real needs of deprived kids, because the cultivation of an academic elite, which is what most education is about, conflicts with this. We spend a great deal of money on those young people who stay long in schools, and even more on students of higher education. The price we have to pay is in that group whose voices we have just heard. It seems that the humiliation of needy kids is the expense we are happy to incur so that our

Jeremy will be sitting here in 20 years' time, hastening on to those leadership positions which presumably by that time we will have vacated.

The second thing that comes out of the interviews we have heard is a very keen awareness of the economic and social forces which put these children where they are. Their comments are an interactionist's dream. They brim with a legitimate resentment that translates itself early into truancy and school-refusal, and then goes on to vandalism, violence, and crime. The three older boys whose voices you heard have spent some 17 years between them in institutional care, and two of them are not yet 20. In the year since the tape was made, two of these lads have been back in prison, one of them twice. The chance of changing their behaviour, I suspect, is now absolutely nil, because there is no reason why they should change. They have quite integrated identities which we have helped to build up. Asking them to change their ways is rather like asking me to go and run a Wimpy bar or to be a prop forward!

Our research also suggests one or two other things about the ways in which we approach deprived and delinquent adolescents. Educational-ists, I suspect, tend to have too great an estimate of the efficacy of the establishment which they run, and often underestimate the complexity of the institutional setting. Too many people, in my view, are still looking for solutions in the shape of the right institution. But I am afraid that all round success is simply impossible for you are always going to have somebody who suffers.

In ordinary schools, an academic stress will depress a concern with social areas and there will always be a group who cannot cope. In the case of treating delinquents, the conflict in aims of community home schools is even clearer. If, for example, the school develops close relations with the local community, the neighbourliness can stigmatize the children, yet if you isolate adolescents it makes it quite impossible for them to readjust after they leave. Because of the conflicts inherent in institutional structures, it is impossible to produce a system which is going to achieve every possible success. For day schools, this means that while we may succeed in catering for the majority of pupils, we cannot at the same time meet the needs of very deprived groups. Our priorities for one group work against what is needed for the other.

This conflict means that the provision we have to make for children has to be varied. I have always found, when talking to teachers, that there can be a quite bizarre gap between what they say they are doing and what they actually choose to undertake. I suspect, therefore, that schools are more about social allocation—that is, preparing children for adult roles—than about education. We socialize young people into bits of our class system more than we care to admit. For example, for the handicapped delinquent we provide realistic trade aspirations, whereas in the public schools, distanced relationships are stressed for intending bureaucrats. In the progressive schools, one finds the endless expressive chatter which seems so absolutely essential for any creative enterprise, and so on. Sometimes, in fact, the real functions of schools come out in a most bizarre way. I can remember once visiting an exclusive preparatory school and coming across a little vocational handbook telling little boys how to go to the lavatory—in court dress!

Schools are, therefore, about fitting people into society rather than widening the spirit. That is why, for me, Winchester and Bedales are very much the same, although they appear superficially different. All of their leavers are destined for the same bits of our society. That is also why the National Nautical Approved School has nothing in common with the great institution which at first glance it resembles—Dartmouth Royal Naval College.

The interviews I have quoted indicate that deprived children fully understand these differences in destination. Because they are so aware, it must make practically meaningless many of the high-sounding phrases and moral edicts which we purvey to them in the shape of education. They know these to be phoney yet only in recent years have they developed the political and economic muscle to make their views heard.

I have said something about deprived children, and the institutional care which we offer them. They have also said something to us. In closing, are there any comforts we can gain?

One could, of course, make the usual plea for a redistribution of resources, particularly into housing and deprived areas. However, we know that this is very unlikely to happen, and in order to be relevant our discussions have to be more practical.

First of all, we can try to take deprived children out of impersonal institutional structures. I know that this might be stigmatizing for them but I believe that a stigma which is clear is better and easier to cope with than the terrible humiliations which most of these lads will suffer. We can also try to keep the most difficult adolescents out of residential care, because this is expensive and not very effective.

I think also that each of us can be much more honest about these children when we are responsible for them. Much of the behaviour of deprived and delinquent children is not only quite logical to them but it is also quite legitimate, and, in its own way, highly creative and innovatory. Yet, because of our social position, we find this behaviour unacceptable. I think, therefore, we should be quite honest about this and take a more straightforward line with these lads. A truthful stance would be, 'I dislike your behaviour because it offends me. You're unlucky because I'm not going to put up with it and I've got the power to do something about it. I can assure you that this will be uncomfortable for you. I agree with you that it's unfair.' I suspect that this more honest approach would at least give our 'dustbin men' some semblance of choice and recognize them more as people in some charge of their own destiny.

I think, also, that we could do a lot more to try and accept them for the warm, likeable, spontaneous, and very exciting young people that they are. I think that we should strive to find them jobs; we should also try and provide them with homes. We should certainly give them all the help we can and we should not shelter behind the stereotypes which we tend to entertain, that they are difficult and unrewarding thugs. These stereotypes merely protect us from what we are really doing and hide the fact that we have made our way in the very same system which has crucified them.

I find it nice to come to Dartington, just as it was marvellous to work in Cambridge. After all, both are campuses of amenity and beauty which, along with most other institutions in this country, are a microcosm of the wider society, with their wide inequalities of income, status, and life-style. By accepting stereotypes about deprived and delinquent young people, we are sheltered from moral unease. The 'dustbin men', I suspect, are where they are, simply because our Jeremy is where he is.

Note

1 Equivalent to social security allowance in the USA. Ed.

References

Abel-Smith, B. and Townsend, P. 1965, *The Poor and the Poorest* (London: Bell).

Becker, H. 1964, *The Other Side* (New York: Free Press).

Bernstein, B. 1972, *Class, Codes and Control* (London: Routledge & Kegan Paul).

Bowles S. and Gintis, H. 1976, *Schooling in Capitalist America* (London: Routledge & Kegan Paul).

Central Advisory Council for Education, 1967, *Children and their Primary Schools* (London: HMSO).

Coates, K. and Silburn, R. 1970, *Poverty: The Forgotten Englishmen* (Harmondsworth, Middx: Penguin).

Cornish, D. and Clarke, R. 1975, *Residential Treatment and its Effects on Delinquency* (London HMSO).

Davie, R., Butler, N. and Goldstein, H. 1972, *From Birth to Seven*, (London: Longman).

Department of Health and Social Security and Welsh Office, 1977, *Working Together for Children and their Families*, (London: HMSO).

Douglas, J. 1964, *The Home and School*, (London: MacGibbon & Kee).

Fogelman, K. (ed.), 1976, *Britain's Sixteen Year Olds*, (London: National Children's Bureau).

Hall, S. and Jefferson, T. 1976, *Resistance Through Rituals* (London: Hutchinson).

Halsey, A. (ed.), 1972, *Educational Priority* (London: HMSO).

Hargreaves, D., Hester, S. and Mellor, F. 1976, *Deviance in Classrooms* (London: Routledge & Kegan Paul).

HMSO, 1967, *Children and their Primary Schools*, (London).

HMSO, 1975, *Report on the Work of the Prison Department*, (London: Cmd. 6542).

HMSO, 1974, *Report of the Committee on One Parent Families*, (London: Cmd. 5629).

Lambert, R., Millham, S. and Bullock, R. 1975, *The Chance of a Lifetime?* (London: Weidenfeld & Nicolson).

Lemert, E. 1967, *Human Deviance, Social Problems and Social Control* (New York: Prentice-Hall).

Liverpool Planning Department, 1970, *Social Malaise in Liverpool*.

Matza, D. 1964, *Delinquency and Drift* (New York, Wiley).

Midwinter, E. 1972, *Priority Education* (Harmondsworth, Middx: Penguin).

Millham, S., Bullock, R. and Cherrett, P. 1975, *After Grace—Teeth* (London: Human Context Books).

Millham, S., Bullock, R. and Hosie, K. 1978, *Locking Up Children* (Farnborough: Saxon House, 1978).

Morton, D. and Watson, D. 1971, 'Compensatory education and the contemporary liberalism in the United States: A sociological view', *International Review of Education*, **XVII**, 289–307.

Mungham, G. and Pearson, G. 1976, *Working Class Youth Culture* (London: Routledge & Kegan Paul).

West, D. and Farrington, D. 1973, *Who Becomes Delinquent?* (London: Heinemann).

Willis, P. 1977, *Learning to Labour* (Farnborough: Saxon House, 1977).

Aspects of Education
Edited by M. Braham
© 1982 John Wiley & Sons Ltd.

Chapter 12

Towards a Poor School

*Colin Ward**

> The technological society has deliberately cultivated a careless, consumptive, egoistic and slovenly human being. The frugal society . . . must start with redirecting our attitudes and re-educating our values.
>
> Henryk Skolimowski[1]

Perhaps the best-known contribution made by John Dewey to the endless debate on education was his remark that 'what the best and wisest parent wants for his own child, that must the community want for all of its children'. But perhaps the best and wisest of parents are the very ones who are least able to specify their hopes in this respect, and the more they perceive and acknowledge the uniqueness of each child, the less likely would be their hopes for any particular child to have any general relevance. Unless, that is, they take refuge in generalities of universal application. They might want their child to be happy, to be fulfilled, to be autonomous, or to 'make a contribution'. But who doesn't? What guide to individual or collective action could we derive from such aspirations?

I have a friend, a Paraguayan anarchist, whose children were named according to parental convictions. Regardless of sex or custom, the first was named Liberty, the second was called Equality, and the third was named Fraternity. (If you are wondering what the fourth child of the family was called, I have to tell you that he was called Ché.) It is hard to guess which of the family would grow up most embarrassed by this imposition of ideology on nomenclature, and I have no idea whether he

---

* Former Editor of *Anarchy* and later Environmental Education Officer, Town and Country Planning Association, London, and Editor of *BEE, the Bulletin of Environmental Education*.

sought for each child an education compatible with the slogans with which he labelled his offspring. He would be in trouble if he did, because the resounding catch-phrases we have inherited from the eighteenth century may go together marvellously on French postage stamps, but do they go together in life, or in educational policy making? Dr Ronald Sampson of Bristol recently gave an address with the title 'The choice between inequality and freedom in education' and that title at least draws attention to one of our most agonizing and unresolved educational dilemmas.

For it often seems to me that people's social and political attitudes are determined, not on the conventional left–right spectrum, but on the relative values they place on at least the first two characters in this holy trinity. There is a quite different continuum which shapes their approaches to the politics of education as to everything else: that between authoritarians and libertarians. In terms of the ordinary crudities of party politics, you can, for example, place our representatives in either of the two main parties on this continuum, and you might very well find that in one of those two parties the egalitarians are always on the back benches, while in the other the libertarians are usually to be found there. In the politics of education in Britain, people's devotion to one or other of these principles leads them into some very sterile posturing, and it often lays them open to uncomfortable changes of hypocrisy since sometimes what they want for their own children is something other than what they want for all the community's children.

The pathos of the battle for equality in education is that it revolves around the principle of the quality of opportunity to be unequal. The last word on this particular issue was said many years ago in a deceptively modest little book, disguised as a satire, *The Rise of the Meritocracy*, by Michael Young. This book looks back from the twenty-first century at our own day as the period when 'two contradictory principles for legitimising power were struggling for mastery—the principle of kinship and the principle of merit'. Kinship implies that you are the child of your parents and consequently have access to the opportunities they can provide. In Michael Young's satire, Merit wins in the end, with the perfection of intelligence testing, and consequently with earlier and earlier selection a new, non-self-perpetuating elite is formed, consisting of the 'five per cent of the population who know what five per cent means'. The top jobs go to the top people, and Payment by Merit (M equals IQ plus Effort) widens the gap between top and bottom people. The people at the bottom not only are treated as inferior, they *know* they *are* inferior. But to select the few is to reject the many, and in the meritocratic society new tensions arise. By the end of the twentieth century, although the new working class no longer includes people of outstanding intellectual capacity (since they have all been creamed off by meritocratic selection), a populist movement arises, consisting of dissident intellectuals, mainly women, allied with the disruptive proletariat, declaring in the Chelsea Manifesto of the year 2000 their belief in the classless society.

Needless to say, the manifesto cuts no ice with the meritocrats of the year 2000, though it becomes a rallying point in the bitter insurrection in 2033.

The Chelsea Manifesto declared that

The classless society would be one which both possessed and acted upon plural values. Were we to evaluate people not according to their intelligence and their education, their occupation and their power, but according to their sympathy and generosity, there could be no classes. Who would be able to say that the scientist was superior to the porter with admirable qualities as a father, and the civil servant with unusual skill at gaining prizes superior to the lorry driver with unusual skill at growing roses? The classless society would also be the tolerant society, in which individual differences were actually encouraged as well as passively tolerated, in which full meaning was at last given to the dignity of man. Every human being would then have equal opportunity, not to rise up in the world in the light of any mathematical measure, but to develop his own special capacities for leading a rich life.

Well, my own experience is that the same people who would give an enthusiastic ideological assent to the propositions of the Chelsea Manifesto complain most bitterly when they discover that their children can earn more working for the district council's cleansing department than they can in the lower ranks of professional employment; yet in the strike of toolroom workers at British Leyland in February 1977 they would bitterly criticize the strikers who asserted that with their years of training and immense skill they would only earn the same as foremen of the lavatory cleaners. Other people's defence of pay differentials is always marked by sordid self-interest: our own is always above reproach. Education is not a path to social equality.

What do we say about liberty, the first of the holy trinity? As a political issue this is construed as parental freedom of choice in schooling for their children. As an educational issue it means, among a great many other things, the absence of coercion of the child: the goods are displayed in the educational supermarket and the customer selects or rejects. I am afraid that, with the exception of a few heroes, known by name to most of us, we are as guilty of hypocrisy in the name of this great abstraction as we are in the name of equality. In the publicly provided education system we have a book of martyrs to make the point, among them Mr Duane, Mr MacKenzie, and Mr Ellis. In the privately provided sector we know how, at some stage in adolescence, parental interest in the sacred freedom of the child diminishes until the child is removed suddenly to attend a cramming establishment to achieve whatever educational qualifications are necessary to keep open the doors to a growing number of adult careers.

Martin Buber, looking into the candid eyes of a rebellious pupil, remarked, 'I love freedom, but I don't believe in it.' His remark epitomizes the position of the modern progressive parents. They do love freedom so long as it does not interfere with the chances of their children in the occupational status race. It is nothing to do with the education system or with the philosophy of education, but it is a fact that in most high-status jobs the qualifications for entry as well as the length of training have been raised and extended to a ludicrous extent in order to up-grade that occupation. I need only to mention one occupation, that with which I am most familiar, the profession of architecture. To be accepted for professional training involves at the outset, in terms of the English education system, three 'O' levels and two 'A' levels, preferably in approved subjects, followed by six years of professional training, after which the successful aspirant finds himself preparing schedules of doors and windows for some building in the design of which he has had no hand. Now within living memory—and I think you will probably agree that architecture has been of an aesthetically and technically higher standard within the lifespan of some living people—it was totally different. Sir Clough Williams-Ellis, who is still alive,[2] confided to Sir Edwin Lutyens that he spent a term at the Architectural Association in London, learning his trade. 'A term,' said Lutyens, horrified. 'My dear fellow, it took me three weeks.' Was Lutyens a better or worse architect than the people who by a restrictive Act of Parliament are today exclusively entitled to call themselves architects? The first architect I ever worked for learned his trade at an age when we still by law imprison children in the compulsory education machine, drawing full-size details in chalk on brown paper on a barn floor here in Devon, for the building of Truro Cathedral for the man to whom he was apprenticed, Sir John Loughborough Pearson, RA. Go and look at the building and see if it leaks.

What I say of an occupation of which I have intimate knowledge applies, I am certain, to the whole range of employment. I deliberately mentioned various architectural knights to indicate that I am not generalizing from the experience of the riff-raff of the architectural profession who all, no doubt, have been through the academic treadmill. In this I am saying, as in so many other spheres of life, professionalism is a conspiracy against the laity, and if it is the reason why we have tacitly abandoned out educational belief in liberty, we need to be quite clear that it is these external circumstances rather than our educational ideas which have forced us into this position.

For motivated families, the belief in liberty has been modified by the requirements of occupational entrance, and this view has spread from the intelligentsia to the skilled working class. Anyone from a city like Glasgow, Newcastle, or Belfast will tell you how the educational qualifications for an engineering apprenticeship have risen to impossible heights within the last decade. You need two 'O' levels to be employed with a car-washing machine in South Shields. No doubt you occasionally wash the cars lent by the Department of Education and Science to members of Her Majesty's Inspectorate so that they can get around to schools and tell teachers about the need to encourage children to aim at jobs in Britain's manufacturing industries.

Poor families and poor children interpret liberty in education quite differently. When the sociology graduate from Keele University drifts into teaching because we are overstocked with sociologists, and announces to his class that he wants them to feel free to express their own view of the situation, those amongst his conscripts who can actually hear his voice conclude with resignation that he does not really care about *them*. They conclude that in his opinion they are not worth teaching, and in their minds this is why he adopts his *laissez-faire* attitude. 'He didn't care whether we learned anything or not', is their verdict on the now-departed teacher. We have written off liberty as an educational goal.

What are we to say about fraternity as one of the aims of education? It is a concept even harder to define than the other two. Looking for a way of coming to terms with the idea, I am helped by a passage I read recently from André Malraux's book, *Lazare*. He says,

People think they understand Fraternity because they confuse it with human warmth. But in point of fact it is something much deeper, and it was belatedly, and almost apologetically, that it was added to the blazon of the Republic, whose flag at first bore only the words Liberty and Equality . . . . The word Liberty has still the same ring to it, but Fraternity now stands only for a comical utopia in which nobody would ever have a bad character. Men believe that Fraternity was just tacked on, one Sunday, to feelings like Justice and Liberty. But it is not something that can be tacked on at will. It is something sacred, and it will elude us if we rob it of the irrational element that lies hidden within it. It is as mysterious as love, it has nothing to do with duty, or with 'right thinking'. Like love, and unlike liberty, it is a provisional sentiment, a state of grace.

I am sure that Malraux betrays some ignorance of the history of ideas in his own country in making these remarks, but that is not my concern. Can we get closer to the meaning of fraternity? Peter Kropotkin chose to define it as 'mutual aid', and in his book of that name he remarks that

to reduce animal sociability to *love* and *sqmpathy* means to reduce its generality and its importance, just as human ethics based on love and personal sympathy only have contributed to narrow the comprehension of the moral feeling as a whole. It is not love of my neighbour—whom I often do not know at all—which induces me to seize a pail of water and to rush towards his house when I see it on fire; it is a far wider, even though more vague feeling or instinct of human solidarity and sociability which moves me . . . .. It is a feeling infinitely wider than love or personal sympathy—an instinct that has been slowly developed among animals and men in the course of an extremely long evolution, and which has taught animals and men alike the force they can borrow from the practice of mutual aid and support, and the joys they can find in social life.

Well, he's right, isn't he? But when the sense of fraternity, or solidarity, is cultivated in educational institutions, it is frequently in opposition to the institution itself. Teachers know that the fraternity is that of the peer group and that the values it represents are profoundly anti-educational. 'I have the greatest difficulty in restraining them from tearing up each other's work at the end of the period,' a hard-pressed secondary school teacher told me. Indeed, the closer we get to the classroom, the more diminished is our faith that the school can be the agent of social change or the vehicle for social justice. In many parts of the world there is still a hunger for schooling. Immense sacrifices are made by parents to achieve it for their children. They and their children would find unbelievable the size of education budgets in the schools of the Western world and the low esteem in which our schools are held by their scholars.

Thirteen years ago I wrote an article called 'A modest proposal for the repeal of the Education Act', and it was later blessed in the symposium 'Children's rights' as 'the first time anyone in England had dared to formulate out loud, even to a possibly friendly audience, what many of us had begun to hear as a question in our heads'. That reference to a friendly audience is important because it is easy to be misunderstood. At a time when teachers are joining the ranks of the unemployed, and when their unions as well as those of students are demonstrating under banners reading 'Fight the Education Cuts', am I not grotesquely misjudging the present climate of education in putting on my banner the slogan 'Towards a Poor School'?

Let me declare my vested interest in having rich schools. I earn half my living producing a bulletin for teachers called *BEE, the Bulletin of*

Environmental Education. It costs £4 a year—a modest sum—and in the last year the curve of circulation growth has completely flattened, as our renewal notices keep getting returned with sad little notes saying, 'We like it very much. It's marvellously useful, but we have had to cut our spending drastically.' I always say that they ought to ask their classes to subscribe their pennies, on the grounds that getting our bulletin will improve the quality of the teaching they are subjected to, but no one takes me seriously because it is a basic educational principle, isn't it, that no one should raise a penny for his own education?

I earn the other half of my income running a project for the Schools Council, which is the body concerned with curriculum development in England and Wales. Our project is called 'Art and the Built Environment'. Can you imagine anything more frivolous, while the nation's economy goes down the drain? Not only is our project one of those marginal frills, by the standards of the education industry, but its sponsor, the Schools Council, is itself vulnerable. The notorious Yellow Paper—the report to the Prime Minister from the Department of Education and Science, which was leaked to the press—described its performance as 'mediocre'. So I have a strong interest in an education system rich enough to support marginal activities—or activities which in the eyes of the system are marginal.

In what sense do I see virtues in the idea of a poor school? There is a Polish stage producer, Grotowski, who wrote a book called *Towards a Poor Theatre*, implying that the theatre would get a new lease of life if it shed all the expensive trimmings of the proscenium, elaborate lighting and equipment: all that audio-visual gear. (Actually there is a parallel in school here. Do any of our great drama teachers—people like Dorothy Heathcote in Newcastle, for example—have any use for the elaborate theatre equipment with which many schools encumbered themselves in the days when we thought we were rich?) Similarly there is a movement, as I understand it, in the Christian church, known as 'Towards a Poor Church', a kind of echo of all those religious reformers who have haunted that religion, with their bare feet and shaggy beards, urging their fellows to abandon all that expensive architecture and ecclesiastical silverware in order to free themselves to become receptive to the Message. (Actually there is a parallel in school here, too, with those earnest members of the Church of England who think that the only thing that can save the church is disestablishment—the severing of its official connection with the state. Many teachers of what we call religious education in school believe that the only thing that can save the reputation of their subject—which in this country is the only school subject established by law and at the same time the only one we can opt our children out of—is the ending of its statutory existence as well as that of the common act of worship which is supposed to take place in morning assembly.)

Whatever we may say when we lobby against cuts in educational spending, let us reflect between friends on the implications of educational poverty. And before we get self-righteous about it, let us think about the implications of the Houghton pay award to teachers a couple of years ago. Cause and effect there may or may not be, but before Houghton, when teachers were complaining of their poverty, there was no job shortage, there was a teacher shortage. Many schools had a terrifying turnover of staff every term. In 1974 many urban schools were sending children home because there was no one to teach them. I read two items about the same city in the same newspaper on the same day that year, one of which reported the sending home of school-children for this reason while the other reported the rounding-up by the police of truants, collected off the streets. After the Houghton pay award, the huge staff turnover stopped: the oldest inhabitants of the city school became the staff once more instead of the fifth-year conscripts, and the supply of jobs dried up. As the schools became poorer, they became more stable as institutions.

The truth is that in the boom period, now over, education was oversold. Every additional bit of expenditure, every increase in student numbers at the upper and more expensive end of the system, every new development in educational technology, was a step towards some great social goal. But it has not delivered the goods. Professor A. H. Halsey, writing in *The Times Educational Supplement* (21 January 1977), remarks that

We live today under sentence of death by a thousand cuts (that is, of all things except the body of bureaucracy). In education the position is one of extreme relative deprivation, not only because of the financial background of a sudden halt to previously mounting largesse, but also, and more seriously, because of the collapse of *belief* in education either as the best investment for national production, or the great redistributor of chances to the traditionally disadvantaged.

Nor is this simply a British phenomenon. Fred M. Hechinger, the author of *Growing up in America*, also writing in *The Times Educational Supplement* (5 November 1976) says that, 'America is in headlong retreat from its commitment to education. Political confusion and economic uncertainty have shaken the people's faith in education as the key to financial and social success.' Among the people or trends which he blames for this changed circumstance are the right-wing backlash and what he calls the 'desctructive' influence of the deschoolers like Ivan

Illich and the views of critics like Edgar Z. Friedenberg, John Holt, and Christopher Jencks. I think, on the contrary, that these people have had an immensely liberatory effect on our ideas about the way that the intelligentsia lapped up the deschooling literature of a few years ago—the works of Paul Goodman, Everett Reimer, and Ivan Illich—but when, at the same time, the schools were sending home pupils for lack of teachers, they failed, with a few exceptions in the 'free school' movement, to make the connection. The community did not seize the occasion to use the wonderful resources of the city to provide an alternative education for the kids who were wandering the streets. They just waited for the statistics for such offences as shoplifting, vandalism, and taking-and-driving-away, to rise—which they did. At the same time in the universities, well-educated Marxist lecturers were explaining how the education system in our society was simply a device for preparing us for our particular slot in capitalist industry. The government, as though anxious to prove them right, has set off a moral panic about the failure of the education system to meet the needs of industry.

My friend, Stan Cohen, wrote a book about the shaping of stereotypes in the public mind on such themes as 'mods', 'rockers', 'skinheads', and 'greasers', and gave it the title *Folk Devils and Moral Panics*. I would extrapolate from that title the notion that whenever you have a moral panic you have to find a folk devil. We have a moral panic about the state of education, so we find a folk devil in all those soft options that the kids are fiddling around with instead of bashing away at literacy and numeracy and getting ready for the world of work. This particular moral panic was set off by a speech from the Prime Minister, but the process that Cohen calls media amplification has been at work, so that what he actually said was considerably less denunciatory than the accompanying chorus off-stage. When Mr Callaghan made his speech at Ruskin College, enormous attention was focused on the occasion. This was not because of the nice irony that that particular college was founded to give a liberal education to working men, thus ensuring that they would never go back to what Eric Gill called the 'subhuman condition of intellectual irresponsibility' to which we condemn industrial workers, but because of the leak to the press in the previous week of that Yellow Paper—the document prepared by the Department of Education and Science to brief the Prime Minister—which swiped away at all the sacred cows of education except, of course, the Department of Education and Science and Her Majesty's Inspectorate. I must say that I found nothing objectionable about the Prime Minister's speech, but I cannot help feeling both cynicism and anger at the timing of this particular moral panic.

Is it because the government feels conscious that the rival party seems to be stealing its thunder in the public discussion of education? Or is it part of a smokescreen to divert attention from the fact that the cash is running out of the budgets of local education authorities? Well, never mind chaps, let's concentrate on the basics. It's back to 1870, the year of the Act of Parliament which made schooling free, universal, and compulsory, and also the year which marked the beginning of Britain's industrial decline. 1870? Well, just ask an economic historian. Isn't the educational industry, in fact, just the latest scapegoat for the state of the British economy?

The Prime Minister in his Ruskin speech said that he wanted to open a national debate on education, and remarked that 'the debate that I was seeking has got off to a flying start even before I was able to say anything'. Too true. I found it hilarious to learn from *The Guardian* on 14 October 1976—the week *before* Mr Callaghan's speech—that 'a multi-million pound emergency programme to monitor standards in primary and secondary schools has been started by the DES', just at the time when the schools themselves are being obliged to make multi-million pound cuts in their own spending, and just when education committees are solemnly debating reducing the calorific value of school meals as well as raising the price of them. Professor Halsey was absolutely right in suggesting that the last thing that would be cut was the educational bureaucracy. I read that week in the Sunday papers that the Welsh Secretary, Mr John Morris, has also pre-empted the result of the debate by giving 'clear uncompromising guidance . . . circulated to every head teacher in the Principality', saying that 'The priority must be tilted towards the engineer, the scientist and the mathematician. And in addition our children must be taught the languages of Europe to such a degree of proficiency that they can sell and service our products in the countries of our trading partners. . . .'

I am deeply suspicious of all this talk. I do not believe that the roots of or the cure for our chronic economic malaise are to be found in the education system and, if it is true that the young do not like industrial jobs, at either a shop-floor or a graduate level (and it is symptomatic of the superficial nature of the debate that it fails to distinguish between the two), I think it ironical that instead of wanting to change the nature of industrial work, of wanting to make it an adventure instead of a penance, we should want to change the nature of the young. Actually it is not even true that we are short of graduate engineers and we are certainly not short of shop-floor fodder.

There must be many teachers who went through the boom years without even knowing that they were in them: they found themselves committed to a policy of make-do-and-mend as usual, and never got their hands on the money because it was being spent somewhere else. No one here who is a teacher will deny my assertion that the characteristic situation is for the teacher to say all year that he would like this or that set of books or piece of equipment, and be told that there was no cash, while three days before the end of the financial year the head of department would say, 'You've got four hundred pounds to spend by the end of the week. Let me know what to order before the end of the afternoon because otherwise we'll lose the money.' I was in a school the other day, in an Art and Design Department, where thousands of pounds were available to spend on machinery, but the art teacher had only £38 to lay out on paper, paint, and other expendables. He could have kilns but no clay. As an advocate of the use of the local environment in education, I have often come across the situation where the teacher can easily get an illuminated terrestrial globe to suspend from the ceiling, but found that it was not in order for him to buy a class set of street maps of the locality.

One of the ways in which hierarchical systems work is by withholding information on the budget. We see this at a national level where the Chancellor of the Exchequer has it all in his black box to reveal to a waiting nation on budget day. Secrecy is made into a fetish and politicians have been disgraced because of budget leaks. But should not the nation's budget be the subject of earnest discussion throughout the country for months before? It is the same with the education budget and the budget of the school itself. I am willing personally to join in the scramble for slices of the diminishing cake, but which group of supplicants, all shouting 'me too', do I join? This is what is happening at the ludicrously stage-managed regional conferences being held by the DES and the ministers around the country, where every kind of special and sectional interest is being given the opportunity to say 'me too'.

I would rather join a different campaign. My bit of graffiti would say 'Open the Books'. Just what is the school's budget, and how is it to be allocated? What subject interest is starved just because it does not use a lot of prestige equipment? Just what is the authority's budget and how much of that goes in administration? Just what is the nation's education budget and how much of it is spent by the DES on itself? A year ago, John Vaizey, in one of his provocative little contributions to the education press, asked, 'Do we really need the DES?' Exactly what function, he asked, has the department, when the local authorities themselves have inspectors and subject advisers, and when we have a theoretically decentralized education system? Her Majesty's inspectors are always blandly telling us that they have no control over the curriculum. If you took a conspiratorial view of politics you might think that the Yellow Paper is the department's attempt to assert, in the face of Lord Vaizey (who is, after all, one of our foremost authorities on the economics of education), that it *has* a function, or is going to make one for itself.

Some people will remember a frivolous little book called *Parkinson's Law*, whose author commented, among other things, that, as the Navy had fewer and fewer ships, the Admiralty had more and more employees. Much more recently there is the instance of the National Health Service, which is the largest single employer in Britain. In the ten years before its reorganization, its staff increased by 65 per cent. Its medical staff, however, increased during this period by 21 per cent, and its domestic staff by 2 per cent. The truth is, unpalatable as it must be for those people who believe in government action and government funding for every task which society has to fulfil, that the governmental mechanism develops a momentum of its own: it secures and guarantees its own future. You will have seen photographs in the papers (e.g. *The Sunday Times*, 6 March 1977) of the new office blocks for the administrators and the old Nissen huts for the patients, and you will have read that the staff of the consultants, McKinsey's, who advised on the reorganization of the Health Service two years ago, now believe that they gave the wrong advice. You may have heard on the radio Mr Tatton Brown, who was chief architect for the Department of Health from 1959 to 1971, reflecting that the advice he and his colleagues gave to the Regional Health Authorities was not the right advice on hospital design. As you know, the pundits of hospital organization were advising the closing of those little local hospitals in favour of huge regional complexes like Addenbrooke's and Northwick Park. Now suddenly they have swung around to praising the local cottage hospital as being manageable, friendly, community-oriented, and economic. But the machine they set in motion is still condemning local hospitals to death. There is an exact parallel in school planning. A series of obsolete assumptions about the size of the sixth form generated the idea of the huge unmanageable comprehensive school, and the rationalizing out of existence of small secondary schools is still in process, long after any teacher believes that there is anything to be gained from doing so, just as the war against selective secondary schools is still being fought long after we have given up the hope that the education system can be used to promote social justice.

The person who worships the state and thinks that any other mode of provision is a let-off for the state or a cop-out from the state, when faced by the politics of retrenchment, can only protest and wave his banner.

There is, for example, in the world of preschool education a deep ideological division between those who believe in the provision of day nurseries and nursery schools by local education authorities, on principle, and those who believe on principle in babyminders and parent-organized playgroups. Every now and then there is a scandal about illicit babyminding, but it was left to an outsider, Brian Jackson, to think up the idea of courses in babyminding for unofficial babyminders. Now, as part of its education cuts, one English county has decided, reluctantly, to close all its nursery schools. The customers are helpless. If the local community had developed its own unofficial network of provision for the under-5s, it would have been better off today.

I was walking through a country town the other day when I passed a building with that little-red-schoolhouse look and, sure enough, there was a stone let into the wall saying, 'These two classrooms were built by public subscription on the occasion of the coronation of King Edward VII, 1901.' Well, I am not enthusiastic about commemorating him or his descendants, but I do think that in education as in many other fields of life we have thrown away a huge fund of energy, goodwill, and popular involvement, in abandoning the principle of voluntary self-taxation to improve facilities, in the name of universal publicly provided facilities. Dependence on government means that we become powerless when some centralized decision-making system says, according to priorities which may be wise or foolish, that we are not going to get what we want through the system. The rediscovery of the voluntary ethic can happen quite quickly: I read earlier this year that parents from the Sussex villages of Ferring and Findon have offered to put up two prefabricated classrooms at Angmering Comprehensive School, because the extra classrooms have been axed by government spending cuts. The *Evening News* (7 January 1977) says that the council's schools committee has recommended that West Sussex County Council accepts the 'revolutionary' idea. As I have indicated, the idea is not all that revolutionary. In the poor world, it would be taken for granted. Illiterate poor parents in the shanty towns on the fringe of a Latin American city would take it for granted that they should build a primary school for their children. However, one of the cuts that Essex County Council has decided on is that no further swimming instruction or maintenance should be provided in pools run by parent-teacher associations. Now that really is a foolish gesture because it will deter other parent-teacher associations from providing swimming pools. The council should have leant over backwards to fulfil its part of the bargain, just to show how valuable it thought parent and teacher initiatives are.

In the situation of a 'no-growth' economy, which to my mind is our situation today and which we are faced with in any conceivable future, there are certain priorities which are self-evident to me. I find, to my horror and amazement, that they are all totally revolutionary. My first priority is that we should put our money at the bottom end of education rather than at the top. Now this really would be a revolutionary change in the order of things. For the greater the sums of money that are poured into the education industries of the world, the smaller the proportion which benefits the people at the bottom of the educational, occupational, and social hierarchy. The universal education system turns out to be yet another way in which the poor are obliged to subsidize the rich. A decade ago, Everett Reimer found that the children of the poorest one tenth of the population of the United States cost the public in schooling $2 500 each over a lifetime, while the children of the richest one tenth cost about £35 000. 'Assuming that one-third of this is private expenditure, the richest one-tenth still gets ten times as much of public funds for education as the poorest one-tenth.' In his suppressed UNESCO report of 1970, Michael Huberman reached the same conclusion for the majority of countries in the world. In Britain we spend twice as much on the seondary school life of a grammar school sixth former as on a secondary modern school leaver, while, if we include university expenditure, we spend as much on an undergraduate in one year as on a normal school child throughout his life. The Fabian tract, *Labour and Inequality*, calculates that 'while the highest social group benefit seventeen times as much as the lowest group from the expenditure on universities, they only contribute five times as much revenue'. No wonder Everett Reimer calls schools an almost perfectly regressive form of taxation. In the scramble for dwindling public expenditure on education, you may be sure that the universities are going to be almost obscenely successful by comparison with the preschool education lobby.

In re-ordering our expenditure, I would invest heavily in preschool education, and in the infant and junior school. My aim would be the traditional, and currently approved one, that every child should be literate and numerate on leaving the junior school at 11. All right, it will take up to the age of 14 to achieve this for some children, but I want to assert that the compulsory prolongation of schooling beyond such an age is an affront to the freedom of the individual and has nothing to do with the aims of education, even though it has everything to do with the restrictive practices of the job market. I mentioned earlier the entry qualifications demanded by the architectural profession. A month ago the RIBA Council solemnly sat and discussed how to make it harder still—like demanding four 'A' levels—so as to restrict entry still further. Do we have to wait until two 'A' levels instead of two 'O' levels are needed to get a car-wash job in South Shields, or do we say enough is enough: this is not what we have teachers for?

I quoted earlier the brilliant satire, *The Rise of the Meritocracy*, written by Michael Young in the 1950s. He was interviewed by one of the Sunday papers this year and explained why he feels that there is no future for secondary schools as we know them. He said,

I think secondary schools in their present form are doomed. They haven't yet managed to reflect the new kind of family. The father used to be the fount of authority. Today, that authority is greatly diminished partly because it's shared. Schools and universities borrowed authority from the authoritarian father and now that it's no longer there to be borrowed, children in secondary schools are not going to accept it. There has to be a reduction in the school-leaving age and a move over to half-time education. People will be learning at home, at the workplace and not forced into institutions which use a bogus authority.

Dr Young has the honesty and the poor taste to bring up the subject of the crisis of authority in the secondary school: a crisis that ensures that much of our expenditure on teachers and plant is wasted by attempting to teach people what they do not want to learn in a situation that they would rather not be involved in. A poor school could not afford such waste and frustration of both teachers and taught. The school has become one of the instruments by which we exclude adolescents from real responsibilities and real functions in the life of our society. We have in the last year of secondary schooling pathetic attempts to give 'relevance' by providing 'work experience' courses aimed at aclimatizing the young to the shock of going to work, or by providing courses in colleges of further education with such titles as 'Adjustment to Work', for the benefit of those unable or unwilling to hold down a job. The Trades Union Congress and the Confederation of British Industry have joined forces in backing a project for informing school-children about industry. Arthur Young, the headmaster of Northcliffe High School in Yorkshire, has for years been trying to find the right equation between learning and earning. He values the efforts of his pupils to earn money for themselves and has sought, within the narrowly prescribed limits of the law, to provide opportunities in and out of school for them to do so. He remarks of work experience projects that they

have never really got off the ground because of the legal, insurance and trade union problems that hedge them around. I have always thought that the schemes proposed were phoney—the most important aspect of work experience is being neglected completely—the wage at the end of the week.

Like Michael Young, Arthur Young sees an urgent need to change the relationships in the secondary school. Describing the efforts made to provide actual cash-earning experiences for the most unlikely lads at his school, and the effect it has had on their attitudes to running their own lives, taking decisions, budgeting, fulfilling obligations, dealing with strangers, as well as such mundane things taken for granted by the middle-class child as using the telephone, he remarks,

> We have to overcome the ridiculous idea that giving children the chance to earn money in school is somehow immoral. . . . In the changing situation in education, pupil–teacher relationships and roles are the essence of much heart-searching and debate. We might do well to compare the differences in an earning–learning situation between master and apprentice and in the traditional school situation, captive scholars facing chalk and talk across the barrier of the teacher's desk. The comparison of relationships between newsagent and paper-boy and between paperboy and schoolmaster might also be revealing.

The carelessly rich school, greedy for resources, has no need to be a productive institution. The poor school could not afford not to be a productive workshop and belongs to a society in which every workshop is an effective school. Don't think I am denigrating or down-grading the teacher. Far from it. A poor school could not afford to have its spending kept out of the individual teacher's hands. A poor school needs to know what it is paying for. In the 1960s educational spenders were swept away on a tide of commercially inspired expensive options like program-med learning and teaching machines, which are greeted with a cynical laugh in the 1970s. The expensive hardware of educational technology has become an irrelevancy and an embarrassment in this decade. I want the school to have a clearly stated published budget with a personal allocation to each member of the staff to spend as he or she sees fit. The teacher should be responsible for his own spending. He can do it wisely or foolishly on such materials and equipment as he desires. He can pool it with others, he can carry it over to next year.

The poor school would be self-catering. Why shouldn't the school meals service be in the hands of the pupils? Why shouldn't every secondary school include a day nursery run by the pupils? The poor school would be too valuable a community asset to be open for a small part of the day and for a restricted age band. Already we are feeling our way towards such an institution through the concept of the community school and the community college. When we consider now little the massive educational spending of the last decade did to enhance the lives or life-chances of the children in what is known as 'the lower quartile of the ability range' in secondary education, we may perhaps hope that the new age of frugality will lead us to devise appropriate educational experiences in a climate where we make fewer grandiose claims for what the school can do. By settling for less, we might even achieve more.

Notes and References

1 Henryk Skolimowski, 'The earth and its friends' (London: British Broadcasting Corporation, Radio 3, 26 November 1976).
2 Sir Clough Williams-Ellis died on 9 April 1978. Ed.

Aspects of Education
Edited by M. Braham
© 1982 John Wiley & Sons Ltd.

Chapter 13

Teaching, Learning, and Coping in 'Progressive' Schools: A Discrepancy Analysis

*Michael Huberman**

Although I have never thought of it in precisely those terms, the bulk of my theoretical and practical work over the past five years has, in fact, been concerned with the creation and study of 'alternative models and scenarios in education'. So it would be useful for me and, I hope, interesting for you to try to pull together some of the strands of that work and to put them in relation to other ongoing work in that field.

Let me mention briefly the areas in which that work has been carried on. First, I have done some basic conceptual research on what is called 'innovation process theory'. The premise of this work is that change can be studied as a *process* from the emergence of a need or problem through to the adoption of a new practice which partially or fully satisfies the need or solves the problem. The process is, of course, very complex. There are hundreds of independent variables in any study of the change process. This, together with the multiple interactions between these variables, makes any kind of conventional prediction or control a very hazardous venture. There are, however, ways of reducing the complexity by elaborating theoretical models which can depict the three or four basic patterns operating in any given innovation. These models—the research, design, and development model; the social interaction model; the problem-solving model; and a more integrated 'linkage' model— have been presented and analysed in R. Havelock's monumental study

---

* Co-founder and co-ordinator, l'École Active, Genève, and Professor, Faculté de Psychologie et des Sciences de l'Education, Université de Genève.

on knowledge utilization (Havelock, 1969) and in my shorter study of innovation process theory (Huberman, 1973). More recently, Havelock and I tried to use the basic conceptual framework of these earlier books to analyse a large sample of experimental projects in education in developing countries (Havelock and Huberman, 1978). Here again, we tried to capture the chronological sequence as well as the factors which appeared to account for the relative success or failure of a project. Most of the most significant and colourful data came from interviews with people who had initiated, administered, counselled, or opposed the experiments and who, for the most part, had enjoyed a lifetime of experience in educational innovation.

A second strand of research has been the analysis of adult learning. Adults learn new skills or attitudes differently from children and they carry on their learning, for the most part, in non-institutional settings and without formal instruction on the part of another adult. In fact, much of adult learning can be subsumed under the rubric of 'socialization', in the sense that people learn new roles as workers, parents, members of community institutions, etc., simply by taking on these roles without very much (appropriate) prior training and by gradually coping with them more successfully over time. This seems very much to be the case in teaching, which is the area in which I have done most of my work (Huberman, 1974). In particular, I have tried to study how teachers become aware of, try out, and adopt ways of organizing classroom environments with which they are relatively unfamiliar or for which they have received very little formal preparation. Most of these environments have entailed the organization of time, space, materials, activities, and children in primary schools (ages 4–12) which purport to implement neo-Piagetian and neo-Freudian theories of learning and development. These schools are variously called 'open', 'informal', 'experimental', 'alternative', 'non-directive', 'child-centred', 'progressive', and 'activity-centred'.

Finally, I have spent much of the past five years founding, coordinating, and participating in the evaluation of one of these experimental schools in Geneva. This school, called l'École Active, currently enrols pupils from the infant level (4 years old) to the midsecondary level (14 years old) and will eventually cover the age group 4–18. The bulk of this paper will be devoted to an analysis of that school, together with some results of research in another primary-level experimental school in Geneva, called the Unité Coopérative d'Enseignement (UCE). The primary interest of many of these data is that they are concrete or 'naturalistic'. That is to say, a number of ethnographic techniques (participant observation, systematized 'ecological' observations, verbatim recordings of classroom interactions, etc.) were used alongside the more conventional psychometric measures. These techniques allowed us to capture much of the richness and situational complexity in the life of these schools which are often lost—or distorted—in studies based primarily on (probabilistic) relationships between groups of discrete, linear, and additive measures.

1. Unfamiliarity, fluidity, social discrepancy

I should like to centre this text on three interrelated aspects of the École Active and others like it, as these aspects relate to the more general theme of how alternative models and scenarios in education are conceived and what happens to the children, teachers, and parents who live in them. The first aspect is the *unfamiliarity* of these settings to the participants. For almost all the parents, teachers, and children, these schools put forward rules, activities, and relationships which are very different from those they have known in their own previous schooling. For the children, the type of activity, the range of choices and constraints, and the nature of their relationships with other children and with their teachers require them to behave very differently from the roles they played in other schools. For the teachers, there has been little preparation in their formal training for the type of classroom management or the freedom from external constraints involved in the experimental school. For the parents, the school experiences of their children have no relationship to their own. Nor are they used to dealing with such public institutions as schools in ways that (a) accentuate their own personal involvement, (b) put them into a highly personal relationship, centred on their children, with an adult who is neither a friend nor a relative, and (c) call on them to collaborate closely with—often pay for the schooling of—a host of other parents whom they would never have singled out spontaneously as likely social or business partners. In Geneva, for example, parents who come to collect their child from any one of the state schools must open a gate on which the following ordinance is written: 'Parents are not allowed in the school during classroom hours'. Almost all the communication between teachers and parents is written (via the report card or, often, by form letter) and is generally mediated by an inspector. By contrast, in the École Active parents are called on to participate in the hiring of teachers, to do remedial work, to manage many of the artistic and handiwork workshops, to supervise children during lunch, to accompany children and teachers on excursions, etc.

A second aspect of the school which I want to mention is the *fluidity* or *lack of formal structure* in the way in which the school is managed. Most 'progressive' schools in the neo-Piagetian or neo-Freudian ('humanist') movement tend to extend the principles of individual learning and growth to cover the rules for administering the institution itself. The emphasis is placed on individual freedom, unique experience, and humanistic values, all in the service of a generous but vague and diffuse set of goals. This means that decision making and management become informal, consensual, and participatory. Little is written down. Decisions are made in face-to-face meetings at which all parties concerned are present. Authority is highly decentralized, so much so that it is often impossible—and here I speak from experience— for the director to prohibit any other person from taking an initiative unless there is a strong pressure group behind the director. Very likely, this form of management is adopted less for its functional or even ideological value than as a reaction against the routinization, bureaucracy (using written regulations, passing information through predetermined channels, delegating responsibility), centralization, and hierarchy present in most other social institutions with which teachers, parents, and children deal on a daily basis. But the point I wish to make here is simply that the novelty or unfamiliarity of the teaching and learning environment for teachers, parents, and children, is accentuated by the near absence of rules or agreed-on mechanisms for administering that environment, apart from the structures which each group—sometimes, each individual—invents for itself.

The third aspect I will be examining can be called *social discrepancy*. This term means simply that the teachers, parents, and pupils in 'alternative' schools are operating in a subculture which is radically different from the surrounding environment. The *parents*, for example, become rapidly aware that the children next door or their nieces and nephews are doing different work at school and that the work appears to be more demanding and more systematic. The parents are also aware that they are being asked to help decide on what should be taught their children and by whom in a society where nonprofessionals are, in general, not consulted—nor given the impression that their opinions are relevant—in advising specialists on how to manage clinics, hospitals, courts, schools, and other social services. As for the *teachers*, they know from their own experience that the state schools are using a different curriculum, different materials, different modes for evaluating pupil progress, and very different rules for managing day-to-day relationships and activities. Finally, the *children* are very much aware that the experimental school is a 'special' place for 'special' children. Their in-school and out-of-school behaviour reflects clearly their sense of belonging to a protected subculture and their suspicion that the world outside the school is hostile.

Let me try now to summarize these three aspects. To use the theme of this volume, the experimental school is an *alternative*; it is *different* from other schools. It is also *novel* for the parents, teachers, and children who work in it. All have very little prior experience of, or training for, the way in which teaching, learning, and relating are being carried on. Nor is any one person explicitly directing or providing rules for the way in which decisions are to be made and activities to be administered. What everyone has in common is inexperience, commitment to a set of mobilizing but diffuse objectives, and membership in a socially marginal institution which the state school authorities did not themselves create as a pilot experiment.

2. Two propositions

There are two questions to be answered here. Who copes successfully in such an environment? What happens to such an institution over time in terms of its membership and management? On the basis of my own experience and of the initial results of our research, I can only begin to answer these questions. Moreover, the answers can at best be brief in such a paper as this one. Here are two general propositions on which I shall elaborate in the course of my discussion:

(a) *Capacity to cope successfully—as a pupil, teacher, or parent—is directly related to the degree of discrepancy between prior experience (schemata, exposure to stimuli, behavioural repertoire) and the circumstances encountered at the school.*

This is particularly true for the children faced with learning in 'non-directive' or 'self-motivating' settings, and I shall be concentrating on this population.

(b) *Those adults and children for whom the discrepancy is large (superoptimal),* i.e. teachers, parents, or children who are required to behave in ways with which they have very little prior experience, *will tend to react in anxious, regressive, and defensive ways. Unless the degree of discrepancy is reduced or differentiated, these participants will compromise the success of the experiment.*

Faced with an overload of unfamiliar stimuli, some children will 'act out' their anxieties by provocatively avoiding or disrupting any activities which teachers or other children try to organize. Others will concentrate on one activity, scholastic or non-scholastic, with which they have felt comfortable in their previous environment and with which they have had a history of success. In both cases, there is an implicit grasping for some kind of security or structure which the child feels will connect this new setting to the one in which he has functioned before. There is here a basic drive for self-maintenance or self-consistency: a need to be continuous and predictable to oneself and to structure the environment in such a way that it consistently provides that continuity. This drive, in fact, can be observed in any systemically 'open' structure or organism as it carries on its transactions with the environment.

The reaction of the teachers for whom 'open', 'informal', or 'non-directive' classrooms are unfamiliar is analogous. Here again we can point to two extreme types of behaviour. Some of the teachers tend to 'go all the way' in organizing their classrooms. They create what Carl Rogers calls a 'maximally permissive field' (his detractors call it 'maximal chaos') in which children make all or most of the choices for them-selves as to what, if any, activities they will undertake and how they will do them. The teacher imposes little structure and avoids situations in which the children will attempt to imitate her or his values or behaviours. In doing this, many teachers rely heavily on a doctrine. The doctrine—an eclectic set of theories derived in part from Piaget, Rogers, Wilhelm Reich, Gerard Mendel, the French school of social psychology close to Lacan known as *pedagogie institutionnelle*, and contemporary anarchist literature—provides justification and support. It appears to help the teacher to maintain her level of energy and self-respect in the face of unpredictable behaviour on the part of the children, anxiety on the part of the parents, and open hostility on the part of other teachers or state school administrators. In the classic dialectic of cognitive dissonance, the doctrine grows stronger as the situation gets more critical.

In some cases, however, there is no explicit doctrine, but rather a deeply ingrained way of dealing with children which reflects the personality structure of the teacher and which she has had to repress during her career in conventional state schools. I suspect, in fact, that doctrine or theory is far more shallow for practitioners in education than we realize. Being with children is such an intimate, primary relationship that our ideas of how it ideally should be carried on cannot help being shaped by the ways in which we feel psychically and somatically comfortable doing it. Perhaps this is why doctrinal debates on non-directive and directive schooling are so emotionally charged—they involve our defending our own spontaneous, organic ways of relating to other people, i.e. defend-ing our own identities. This may also explain in part why teacher training based on a limited number of models (as evidenced in lesson plans, manuals, prescribed ways of grouping pupils, the type of classrooms, and master teachers used during internships) is perceived in some cases as inadequate or even humiliating and by other teacher candidates as highly appropriate and useful. In one recent study carried out in Geneva, it appeared clearly that when the training model did not correspond to a teacher's spontaneous manner of working with children, she would reject or 'shed' that model once she felt in control of her own class and would revert to the earlier, more personally congruent form of teaching which she had tried out (often unsuccessfully) in her first year of teaching practice and for which she had been criticized by her instructors.

There is a second type of reaction on the part of teachers placed in highly discrepant situations which corresponds to the children's regressive behaviour mentioned earlier. It takes the form of a brief, unsuccessful attempt to carry out a child-directed form of classroom management, followed by a very rapid reversion to the type of activities and relationships with which the teacher is the most comfortable, that is, those which give the most predictable results, which allow the teacher to feel that she can *control* and *anticipate* the behaviour of the children. Since the institution is so lacking in structure and since the child-centred classroom is more disorderly and unmanageable than she had anticipated, or what she imagines to be the case in other classrooms in the school, the teacher quickly closes off her class. She cuts down on exchanges, vertical grouping, between-class projects and visits, and goes back to the only kind of classroom management of which she is certain. She then, very cautiously, tries out a very modest, circumscribed experiment (setting up an activities corner, having the children define and carry out a project, inviting a parent to teach pottery or dance), then another slightly more ambitious one.

All this time, these teachers are on the defensive *vis-à-vis* the more 'progressive' and highly vocal teachers and parents who look on any deviation from the institutional doctrine as 'reactionary', 'cowardly', 'treacherous', that is, in normative terms. This situation leads inevitably to conflict between teachers—often, but not always, between the less experienced (absolutist) and more experienced (cautious)—in which the parents rapidly take sides. As these is no stable or legitimate institutional structure for mediating these conflicts, the school may tend to disintegrate through a process of internal friction. Several of the examples mentioned by Deal (1975) in his analysis of alternative secondary schools follow this scenario, in virtue of which Deal estimates the average life expectancy of alternative secondary schools in the USA

to be 18 months. Smith and Keith (1971), in their ethnological study of
the 'Kensington' school, tell a very similar story. Figure 1 is one of the
summarizing flow-charts from that study, in which there appear some
of the elements I mentioned earlier.

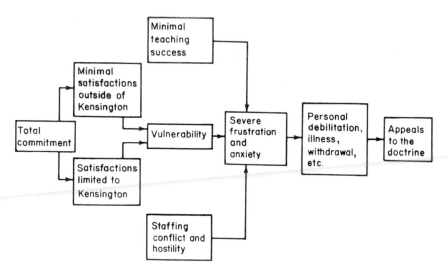

Figure 1   The consequences for the teachers of 'total commitment' to an
experiment in child-centred education at Kensington (from Smith and Keith,
1971, p. 105)

This brief sketch brings out two points which I will be making
throughout this paper. First, there is simply *no way of telescoping
successfully the time needed to assimilate and accommodate to the changes
involved in teaching or learning in 'non-directive' schools* on the part of those
children and adults whose previous experience has been radically
different. These environments will necessarily be perceived as threatening, even if the protagonists create them or come to them willingly, and
it will take a long time before the teacher or child is ready to go beyond
the phase of defending and protecting himself and to begin to explore
actively that environment. The greater the discrepancy, the longer the
period of adaptation and the stronger the likelihood that the person will
leave the setting before any positive form of adaptation has taken place.
The second point is that *the adult's strategy of telescoping the period of
adaptation by reverting to a pedagogical doctrine is essentially an unhealthy and
ineffective device* for dealing with anxiety which generally results in
intra-personal and inter-personal conflict and breakdown.

It is worth noting here that we often take intuitively into account the *pupils'* needs for general and protected exposure to changes in the classroom but not those of the *teachers*. The assumption is that the child is somehow more 'fragile'. This is another way of saying that his mental and emotional development is more receptive to and affected by environmental influence than would be the case with adults. But if we make this claim, then we are also saying that the child has a greater capacity to learn, a greater neuropsychic plasticity which allows him to make more rapid and more frequent changes in his responses to novel stimuli, than the adult. The implication is, then, that adults are, in fact, more fragile, in the sense that changes are relatively more difficult for them to assimilate and extreme changes far more difficult for them to accommodate to. There is empirical evidence, for example, that parents often react more severely (by withdrawing, falling ill, etc.) than their children to rapid and successive changes in activities, climate, language, social partners, place of residence, and the like (Holmes and Rahe, 1967).

In our study of educational innovations in developing countries, Havelock and I found a regular pattern in which administrators systematically underestimated the time and support needed for teachers to learn, try out, and adopt new curricula, ways of classroom grouping, use of new materials, changes in within-school and school–village relationships. This is not in itself surprising. Administrators are continuously prescribing changes for others, the type and magnitude of which they would *never* dream of prescribing for themselves. This occurs, in developing countries no more than in 'developed' countries, whenever the managers are separated from the actors or are, more generally, making decisions for other people to carry out.

But we also found that teachers will voluntarily accept to be put, or even put themselves, in the same situation. That is to say, they undertake an innovation for which (a) they have no clear idea of what it entails specifically in terms of organizing time, space, and children in the classroom; (b) they do not have the capabilities either to implement the change as planned or to deal with unanticipated events in the course of implementation (and the less prepared the teachers are, the greater the number and the gravity of these unanticipated events); (c) they have no regular access to sources of support or expertise to help them through difficult moments. It is no wonder that the resulting rate of adoption is so low. In this kind of situation, a teacher will, of necessity, reduce the degree of novelty and uncertainty to a tolerable level. This results in very little actual change—carefully camouflaged from administrators and from hit-and-run evaluators—and in increased resistance to future experimentation. In our conclusions, Havelock and I have tried to identify and describe the optimal conditions for teacher learning and change in innovative settings. Gross *et al.* (1970a) have carried out a similar analytic and prescriptive study based on an American case.

Having looked briefly at the children and teachers, let me spend a moment on *the parents*. The reactions of parents for whom the schools' programme of learning activities, institutional structure, and form of interpersonal relationships are highly discrepant tend to take the following forms:

(a) Expressions of blind faith in what the teachers and children are doing. This faith is based either on the school's implicit or explicit doctrine or on a strong compensation motive: 'I was miserable in school for being forced to do things I detested. I want my child to be happy and to like learning.'

(b) Other symptoms of cognitive dissonance: vilifying the state schools ('they beat the children', 'teachers who work there hate children', 'it's like a prison for the children', 'it's run for the interests of the administration; they forget that schools are meant to serve children and teachers'); refusing to give credibility to any negative information pertaining to the experimental school ('these are just temporary problems', 'it's still a paradise compared to the state schools'); maintaining an almost magical view of the institution ('my child isn't doing much, but I know that something important and necessary is going on').

(c) A basic intolerance. Blind faith rests on an edge of heavy anxiety. Those who betray our blind faith, as indeed they inevitably must, become overnight our adversaries. This is because they have disappointed us at a time when we were highly dependent on them and because we cannot forgive them for being able, or pretending to be able, to solve (our) problems which we feel we are unable to solve. One of the most fascinating phenomena at the École Active has been what I would call the 'demand for immediate perfection'. Many parents expected that their children would spontaneously learn to read, write, and count with no external constraints. They also expected that the children would show immediate and observable signs of increased self-reliance, self-acceptance, social poise, and artistic sensibilities. They wanted a school in which all decisions were to be made consensually and without the necessity of such mechanisms as delegation of authority to representatives or to a director. At the same time, they expected these decisions to be made rapidly, efficiently, and without conflict. The school was to be, in all respects, a social and moral haven, the one universe in their lives in which everything lived up to their aspirations for themselves, their children and their political beliefs.

This kind of expectation is, of course, intolerable for all parties. In particular, the teachers feel an enormous pressure to produce immediate results in a situation for which they feel almost totally unprepared. Given the level and intensity of the parent's expectations, the teachers do not feel free to admit their lack of preparation (without appearing to be imposters). They also know that such expectations are unrealistic: the parents cannot fail to be disappointed and are likely to lay the blame on the quality of teaching. Feeling that they have no time to get ready, that they will not be permitted to make errors, and that they have no hope of meeting the demands of the parents, the teachers become resentful and defensive. This reaction, in turn, surprises the parents: 'We think the teachers are doing a marvellous job with our children; why are they afraid of us?' 'What are they trying to hide?' 'We have an articulate group of parents and an extraordinary group of children, but perhaps the teachers aren't up to the challenge.' 'We've given them our children for a very important experiment. *We* are the ones who are taking the greatest risk. Yet the teachers seem to be the most fearful.'

Blind faith, cognitive dissonance, unrealistic expectations, and recourse to doctrine are manifestations of the same syndrome: the need to decrease the level of anxiety when faced with an unfamiliar situation in which one anticipates failure. Having no *experience* of the situation yet leaping into it, or committing one's children to it, calls for turning to others who one assumes do have experience. Yet a characteristic of most alternative schools is that, almost by definition, *no one* has very much experience. Those who do are likely to point out the shortcomings of the doctrine and their point of view may, as a result, be considered less legitimate thereafter.

This phenomenon comes out very clearly in our interviews with parents at the École Active. To cite from one: 'You have to remember that the only knowledge we have of child-centred learning comes through books and discussions. It is all *intellectual*. Our own education was very different. I think our children's education was, up to now, closer to ours than to what they are doing at the École Active. Besides, we don't see any more grades or homework. We don't know exactly what the school's programme is. So we don't really know what the children are doing at school and what the real differences are from the state school . . . .. Still, we *know* it's the right choice for them and for us.'

3. The assumptions and environment of progressive schools

I should like now to go back over some of these points in greater detail. In particular, I will be documenting my remarks with some of the results of our study on experimental schools in Geneva, notably those results which intersect with other empirical research in England and North America.

Let me start by reformulating the basic hypotheses of this paper. Implementing educational alternatives entails creating discrepancy from previous behaviours for many of the persons involved. The more ambitious or doctrinal the alternative, the greater the degree of discrepancy is likely to be for a greater number of persons. When the conditions allow for a gradual and non-threatening manner of 'trying out' the alternative—being able to rehearse the most difficult parts beforehand, having sustained support from other people, stretching out the period of adaptation—the new behaviours can be successfully and durably consolidated into the behavioural repertoire of most of the participants. Given, however, the doctrinal basis of the alternative, as well as the lack of prior experience on the part of its initiators, there is a tendency to impose non-differential conditions on all participants. This maintains a high degree of discrepancy for most people between the demands made on them by others and their image of themselves. As a result, these demands are perceived as threatening. Demands perceived as personally threatening produce defensive behaviour which takes several forms (abandon, regression, aggression), all of which compromise the success of the alternative.

Of course, there is a fund of simple common sense behind these elaborate propositions. When we are not yet able to do something we want to do and are no longer willing to stay at our former level of competence, we are dissatisfied. When we are willing but not able to go back to our point of departure, we are often anxious. In psychodynamic terms, this is called 'separation anxiety'. We feel that we do not possess the capability to deal with a new situation and fear that the outcome will be painful. By failing, we will be punished (or punish ourselves), and lose thereby parental love without which we shall feel alone and unprotected.

To take the proposition one step further, when someone whom we admire or fear tells us explicitly that we *should* be able to do now what we know we cannot do and that we *cannot* go back to what we were doing before, we are far more 'separation anxious'. In the Geneva experimental schools, and in several similar experiments, this was the message being communicated continually from the teachers to the children, from the parents to the teachers, from the founders of the school to the teachers, and between the teachers themselves.

Let me try to illustrate this point in relation to the behaviour and development of children in 'progressive' or 'child-centred' classrooms such as those in our school and those analysed by Smith and Keith (1971), Bennett (1976), Gross *et al.* (1970a), McPartland and Epstein (1973), and Franks (1976). As I read the objectives of these schools, there emerge a series of assumptions about how children optimally learn and develop. Here is a small sample:

Children are 'naturally' or innately curious. They will explore their environments, even in the face of obstacles and frustrations, without intervention on the part of adults, provided they are not threatened.

The environment which best facilitates mental and emotional development is rich (in materials and possibilities for manipulation and experimentation) and maximally permissive in such a way that it does not interfere with the spontaneous process of maturation.

The child is himself in the most strategic position to know and to select the components of his environment which are the most conducive to his developmental needs and growth.

If a child is absorbed in a task, significant learning is going on.

It happens that there is a good deal of empirical evidence to support many of these assumptions: Piaget's studies and subsequent theory of the equilibration process, White's research on competence motivation, the so-called 'cafeteria experiments' conducted by Davis, Berlyne's work on epistemic motivation, McReynold's research on cognitive innovation, etc. Most of this work, however, has been carried out in preschool or non-school settings, and was not controlled for a number of inter-individual differences. I shall have occasion to come back to this point. For now, however, let me try to give some sense of the implications of putting these assumptions into practice. First, at the level of the teacher's role, here is a typical list of expected teaching behaviours, taken from the Gross *et al.* (1970b, p. 694) study:

1. Teachers were expected to behave in ways that would assist children to learn according to *their* interests rather than in terms of a prescribed curriculum;
2. Teachers were expected to emphasise the process, not the content of learning, and to allow pupils maximum freedom in choosing their own activities;
3. Teachers were expected to see that the classroom was saturated with

a variety of educational materials, primarily self-instructional in
nature, so that children could pursue their own interests;

4. Teachers were expected to act as facilitators of learning between
   children and materials and to encourage teaching of children by other
   children;

5. Teachers were expected to allow pupils to decide the materials they
   wished to work with, how long they would work with them, and
   with whom they wished to relate;

6. Teachers were expected to give pupils primary responsibility for
   directing their own learning and to assist them only when they
   perceived that their help was needed.

In our own research at the École Active, there were two teachers who
corresponded closely to this profile. We observed all the teachers via a
time-sampling technique and took verbatim, as well as anecdotal,
records of their speech, gestures, and interactions with the children. The
transcriptions were used both to provide feedback to the teachers and to
derive a more quantitative profile of each teacher on six scales. This
profile was then correlated with the children's scores on a stick-figure
test of positive and negative self-image. For each scale, there are a
number of behavioural indices. For example, a teacher scored as
'affectionate' (*chaleureux*) would have been observed often to be smiling
at the children, showing affection (putting his arm around a child,
sitting close to a child when working with him, etc.), and making
personal remarks to the children (little compliments, questions, comments which are not strictly centred on the work at hand). Teachers
scoring high on 'calm' (*détendu*) had little tension or impatience in their
voices, had fluid movements and gestures, and had relaxed expressions
on their faces. Below are some illustrations of the behavioural indices
comprising the remaining four scales:

Supportive (valorisant)

listening to the children attentively when speaking with them;
using the children's first names when speaking with them;
looking the children in the eyes when speaking with or listening to
   them;
making compliments on ongoing or completed work done by the
   children;

Flexible (souple)

integrating the children's suggestions into an ongoing activity;

using materials brought in by children (for discussion, for putting up on the wall, for suggesting an activity);

agreeing to change one's mind (concerning a decision) or one's plan (for an activity);

giving the children latitude in the choice of their seats, their movements, the time needed to complete an activity, and the choice of the mode of work (individual or group);

reacting differentially (e.g. authorizing a child to change activities, giving out criticism or sanctions) rather than absolutely as a function of a particular situation.

Structuring (structurant)

going towards the children (rather than waiting for the children to come to the teacher for help or instructions);

helping children spontaneously (i.e. without a specific request) who appear to be in difficulty (blocked, tired);

rapid intervention in the case of perturbations in the classroom;

rapid intervention in the case of children being unoccupied;

giving clear instructions when initiating an activity;

helping children to organize their own activities;

making certain that decisions are respected concerning activities undertaken and the rules for talking, working, moving about, etc., in the classroom.

Challenging (stimulant)

giving encouragement to the children (by gesture, expression, or words) in their ongoing work;

encouraging children to undertake more complex or more difficult tasks, while communicating an expectation that the child will succeed at the task;

encouraging children to go further in exploiting their ideas, interests, or projects.

Let us now examine the profiles of the two teachers mentioned earlier on the six scales of our grid. One can see from a rapid survey of the graph in Figure 2 that the teachers spend much of their time giving positive reinforcement to and trying to adapt to the interests and desires of the children, while apparently imposing few demands or constraints on them. The implicit, and often explicit, message they transmit is, 'I like you . . . . You are someone worthy of affection and attention . . . . What you are doing is important . . . . You know what is best for you

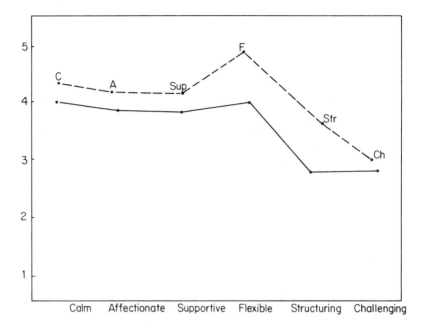

Figure 2   Mean scores of two teachers on six scales of an environmental climate grid (26 observations)

and what you want to do . . .. You don't need me to help you or to activate you to work, but if you do need me, I am available.'

There is little doubt in my mind, and the results of our research tend to confirm this, that many of these messages make children feel more comfortable and more justified in liking and accepting themselves. This in turn helps them to try out new and more difficult tasks. All the more so in that many of these children had been exposed daily and intensively—that is, without the possibility of avoiding the situation—in the state school to very different messages. The basic one was: 'I do not like you because you are not willing to be like me and to respect the kinds of things which I care about. Therefore, there is no reason why someone (as impartial, as normally interested in the welfare of my pupils, as diligent, as powerful) like me should treat with consideration someone (as disrespectful, as stubborn, as sullen, as disorderly, as unmotivated) like you.' The social psychological construct of 'reflected appraisal'—the child internalizing as his own judgement of himself the judgements which significant adults in his life make about him—can be empirically validated here in the initial (and negative) self-concept of many children who come to the École Active or the Unité Coopérative d'Enseignement after a few years of conventional state schooling, and in their subsequent, far more positive views of themselves after a few years (sometimes a few months) of daily life in classrooms managed by these two teachers and others like them. Moreover, this change in self-concept is reflected in their behaviour. Briefly summarized, they begin to behave as if what they are doing and saying were worthwhile and merit other people's interest as well. The process then becomes circular: since these things are worthwhile and they interest other people, the child comes to have confidence in his own internal judgement. He then tends to take more risks (trying out new activities), to tolerate frustration or ambiguity more successfully, to give his opinion or his contribution more freely in groups, to work more co-operatively, etc.

Except that it is not quite that simple. Let me go back to the last part of the message which the teachers in the experimental schools convey to the children: 'You don't need me to help you or to activate you to work, but if you do need me, I am available.' This message derives, in part, from the assumptions about the optimal conditions for children's development mentioned earlier (p. 187). These assumptions, in turn, are founded on two theoretical bases. The first is Piagetian. *Very* schematically, the research by Piaget and the Geneva school shows that cognitive development—the elaboration and recombination of action or operational schemata into increasingly more complex and differentiated forms—occurs 'naturally' or 'spontaneously' (ontogenetically) through an interactive process of maturation and of transactions with the surrounding environment. In this process, the child is 'active'; he constructs his mental schemata (i.e. his intelligence) through a process of reflective abstraction (*abstraction réfléchissante*), which is self-regulating.

When this theory is applied to cognitive activity in schools, it is formulated typically in the following way:

If a school emphasises thinking, its structure must focus on the child's intrinsic motivation, as was done in the Tyler School. The children understood that what counted was their own activity and that high-level functioning was its own reward. We wanted the children to be pleased with their own accomplishments, not to do things in order to please the teacher. We wanted them to rely on their own internally controlled evidence, not vacuously look at the teacher's face for approval or disapproval. We wanted, above all, to leave the children free to move into those situations they found rewarding. In sum, our aim was to respect the children's individual capacities and differences and leave them in control of the situation.

In behavioural terms, the child provides his own schedule of intrinsic rewards and reinforcements. The teacher is an occasion of, not an implanter of knowledge. Whatever the terminology, the teacher must be firmly convinced that thinking cannot be taught as a subject matter and is not an object of knowledge that is remembered and can be forgotten. Piaget's theory provides the necessary framework that can give the teacher this reasonable assurance. (Furth, 1975, p. 23)

The premise here is that external situations are under the control of internal human mechanisms. The child has an internal 'need to know' which causes him actively to seek out and select from the surrounding environment.

This does not mean, however, that the conditions of the environment will not effect significantly the quality and rate of the cognitive process. This is a point which Piaget and collaborators have made consistently (see Piaget, 1967, especially pp. 38–42, 145ff). Nor does the proposition address itself to what psychogenetic research calls 'social learning', that is, the learning of specific codes and conventions. It happens that much school-based learning, notably grammar and spelling and, to some extent, mathematics, is social learning.

The second theoretical foundation is neo-Freudian, in particular the writings of such 'ego', 'humanistic', and 'phenomenological' psychologists as Hartmann, Goldstein, Lecky, Rapaport, Angyal, Erikson, Allport, and Maslow. Educators have tended to focus on the more contemporary and more accessible works of this school, notably on those of Carl Rogers. The operational construct in Rogers's work is 'the need for personal regard'. These needs refer to such attitudes as warmth, liking, respect, sympathy, and acceptance. If the parents meet these needs 'unconditionally', the child will feel 'prized' by his parents. He will then have no need to deny experiences. However, if the parents make positive regard conditional, the child will be forced to disregard his own experiencing process whenever it conflicts with the self-concept he feels it is necessary to maintain. This is the source of what Rogers calls 'incongruence' between organism and self and between self and experience.

The child learns to have a basic distrust for his own experiencing as a guide to his behaviour. He learns (introjects) from others a large number of values and adopts them as his own, even though they may be widely discrepant from what he is experiencing. Because these concepts are not based on his own (organismic valuing process) . . . they tend to be fixed and rigid, rather than fluid and changing. (Rogers, 1969, p. 245)

It follows that the imposition of adult models and expectations is neurosis-producing. If we look back at our six scales of teacher behaviour, the fifth (structuring) and, in particular, the sixth (challenging) imply very clearly that positive regard is conditional, that the teacher expects the child to try a new or more difficult activity or to persevere at a task which the child might not have expected of himself. Our two teachers have correspondingly lower scores on these scales (see Figure 2).

4. Why it isn't so simple

When I said earlier that it wasn't that simple, I meant that the effects of an environment that is maximally permissive and unconditionally accepting are not always consistent with the theory. Let me illustrate this point with two examples from our research. Below is an abridged excerpt from an observation made in the UCE in Geneva (third-grade class). The teacher, whom we shall call Olivier, has a profile on our scale which is very close to that of the two teachers mentioned earlier. The observation focuses on one of the pupils, Valérie, as she works at a table with five other children. She is doing an exercise in her workbook of modern mathematics (sorting into logical categories and sub-categories groups of flower petals which have two or three properties in common).

15:34 Val. turns round. Looks around her at other children in the room.

15:36 Still looking around. Gets up, goes out of the classroom. Chats with girl in corridor.

15:38 Comes back into classroom. Sits down. Looks down at exercise. Looks up. Looks around.

15:40 Gets up, goes over to Oliv. Says [the gist of the conversation is that Val. finds the exercise too difficult. Oliv., without looking at the exercise, asks her what she thinks she should do. She doesn't know. Oliv. suggests that she should practise with a more simple exercise in the cupboard which allows her to manipulate individual cards with the pictures on them and to put them on a large sheet in which logical categories are outlined (by 'trees'). She can use these outlines or draw in her own lines] . . .. Val. takes out the material (cards containing pictures of clowns some of whom have their eyes open and others closed, some have a bow tie and others do not) and sits down on the floor next to another girl (Elis.) who is doing a similar exercise.

15:43 Val. begins to sort cards. Appears to be concentrating. Inattentive to high level of noise and coming-and-going around her. Oliv. comes over, looks rapidly at piles Val. is making, walks on outside into corridor. Val. looks over at girl (Elis.) sorting next to her. Looks back to her cards and sheet. Looks up. Looks outside at activity in corridor.

15:47 Still looking outside (very little going on there). Oliv. comes back, sits down next to Elis. to look at what she has done. Val. looks on, goes back to her task, looks on again.

15:50 Oliv. discusses task with Elis. (She has got it right.) Oliv. says, 'Very good, Elis. That's the first time you've done such a difficult classification.' Elis. puts away material. Oliv. goes off.

15:51 Val. frowns. Begins to collect cards and fold up sheet. Stops. Lays them out again. Sorts cards into three piles (no apparent system). Looks around. Looks down at piles. Gets up. Goes out to corridor. Comes back into classroom. Looks at clock. Stands over piles of cards and sheet and looks at Oliv. who is talking with a visitor.

15:54 Val. still watching Oliv. Sits down. Re-sorts cards into two piles. Looks slowly at cards in each pile while shuffling them. Appears to be distracted. Another girl (Ar.) takes out material previously used by Elis. and sits down next to Val. Ar. lays out cards and sheet.

15:56 Ar. looks at Val., cards, and sheet. Says, 'I don't understand this at all. Do you?' Val. says, 'No.' Ar. raises hand (to attract attention of Oliv.). Val. looks at her, raises her own hand, lowers it, raises it again.

15:58 Oliv. comes over to Ar. Says, 'Show me what you've done.' Val. looks on, looks away. Starts to sort her cards. Works rapidly. Looks over at Oliv. and Ar., then looks back at her cards and sheet. Picks up cards, sorts them differently. (Still no apparent system in her classification.)

16:01 Oliv. goes off. Ar. looks at Val., piles, and sheet. Ar. comes over, says, 'You have too few in this pile.' Takes Val.'s cards and re-sorts them. Val. is silent, looks on. Looks away. Ar. goes back to her own exercise. Val. looks down. Looks up at clock. Gets up. Goes out into corridor.

16:04 Val. comes back with another girl (Is.). They sit down in front of Val.'s sheet and cards. Is. looks at cards, says, 'There's this kind of clown (with tie) and this kind (without tie). How do we put them on the (classification) sheet?' Val. says (almost inaudible), 'Don't know.' Is. sorts cards. Appears to have found the two categories of classification. Val. looks on. Is. raises hand. Oliv. comes over. Oliv. says (discusses classification system with Is.) . . .. Val. intermittently looks on, looks away toward corridor.

16:07 Oliv. turns to Val. and asks her whether she agrees with Is.'s system of classification. Val. says 'Yes.' Oliv. asks her to explain it. Val. says (explains confusedly and haltingly what Is. has done. Appears to grasp the point that the clowns are with and without tie and with eyes open and closed but does not see how to lay out these sets in a system of classification). Val. not looking at Oliv. while she is talking. Oliv. says, 'Good. Now you can go back and try the exercise you were working on in your workbook. You should be able to manage fine now all by yourself.'

I have reproduced in some detail this protocol because it typifies several of the implications of child-centred classrooms as they are managed in many 'progressive' schools. To summarize and interpret this incident:

—Val. is not able to master the task and appears unwilling to ask Oliv. for help.
—Val. spends 25 minutes sorting the cards with no apparent success. Her explanation at the end parrots what Is. has already said to her or to Oliv.
  —Other children (Elis., Ar., Is.) appear to be able to master the task or, if not, spontaneously to seek out Oliv. for help.
—Val. finally decided to get help by seeking out Is. Is., however, is not able to 'teach' Val., but rather gets quickly involved herself in the activity and works independently.
—Val. is clearly ill at ease throughout the activity.
—Oliv. sends Val. back to the original exercise which she, very likely, will not be able to do since this exercise is more difficult than that of the classification of the clowns.
—Val. appears not to want anyone, save Is., to notice that she is unable to do the exercise.

In particular, Olivier has communicated a series of messages which Valérie is unable to deal with. He has told her that this second exercise should be easy for her to do (it was not), that she should not require his help (she does), that she is sufficiently autonomous to correct herself now and to go on to more difficult work (she cannot). In brief, Valérie is distressed because she feels that Olivier wants her to be capable of doing things she cannot do, and she does not feel free to tell him this. She appears to be afraid that if he discovers her dependence on him, he will be disappointed in her. She feels that the only way to maintain his affection is to pretend that she is more autonomous than she actually is.

I am trying to make several points here. Let me take each in succession.
(a) There is no way in which Valérie will *not* introject Olivier's

expectations for her. Olivier is a significant, nurturant, and powerful person in her life. She spends all day with him doing the most important kind of work which minors are expected to do. In short, she *constructs* her sense of who she is and what she can do by testing her identity and her actions against Olivier. He is, in Piagetian terms, the object in the environment on which she acts in order to solidify and expand her understanding of that environment. In so doing, she will be able to adapt successfully to that environment, i.e. render it predictable, manipulate it to meet her intentions.

(b) The less structure which Olivier provides, the more Valérie feels anxious. She becomes increasingly less able to concentrate on her task at hand. Most of her mental and emotional energy is mobilized to deal with the need to camouflage from others her helplessness. In feeling abandoned by Olivier, she can only punish herself.

(c) This occurs because Olivier *does have* expectations. He is not unconditionally accepting or, at least is not perceived as such by Valérie, which is the key factor here. He is telling her—or more precisely, she is hearing—that he wants her to be a more resourceful person than she feels she is or can ever be. What especially causes her anxiety is the distance between these expectations, which she feels she must meet in order to be loved, and her perception of herself. The best evidence that she has introjected these expectations is her painful, unsuccessful attempt to work alone and, when finally driven to seek help, to seek out another classmate rather than Olivier.

(d) This incident is a good example of the ravages caused by psychological and pedagogical theory. Look back for a moment at the four assumptions about child learning and development (on p. 187). These assumptions do not obtain for Valérie. By maintaining them, Olivier can only terrorize Valérie by holding a normative stance on her behaviour. Paradoxically, this kind of absolutist 'child-centred' doctrine makes abstraction of all the 'childish' qualities (impulses, emotions, longings) in Valérie and forces her into the posture of a self-confident, self-reliant adult. Olivier's premise, that meddling with the spontaneous, process of maturity in Valérie would be an authoritarian and alienating intervention, because it is far more punishing in its demands on Valérie.

(e) The basic problem, which can be attributed also to the influence of theoretical purism, is that Olivier is providing an *undifferentiated* environment for children who are at very *different* levels of capability to cope with the demands of the setting. Elis., Ar., and Is. appear to be far more capable than Valérie of programming and regulating their own activities and needs. They are more able to extract from a complex and distracting environment those tasks which optimally stretch their current repertoire of skills and concepts. These children, however, might be far less at ease than Valérie in a conventional, teacher-directed class-room.

There has been a great deal of research in individual differences between children (as well as between adults) who are exposed to the same experimental setting. In almost all the pioneering studies (Anderson *et al.*, Cronbach and Snow, Wispé, Grimes and Allinsmith, McKeachie, Washburne and Heil, Soar) the evidence indicates that individual behaviour is affected by the match between the structure or 'press' of the environment and a number of personality factors: activity level (including persistence and impulsivity), level of anxiety and defensiveness, valence of passive, dependent modes of response, level of assertiveness and aggression, egocentrism and level of self-esteem, cognitive styles of organizing and analysing information, and the like. These analyses, known as trait-treatment or aptitude-treatment interaction studies, underline the importance of interactions between pupil characteristics, learning objectives, and teaching style in accounting for the variance in scores on performance or attitudinal measures. The basic patterns and relationships are often curvilinear and disordinal: as teacher indirectness increases, the performance of dependent or anxious children suffers and that of autonomous or self-confident children improves. Schematically, we can plot these curves as in Figure 3.

These relationships are, of course, far more complex than is depicted here. To give an empirical illustration, let me show the results of the Grimes and Allinsmith (1961) study. They first identified third-grade

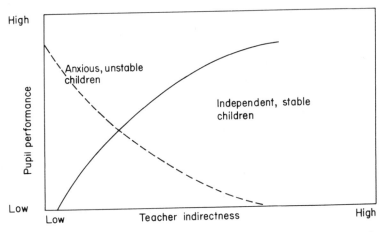

Figure 3   Theoretical relationship between teacher indirectness and pupil performance for two 'types' of children

children who were high and low in 'compulsivity' (orderliness, neatness, conformity, attention to detail) and in 'anxiety'. These children were enrolled in two different schools. One was highly structured or 'traditional' and used the conventional curriculum. The other was less structured and was characterized by a more affectionate, permissive environment. In addition to these differences, the schools used different types of reading programmes. The structured school taught by a code method, the unstructured school by a 'look and say' or 'meaning' method. The reading achievement scores for the four types of children in the two schools are presented in Figure 4. The pattern shows that the

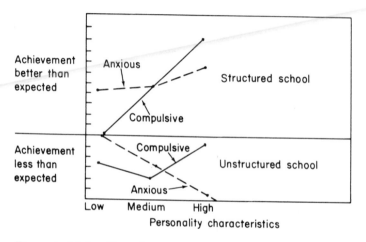

Figure 4 Main effect of school type on reading achievement of anxious and compulsive third-grade children in two school environments (from Grimes and Allinsmith, 1961)

influence of structure in school environment and reading method was beneficial as personality problems increased. Lack of structure was, in particular, inimical to the 'compulsive' pupils.

These relationships also appear in the Bennett study (1976, see pp. 141–148). Bennett reports that levels of actual work are lower in informal classrooms and that the lowest frequency is observed in the 'unmotivated (anxious) introvert' and the 'motivated neurotic'. These types correspond closely to those studied by Grimes and Allinsmith. Bennett concludes—somewhat hastily, in the light of the experimental conditions of his study—that informal classroom environments are unsuitable for anxious pupils.

The problem with all these studies, including our own, is that an enormous amount of within-group variance (individual differences) is

being lost in the amalgamation of children and teachers into oversimpli-
fied types and groups. Most sensitive and competent teachers will
intuitively take personality differences into account. They will provide
more structure for anxious children and give more leeway to independent children. The differences in treatment necessarily disappear in
most measures based on frequency counts, ratings, and ranking scales
and on grouped or mean scores. In fact, sensitivity to and provision for
individual differences are far more likely to occur in 'informal' classrooms than in highly structured classrooms, if only because of the
flexibility allowed in the former by the curriculum or the personality
structure of the teacher (in particular, her tolerance of ambiguity,
novelty and variety). Where this typically does *not* occur is in cases like
that of Olivier, whose doctrinal justification for what he is doing enables
him not to see or not to acknowledge the effects of an undifferentiated
treatment. His response to our observations was, 'It's just a matter of
time until Valérie and the others like her in the group come around and
take themselves in hand. To give them more structure now would be
doing them a disservice.'

My point is that Olivier has miscalculated Valérie's experience and
threshold of tolerance to unstructured environments. The distance
between the demands of the environment and her customary demands
on herself is too great for her to expend any psychic energy on other
tasks than that of protecting herself. Olivier makes the situation more
painful by clearly communicating norms of self-reliance and by reinforcing positively those who behave autonomously. The operative principle
here is optimal *discrepance*. As Harvey (1966, pp. 63–64) writes:

> To be maximally effective for producing articulated and integrated cognitive
> systems the input must always be optimally discrepant from the intra-subject
> baseline in relation to which they are gauged and assigned their psychological
> weight. If the discrepancy is too small or *suboptimal*, boredom may result . . . . If
> the baseline event discrepancy is too great or *superoptimal* for the particular
> subject at the particular time of stimulation, avoidance of novelty and tendencies
> toward constriction of the baseline on subsequent occasions might also result. If,
> on the other hand, the situation presented to the subject is *optimally discrepant*, it
> will be perceived as a positive challenge, will give rise to exploration and will
> contribute toward the system being articulated and expanded to include the
> previously deviant input.
>
> Of course, what is optimal stimulation or discrepancy for one subject might
> well be too much for a second and too little for a third.

There is further confirmation of this thesis from recent research in
Geneva (Piaget, 1974; Inhelder, Sinclair, and Bovet, 1974) on the
stimulation of 'cognitive conflict' through the presentation of tasks of

moderate novelty, as well as from the classic experimental studies of Hebb and Berlyne. In addition, many of the paradigms for behavioural change in psychodynamic theory contain the same theoretical premise.

5. Apathy, modelling, and intrinsic motivation

Valérie's behaviour in an informal classroom illustrates one dramatic effect of 'superoptimal discrepancy'. I wish to mention another effect which is both more easily and more frequently observed. Let me cite from two of the studies on progressive schools mentioned earlier: the Kensington study (Smith and Keith, 1971) and the Cambire study (Gross et al., 1970a):

An early and continuing problem was that the majority of children were unable to devise and to carry out individual plans of work . . . .. In addition, the children lacked adequate skills to work, together in groups . . . .. The wandering about in the gym continued and was accompanied by clay throwing, paper aeroplanes, further misuse of materials and a general restlessness. (Smith and Keith, 1971, p. 156)

In the words of one teacher, 'I never was able to instigate enthusiasm in these kids while keeping the noise level down and I never knew how to get them to use their time for learning instead of playing. The children were beginning to abuse freedom; they wouldn't do any work; they wouldn't record what they had done; many became discipline problems who weren't in the beginning . . .'. Nine out of ten [teachers] said that their pupils had 'just played around with materials' or 'made no effort to learn something from the materials'. (Gross et al., 1969, p. 698)

In our observations at the École Active and at the Unité Coopérative d'Enseignement, many of the same features are found. In classes scored as low on dimensions of teacher structuring and challenging, there was a high frequency of such behaviours as the following:

interruptions of pupils at work by other pupils;
noise, milling about, pupils coming and going in the classroom;
children at work on tasks which were either too simple or too difficult for them;
long periods of chatting;
slow progress at, frequent interruptions of, outright abandon of an activity;
children looking into space for long periods of time;
children copying answers out of their neighbours' workbooks;
high number of errors, etc.

Very often, there was an 'eye of the storm' phenomenon: a quiet, active group of children near where the teacher was sitting. As the circle widened, there was an increase in unoccupied, distracted, or agitated children. Here and there, a few isolates worked industriously in little islands in the midst of a sea of noise and movement.

This is, of course, the battle ground between educational conservatives and progressist 'true believers'. Descriptions such as the preceding, together with comparisons on standardized achievement tests, are often considered sufficient basis to discredit the 'open school' movement. The response of the progressists is that these measures are unfair (they do not measure the more fundamental changes, notably those in self-concept) and ephemeral (comparisons are made at the end of a year or two, whereas the more fundamental changes, which will affect in the long run scores on aptitude and achievement tests, take far longer). My own bias, which comes largely from four years of experience at the École Active, from visits to other schools, and from the findings of our research at the École Active and the UCE, is that the burden of proof still lies on those progressists of the Rogerian school who, like Olivier, assume that optimal mental, emotional, and social growth will take place for the majority of children in unstructured environments. There appear to be few children who flourish in that kind of environment, even after three or four years, and these are largely the children who functioned well or reasonably well from the outset. Time of exposure may be a necessary, but it is not a sufficient, condition for the majority. There is no clear evidence that these children become measurably more self-accepting, self-reliant, self-confident, or self-disciplined over time for having lived in maximally permissive classrooms.

I have already dwelled at length on what I think is the basic explanation for this phenomenon, namely the size of discrepancy for most children between the circumstances to be accommodated to and their present repertoire. In terms of 'readiness', many children lack either a sufficient amount of experience or level of maturation to perform in the way in which adults would have them perform.

Let me give two final illustrations. During one of the observations, a teacher in the École Active says to a child (8 years old), 'Xavier, you said you wanted to work this morning. Now you're just bothering the others. No one is forcing you to work. You decided it yourself, and now you're not holding to your own agreement.' My point is that Xavier is lacking the necessary impulse control, the sharp delineation between future and past, a personal history of deferring gratification and the logical sophistication involved in making and maintaining such behavioural 'contracts', all of which are required for him to hold to his own agreement. He needs the teacher in order to be able to hold to that agreement, and his deviant behaviour may itself be the only way he is able to express that need in the circumstances. Or, as another group of children observed in one of our interviews: 'Sometimes we just aren't able to stick to the work we begin. There are so many things to do, and they are all interesting. Especially when our friends are working on something interesting. So we take up a lot of things and then we leave many of them off without finishing them.'

I have also suggested a second explanation. It may well be the case that, as a general rule, unconditional positive regard and maximally permissive environments are inimical to optimal mental and emotional development. As I argued earlier, they do not facilitate the necessary confrontation with the environment (action on people and objects which resist; internalizing, then discarding those parts of another model which are incompatible) from which mental and emotional structures evolve. In Piagetian theory, the environment is constantly disproving, resisting, frustrating each new-found solution to a problem confronted by the child, and this very process of 'object resistance' obliges him to seek a new solution at a more complex level, only to find that solution inadequate for a more elaborate problem. Erikson (1950) speaks very convincingly of developmental 'crises' in his analysis of ego growth. I am also drawn to Coopersmith's work on the antecedents of self-esteem (1970). Whereas children from highly permissive families did not show high levels of self-acceptance and self-reliance, these qualities were prevalent in children whose parents provided clearly stated rules, limits, and standards of behaviour, while showing affection and respect for their children. Coopersmith's conclusion is worth citing:

The findings from these studies indicate . . . that children develop self-trust, venturesomeness and the ability to deal with adversity if they are treated with respect and are provided with well-defined standards of values, demands for competence and guidance toward solutions of problems. It appears that the development of independence and self-reliance is fostered by a well-structured, demanding environment rather than by largely unlimited permissiveness and freedom to explore in an unfocused way. (p. 349)

In our research, Coopersmith's theoretical position is reflected in the six scales of our observational grid for measuring the degree to which classroom environments contribute to the development of a positive self-image in children. Theoretically, teachers who score high on all scales—whose profile is high and horizontal on the graph (see Figure 2)—will create optimal environments for learning and growth. We do not yet have conclusive evidence that this is the case. But most of the observations indicate that 'structuring' and, in particular, what we have called 'challenging', behaviours on the part of the teacher are conducive to sustained interest, satisfaction, and productivity on the part of the children. Nor do these behaviours appear to produce a corresponding decrease in independence, self-expression, risk taking, internal locus of (fate) control, or co-operation between children.

Finally, I would like to suggest that (we) protagonists of such alternative models of education as 'progressive' schools are often blind to the influence of institutional settings so that we lapse into the kind of doctrinal incoherence which we would do well to correct. In arguing this point, let me go back to the illustrative list of assumptions concerning the optimal conditions under which children learn and develop (see p. 187). As I mentioned briefly in that section of the paper, these assumptions, together with the theoretical and experimental studies on which they are founded, are held in a sort of sociological vacuum. For example, if a child continuously explores his environment without adult intervention and in the face of frustrations, we can hypothesize that he is being propelled by an intrinsic 'drive' for mastery over that environment. But a number of other hypotheses are also warranted. For instance, that his parents do not stop or inhibit him. That his parents give him encouragement and praise each time he tries out something he has never done before. That his parents and siblings do a lot of exploring themselves which the child observes. That his parents do not scold him for touching or breaking household objects, etc. Without these attendant conditions, it is likely that many children will *not* explore their environments as spontaneously and consistently as postulated in the initial assumption. In fact, a great deal of empirical research on *preschool* parent–child relationships supports my hypothesis.

Let me say right away that I am *not* questioning the basic construct validity of intrinsic motivation in children. I would agree that when we say 'intrinsic' we mean what biologists refer to as 'characteristic of a species' and that a child's or adult's responses are not exclusively—or, of necessity, even primarily—a function of external situations. I am saying, however, that this construct is by no means as empirically sharp or unequivocal as is often claimed. The environment has a *press*. It makes explicit and implicit demands. It tells the child what he can and should do. To the extent that this press is consistent and coherent, the child, who is dependent on that environment in order to be loved, protected, and sustained, will internalize these demands. They will become his own demands on himself. Even if he does not internalize many of these demands, he will adapt his behaviour to them in order to meet his own needs. Much of the research on observational learning, status envy, and super-ego development lends credence to this theory. As does personal experience as a parent or teacher.

Up to now I have tried to establish three points. Firstly, children will freely explore and manipulate their environments *provided* the significant persons around them facilitate, encourage, and model this kind of activity themselves. Secondly, children will tend to explore and manipulate *in priority* those things in the environment which their parents or teachers give importance to and manipulate themselves successfully and with pleasure. Finally, children will be sensitive and responsive to *other demands* made on them by significant persons in their lives.

Let us look at a hypothetical group of children who come to the École Active or to another progressive primary school. The basic message they hear from the teachers is 'You are here to learn and grow. You will be deciding to a great extent what you do and how you do it. Of course, the choice is limited. This is, after all, a school, and most of the things to do turn around reading, writing and counting.'

The reaction of the children varies greatly. Some, as I argued earlier, have experienced a home and previous school environment in which the message has been radically different. We can expect their behaviour to be 'regressive' or 'disruptive', at least initially.

Others will find the atmosphere congenial. They will behave more or less as they do at home. They will try out the available games, materials, and activities. They will turn to the teacher for aid and companionship. They will seek out those activities which the teacher does best and will probably ask the teacher to do them more often. To the extent that their parents have provided the model in their own behaviours or have given importance to it, these children will 'spontaneously' try to master the basic curriculum in reading, composition, grammar, spelling, and maths. However, they will probably not work as diligently or as systematically on this mastery as they would have done in a conventional school. They will fix on a level of mastery with which they themselves are satisfied, which appears to satisfy their parents and teacher and which is equal to or, ideally, slightly better than that of those classmates whom they admire the most.

Within a few months or, at least, within the first two years, the parents of both groups of children ('highly discrepant' and, in appearance, 'optimally discrepant') are likely to intervene at home and at school. For obvious reasons, the parents of the first group are unhappy. What is perhaps more revealing, however, is the reaction of the second group. These parents will tend to express the following opinion:

Our children are happy to go to school and appear to profit from a less constricted programme. They can pursue their interests freely at school and, often, continue to work on them at home. They appear to be more relaxed, more critical, at times more curious and self-reliant than they used to be. But are they working up to their capacities? Aren't they falling behind by comparison with the official school programme?

If this group of parents is asked to elaborate on its misgivings, it will, for the most part, invoke the problem of upcoming selective examinations and the necessity of maintaining the widest possible choice of career for their children. Basically, these parents are saying that they would prefer their children to take up a career of equal or, if possible, of superior social prestige to their own. They can accept their child's making other choices, but do not feel that he is capable of making such choices before mid-adolescence, that is, *after* having passed examinations which may 'stream' him out of the pre-university track. There are definitely exceptions to this point of view among the parents, but they *are* exceptions. For most, the message is: 'Our children need to work harder on basic skills mastery than they are spontaneously willing to do.' In the ensuing weeks, these children can be observed in class 'spontaneously' asking for and doing more schoolwork.

From our research in Geneva as well as from other empirical studies, it would appear that teachers or school directors are likely to respond to this situation in one of three ways. The nature of that response discriminates neatly between the right and left wings of the progressive education movement. The first response, the one made by Olivier and the two teachers at the École Active mentioned earlier, is the following:

I had thought we agreed that your child would determine his own needs and obligations. By forcing him to do more schoolwork, you are imposing *your* values on him, simply because you are anxious about your own social status. You are not willing to let him grow into the person he was organically meant to be; he can only become the person you want him to become. If you do this, you will alienate him from himself. And he is all the more likely to reject this artificial model as soon as he becomes aware of it. When he does you may well lose his love and respect.

This opinion concurs with that of a small group of those parents to whom I referred earlier as exceptions. These people are not worried about, or actively seek, social marginality or downward social mobility for their children. Alternatively, they may simply share Olivier's point of view. My own observations of this subgroup indicate that it is composed of a disproportionate number of psychologists, teachers, and social workers, and that many of these parents appear to have a very low threshold of tolerance for any discomfort, anger, or frustration on the part of their children. The fact that their children were unhappy at the conventional state school was sufficient grounds to take them out.

If the teacher does not follow the implicit instructions of the larger group of parents, they will rapidly swell the ranks of the first, already discontented group. This, in turn, increases the degree of discrepancy for the child between the environmental press at home and that at school, with an attendant increase in anxious or defensive behaviour in both settings.

The second response is similar to the first, with one important exception. The gist is that the child will realize gradually by himself that he is not working to his full capacity in many areas and that no one but he can force himself to make a greater effort. He will then take his own learning in hand in function of his own self-determining goals. Very likely, these goals will imply a general or precise idea of a career that requires success in academic work. Once he is thus motivated and self-directing, the child will be able to cover months of the school programme in a few weeks' time. Parents hearing this response typically increase the number of discussions about careers at the dinner table. They then wait another half-year. At that point, many join the ranks of the malcontents.

The third response is simply that of increasing the environmental press for achievement in the classroom. The teacher begins to reinforce children more often (by complimenting, smiling at, or physically hugging them) when they choose and complete work on basic skills mastery. She intervenes more often and more rapidly when children are blocked, unoccupied, or are distracting other children from their work. She circulates more often among the children rather than waits until they come spontaneously to her. She encourages the children to try more complex or difficult work, stays with them during the initial phase, and gives them information at regular intervals as to how close they are to achieving mastery. In brief, the teacher multiplies the kinds of interventions which I called earlier 'structuring' and 'challenging'.

I would claim that these interventions are as effective at school as they are at home. By modelling the desired behaviours, by providing positive reinforcement for intellectual effort, by setting clear and high expectations for performance, teachers create to a great extent in their pupils the kind of motivation and achievement which leads both to academic success and to positive self-image for a great number of children. Because this is done in subtle and indirect ways (gestures, ways of looking at the children, reinforcing one child in order to stimulate his classmate), an inordinate number of researchers are fooled into concluding that children will initiate and persevere with difficult or unpleasant tasks without adult intervention. They are all the more easily fooled for wanting to be, i.e. this interpretation is both intuitively appealing and is consonant with clinical and experimental studies of early infant behaviour.

My point is that the type of spontaneous and self-directed behaviour postulated in the assumptions of progressive educators is, to a great extent, a function of a specific environment which creates that behaviour. In other words, certain forms of extrinsic motivation are, at the least, necessary for children to continue to display behaviours of intrinsic motivation beyond early infancy. Furthermore, if we agree with Coopersmith's conclusions (see p. 202), it would appear that external modelling, structuring, and challenging are more than facilitators; they, are preconditions for the development of the very intrapsychic qualities on which the assumptions are founded. Let me explain this point. Parental modelling, structuring, and challenging are associated with high levels of self-esteem. Children with high levels of self-esteem are more likely to feel in control of their environment, to tolerate frustration and novelty, to approach others without feeling threatened, to take cognitive risks. These characteristics are all required for children to explore actively their environments, to act without undue dependence on others, to rely on their own internally controlled evidence, etc. We are back to our list of assumptions and objectives of progressive schools . . ..

This brings me to three conclusions:

(a) Teachers who intervene actively in progressive schools by providing structure and challenge may do this because it is the only way for them to reconcile the social pressures for academic achievement with their own pedagogical objectives. They know that if they get excited themselves about and show pleasure in the mastery of reading and maths, the children are also likely to be motivated. If the teachers compliment children or their school work and give them support during the mastery of difficult operations, the pupils are likely to work harder. This is, in fact, possibly the only way in which schools can manage the impossible combination of having children do spontaneously what teachers want them to do. Very likely, these are the politics of maintaining educational 'alternatives' in any society in which the most prestigious, powerful, and remunerative jobs go to those who can master the basic skills of social communication and are trained to solve problems on the basis of incomplete, ambiguous, and abstract information. The only other option for alternative schools would appear to be social marginalization.

(b) Many teachers make themselves miserable in such a situation because they feel the social pressure, yet cleave to the thesis that teacher intervention and stimulation are authoritarian, that the child becomes increasingly passive and alienated as the teacher becomes progressively active. I have tried to argue that this thesis is not only unproved but probably invalid.

(c) The underlying reason why these teachers, and I suspect that they are legion, are unhappy is that they *would like to intervene and to stimulate*. This is probably why they chose to teach in the first place. People who get openly excited about learning to read, write, and count, who marvel at the way in which children make sense of the world, who like to be in the company of children, who like actively to help children who are having difficulties, etc., are obviously most at ease making a living doing precisely that. I suggest that the alternative schools where this kind of teaching is going on are those which live well beyond 18 months and which provide the real evidence which conventional schools have been trying with decreasing success to avoid looking at. And, if my reading of the sociological tea leaves is correct, the traditionalists who persist in not looking are likely themselves, and to be turned to administrators of such 'alternative' schools.

Acknowledgement

The research underlying this chapter was supported by a grant from the *Fonds National de Recherche Scientifique*, of Switzerland.

References

Bennett, N., 1976, *Teaching Styles and Pupil Progress* (London: Open Books).

Coopersmith, S., 1975, 'Studies in self-esteem', in Scientific American, ed., *Psychology in Progress* (San Francisco: Freeman), pp. 342–349.

Deal, T., 1975, 'An organisational explanation of the failure of alternative secondary schools', in *Educational Researcher*, **4**, (4), 10–16.

Erikson, E., 1950, *Childhood and Society* (New York: Norton), esp. pp. 72–108, 247–274.

Franks, D., 1976 *The Effects of Open Schools on Children: An Evaluation* (US Dept of HEW, National Institute of Education).

Furth, H., 1974, *Thinking Goes to School* (New York: Oxford University Press).

Grimes, J. W. and Allinsmith, W., 1961, 'Compulsivity. anxiety and school achievement', in *Merrill Palmer Quarterly*, **7**, 247–271.

Gross, N., Giacquinta, J. and Bernstein, M., 1970a, *The Implementation of Educational Innovations* (New York: Basic Books).

Gross, N., Giacquinta, J. and Bernstein, M., 1970b, 'Failure to implement a major organisational innovation', in M. Miles and W. Charters, eds, *Learning in Social Settings* (Boston: Allyn & Bacon), pp. 691–705.

Harvey, O. J., 1966, *Experience, Structure and Adaptability* (New York: Springer).

Havelock, R. and Huberman, M., 1978, *Solving Educational Problems*, (Geneva and Paris: UNESCO/IBE; New York: Praeger).
Havelock, R. and Huberman, M., 1977, *A Process of Educational Innovation in Developing Countries* (Geneva and Paris: UNESCO/IBE; New York: Praeger).
Holmes, T., and Rahe, R., 1967, 'The Social Readjustment Rating Scale', in *Journal of Psychosomatic Research* (11), 211–216.
Huberman, M., 1973, *Understanding Change in Education* (Paris and Geneva: UNESCO/IBE).
Huberman, M., 1974, *Permanent Education: Some Models of Adult Learning and Adult Change* (Strasbourg: Council of Europe (CCC)).
Huberman, M., 1978, 'La Formation des enseignants entant que modèle d'apprentissage complexe chez l'adulte', in *Traité des sciences pedagogiques*, vol. VII (Paris: PUF), ch.12.
Inhelder, B., Sinclair, H. and Bovet, M., 1974, *Apprentissage et structures de la connaissance* (Paris: PUF).
McPartland, J. and Epstein, J., 1973, *School Organisation and Student Outcomes: A Study of the Effects of Open-environment Schools* (Baltimore: Centre for the Social Organisation of Schools, Johns Hopkins University).
Piaget, J., 1967, *Biologie et connaissance* (Paris: Gallimard).
Piaget, J., 1974, *Recherches sur la contradication: études d'epistémologie génétique*, vol. XXXII (Paris: PUF).
Piaget, J., 1975, *L' Equilibration des structures cognitives: études d'epistémologie génétique*, vol. XXXIII (Paris: PUF).
Rogers, C., 1959, 'A theory of therapy, personality and interpersonal relationships', in S. Koch, ed., *Psychology: A Study of a Science*, vol. III (New York: McGraw-Hill).
Rogers, C., 1969, 'A modern approach to the valuing process', in C. Rogers, *Freedom to Learn* (Columbus, Ohio: Merrill).
Smith, L., and Keith, P., 1971, *The Anatomy of Educational Innovation: An Organisational Analysis of an Elementary School* (New York: Wiley).

Index

211